D0275157

CRIME

CRIME

How to solve it – and why so much
of what we're told is wrong

NICK ROSS

Biteback Publishing

First published in Great Britain in 2013 by
Biteback Publishing Ltd
Westminster Tower
3 Albert Embankment
London SE1 7SP
Copyright © Nick Ross 2013

ISBN 978-1-84954-499-3

10 9 8 7 6 5 4 3 2 1

A CIP catalogue record for this book is available from the British Library.

Set in Adobe Caslon Pro and Old Standard

Printed and bound in Great Britain by
CPI Group (UK) Ltd, Croydon CR0 4YY

MIX
Paper from
responsible sources
FSC® C020471

To Sarah

CONTENTS

CONTENTS

ACKNOWLEDGEMENTS

In the 1980s I was invited to join a government inquiry – they do like to have someone off the telly to add a bit of celebrity and a spurious sense of public access. The committee was a waste of time, largely because the energetic minister who set it up was immediately reshuffled. Politics can have a short attention span. But at the first meeting I found a kindred spirit. He was a professor, unassuming to the point of being bashful, and when he offered an opinion he usually prefaced it with an apology – in fact, he tended to say 'I'm sorry' every time he expounded an idea. But whenever he spoke he had something important to say. He is the reason this book exists.

His name is Ken Pease, a criminologist then at the University of Manchester. But he was unlike any criminologist I had met before. For a start he was not particularly interested in criminals. He wanted to cut crime, which, as we shall see, is a very different matter indeed. It turned out that, like me, he was originally a psychologist, and perhaps that is where the sense of affinity came in.

Years before, I had been appalled on my first day as an undergraduate when my professor disillusioned most of us about our chosen subject. Instead of interpreting dreams, as I had hoped, we would be mapping brains, running rats through mazes and above all learning how to systemise any evidence we found. It was science, something I had never liked at school. But it opened the door to an exhilarating world. Now, in a sunlit conference room in the Home Office, I was being brought back by Ken to apply that same systematic logic to fighting crime.

We began to discuss things outside the committee; indeed, if truth be told, we almost formed a subversive little clique to try to rescue the committee from well-meaning torpor. The National Board of Crime Prevention died of inertia, as did the Crime Prevention Agency Board that followed, but in the two decades since the two of us first met, Ken Pease has remained the dominant figure in my thinking about crime. Most of the insights in this book – assuming you find anything you regard as insightful – have their roots in the work of this diffident Mancunian.

If only I had matched his early enthusiasm for the two of us to write a book together. Somehow it never quite happened and so, years late, this is a solo venture. But Ken has been a guiding light, and though his name does not appear on the cover, his zest and inspiration are all over the place.

There are so many others who have contributed thoughts, and sometimes much more, a few of whom are listed below. Most importantly Ron Clarke and Marcus Felson, two charming professors I first met at Rutgers University in New Jersey, who have been thought leaders in the field and have encouraged and supported me throughout. Then there is Gloria Laycock, whom I first encountered when she was a civil servant briefing our Home Office board. She was a breath of fresh air, and has been a friend and consultant ever since (as well as an exasperatingly independent-minded director of the UCL Jill Dando Institute of Crime Science, a body I nominally chair, which position, I naively presumed, would give me some measure of influence over her). She and her brilliant successor Richard Wortley are doing the things I am merely writing about.

Two other figures who deserve a special mention have, oddly, you might think, no connection with crime or with this book. One showed it is possible to overturn deeply ingrained orthodoxy within a conservative profession. The other proved there are leaders willing to let facts trump ideology. Both might have seemed mildly eccentric at first and both were eventually awarded knighthoods for their achievements.

First Iain Chalmers, whom I first met on a committee reviewing cancer treatments. (Yes, again they wanted someone off the telly.) He is a doctor who realised that the evidence for so-called scientific medicine was often thin – shockingly so in our review of breast cancer treatments in the 1980s. His doubts about received wisdoms, his inquisitiveness and his rigorous concern for meticulous evaluation may have done more to save lives than any other doctor since the war. A lot of the medical lessons translate directly into crime.

Second, Peter Bottomley showed me how good evidence can trump political self-interest. He was minister for roads when I approached him with a radical idea to cut road deaths. The plan was risky. It overturned the convention that accidents will happen. It proposed that most solutions lay in changing roads and vehicles, not the people who used them. It replaced fatalism with targets. It offered the prospect of failure without hope of party political rewards. Yet to my amazement, the minister did more than agree to the plan. He championed it. Like Professor Chalmers he saved thousands of lives as a result. And he broke through my cynicism about politics to convince me there is everything to play for.

There are many others I should thank, including those who disappointed me by having formulated, tested and published ideas long before I thought I had invented them myself. Dispiritingly little of what I say is really original. So thanks too to all those whose experiments or writings I have cited, many of whom took the time to read my proofs and check I had neither misinterpreted nor misquoted them. I should add a special word of appreciation for the growing band of criminologists who (though you will find that I despair of much in criminology) are, like Ken Pease, more concerned with crime than with criminals. And I have come to know and admire those who are truly experimental, like Professors David Farrington and Larry Sherman of Cambridge. I now count many police officers as friends and am delighted to report that, while I have met a few really plodding coppers in my time, most are admirable, many are really smart, and there are some truly brilliant ones as well.

It is too pretentious to claim that I am standing on the shoulders of giants but I am certainly squatting on the discoveries of many very clever people. They might not all agree with my remixes and reinterpretations. They may well not all approve of the robustly emphatic tone this book adopts at times. But I hope they will be pleased to see how I have espoused so many of their ideas.

I hope that my agent will be pleased as well. Caroline Michel of PFD committed herself to this as a story that needed to be told, not just as another title from one of her huge catalogue of authors. She and her colleague Tim Binding persuaded me to press on when I was giving up. And thanks to Iain Dale and Sam Carter at Biteback Publishing, who had faith to bet on it when others didn't.

And then there is my family, my wife Sarah and sons Adam, Sam and especially Jack, who deserve thanks as well as love for ignoring me when I went like a hermit to my study or disappeared on field trips, and then bothered to read the drafts and tell me when things were manifestly unintelligible.

To all the above, and many more, thank you. If as you read the book you find things that are sage, they are probably down to them; when you find things that are not, they are almost inevitably down to me. And perhaps finally a word of thanks to all the BBC licence payers who enabled my career and to colleagues who cast me and kept me on *Crimewatch*, and quite inadvertently got me interested in issues I might not otherwise have cared a fig for.

PREFACE

This is a polemic. It started as a studious and mildly worded tome which grew too long, too academic. People told me: go write an accessible book.

So now you are expected to take much of what I say on trust. I hope you don't. Scepticism is the driving force of human progress. What I say here is based on years of study, a forest of learned papers and over twenty years' experience of working with the police and other crime reduction agencies. But science works by challenge not by faith, by evidence not acceptance, and so should public policy. Almost all the references and footnotes have been stripped out, along with my thanks to experts who informed and inspired me, but you can find them online along with expanded notes and explanations. Do please check them out at **www.thecrimebook.com**.

Most of the lessons I see in crime are applicable throughout the industrialised world but, alas, this is a subject that drives one to parochialism. Each country has different laws and legal systems, different policing traditions, different statistical frameworks and has collective memory of different events. Even the United Kingdom is at its most disunited when it comes to crime, and to avoid complexity I have focused on England and Wales. My apologies to Scotland and especially to Northern Ireland, which was for many years my home.

Also, before we head off we ought to agree what the fuss is all about. What is crime? You might think the answer is obvious and I am not going to waste much time on niggling definitions. But the concept is surprisingly elusive. Crime is certainly not the same as malice, for many nasty things that people do are legal. It is often not intentional, but the result of anger, over-exuberance, carelessness, ineptitude or recklessness. It is not always even wrong, since rules can be capricious and unfair. Sometimes laws, such as those enforcing slavery or persecuting Jews, are later seen to be crimes themselves. Occasionally those who defy the law become heroes, as with the black seamstress Rosa Parks who refused to give up her bus seat to a white man in Alabama but whose $10 fine won her a Congressional Gold Medal four decades on. Indeed, as the British polymath C. P. Snow famously observed, 'When you think of the long and gloomy history of man, you will find more hideous crimes have been committed in the name of obedience than have ever been committed in the name of rebellion.'

Philosophers have argued over this for generations. Some say sanctions should only apply to actions that do harm to others, while others think anything 'immoral' or palpably unsafe should be a crime. Ultimately law is no more than a tool for regulating fashions in human conduct. Yesterday's shameful crime of abortion is today a routine procedure on the NHS, and homosexuals who once faced prison or chemical castration can now get married.

Still, there will always be plenty that we are all ready to call crime and want less of. Throughout this book I shall try to set our net to avoid dredging tiny fish at the margins of criminality, or catching mermaids at the margins of legitimate protest. What we should be concerned about is to cut the agony that people suffer unnecessarily.

There are ways to do it.

www.thecrimebook.com

1

INTRODUCTION

All you need to know, in a nutshell

Crime has been with us since Adam and Eve and, surprisingly, God didn't spot the solution. Rather than punishing the miscreants, it might have been better had he put the forbidden fruit higher up the tree.

The fundamental thesis of this book is that we have been too slow to realise how strongly crime levels are dictated by temptation and opportunity. Human nature remains more or less constant from one generation to another but situations change, and it is those evolving situations that largely determine how much is stolen, how many people are assaulted and how many citizens get hooked on drugs or even child pornography. The message is that if you want to cut crime then you need to spend more time on low-hanging fruit. Removing provocations like the apple in Eden is quicker, cheaper and generally less fraught with moral pitfalls than politicking about how best to treat offenders.

WHY TV CAUSES CRIME

Years ago, at the start of China's astonishing race towards modernisation, I stood on a top-floor balcony in a dusty town with the local mayor and an interpreter. I was a reporter for the BBC and they proudly pointed out the local hospital, a big school and a prosperous cluster of new houses. Why, I asked, were some of the new homes surrounded by barbed wire? The mayor responded sorrowfully: 'Burglaries,' he said. 'Mostly televisions.' I hadn't realised burglary was a problem in China.

'It wasn't,' said the mayor. 'My father never knew it, nor did my grandfather.'

'So what changed?' I asked.

As the interpreter translated, the mayor recoiled slightly as though it were a trick question. After a moment he responded gravely: 'We didn't have televisions.'

This simple exchange struck me as revelatory: television does indeed cause crime, though not in a way I had ever considered before.

Of course in any society there are bad 'uns, the repeat offenders who are socially maladroit, addicted, brought up in criminal families, dissolute, psychologically damaged or even psychopathic. They cause a hugely disproportionate amount of crime and have to be dealt with; but crime statistics do not surge or collapse in response to how well we do that. For the most part such people are depressingly resistant to punishment or help, and generally grow out of it. They are more of a constant in the equation than many people realise. In any case, even recidivists' offending rates are strongly influenced by how much temptation they face and how easy it is to act out their antisocial impulses. At very least they can often be diverted from the juiciest targets to ones that cause less harm.

Charles Rowan and Richard Mayne, Britain's first police commissioners, realised this, and must be rolling in their graves at what has happened since. They set out to stop crime happening in the first place, not detect it after the event. But policing has evolved very much as they feared it might: preoccupied by catching and prosecuting offenders rather than cutting crime. Worse still, police, politicians and the public mix up two quite different aims: justice and crime prevention. They are both important but they have disappointingly little in common. The conflation of the two goals leads to confusion, and human rights tend to get trampled in the muddle.

You do not have to be a sophisticated statistician to recognise that conviction rates and sentencing tariffs rarely correlate with crime, let alone determine its trajectory. Take any of the mass offences which plagued the industrialised world from the post-war period onwards: shoplifting, burglary and car crime. We shall see how each of these rose exponentially until the 1990s before peaking and then falling dramatically. Neither the surge nor the plunge owes much to sentencing changes or even to detection rates.

Most of the different categories of violence followed the same rise-and-fall pattern, albeit often a few years later. They did so more or less equally in jurisdictions with hard punitive systems, such as Texas, and soft ones, as in Denmark. In England, homicide surged before falling to its lowest levels for well over a decade. Yet detection rates remained about the same and conviction for murder continued to attract a uniform life sentence.

Does this mean policing is a waste of time? Obviously not. Imagine a world with no sanctions for behaving badly. But it does suggest something almost as dramatic: *while policing plainly suppresses crime, it is surprisingly tangential to long-term changes in victimisation rates.* For me, as a broadcaster best-known for helping police to catch offenders, this was a light-bulb insight. Just as China had taught me how temptations like TVs provoke crime,

I now understood that conventional policing has few of the tools to control it.

For the most part, offending levels rise when more of us get sucked in and they fade when we don't. It really is true that opportunity makes the thief. To a vast extent it also creates the football hooligan, drink-driver, knife-wielding youth, sex offender, violent lover, fraudster and murderer too. This is why crime rates rise, and it is how we make them fall. It is why burglary and car theft rocketed until we became serious about home and vehicle security. It is how we so radically curbed football violence and road fatalities. It is the reason why so many British politicians got caught with their hands in the till until their expenses protocols were changed. And it explains why Americans seem so crazily homicidal; their murder rate would be broadly the same as ours were it not for all their handguns.

As we go on I shall set out the facts behind each of these assertions. I realise I shall need to be persuasive because this whole approach flies in the face of almost every sociological and political assumption. The traditional view is deeply instinctive and long predates that infamous apple from the Book of Genesis: crime is caused by people's fall from grace into a state of badness. It is up to individuals to stick to the straight and narrow, and they need to be helped to do so with threats of punishment in this world or the next. Nowadays some people may blame social factors too, but the idea that, ultimately, crime is caused by humans falling from the path of righteousness still seems so self-evident as to be entirely beyond challenge.

For front-line police officers it seems axiomatic: offenders are the problem rather than a symptom. Their principal approach to crime, indeed a large part of their training, is to act as paralegals, precisely as Charles Rowan and Richard Mayne hoped they would not.

But all this presupposes that crime really is caused by criminals.

If you think about it for a moment, this is essentially a tautology. It is like arguing that motoring is caused by motorists. It runs the risk of categorising people as though a driver is a distinct type of person, as opposed to a pedestrian or passenger, when in fact the label 'motorist' merely defines an action at a given point in time. Even the most prodigious criminals spend the overwhelming part of their lives eating, sleeping, drinking, going to the movies and behaving within the law as most other people do.

The willingness to see the world as goodies and baddies is so deep-seated that psychologists have a name for it: fundamental attribution error. We tend to denounce failures in others that we excuse or don't notice in ourselves. We blame the person not the circumstance, and by assuming crime is caused by criminals, we also assume the answer must lie in reducing criminality. It is rather like believing we can reduce traffic by cutting back on the sort of people who drive. Instead the best way is to provide alternatives which are more attractive, so people's behaviour defaults to walking, cycling or using public transport.

Yes, there will be petrol-heads who will always prefer driving, and, as I say, there are serial delinquents who often gravitate to crime – but these are a small minority. And even for them, their behaviours are tendencies, not absolutes. Even fanatics make choices dependent on their options.

We can often shape those options. And we shall see that we can get more leverage if we act before the event rather than after a crime has taken place.

Prevention is better than drama

All this calls for the police to be pushed higher up the food chain. Crime prevention is undramatic. Like public health, it lacks the macho theatre of emergency intervention. But it is generally better to avoid a crisis than chase after it with sirens and blue lights. And crime prevention is a very great deal better than relying on the cumbersome, costly and recidivism-plagued courts and prison services. We, as Rowan and Mayne did, should regard the criminal justice system as the symbol of our failures, not the answers to our problems.

As I say, our reverence for the criminal justice system and our beliefs in deterrence and redemption are fundamentally misplaced. Lawyers neither blush if crime rates rise, nor take credit if they fall. Why should they? It is not their responsibility. Magistrates and judges would be aghast at the prospect of being paid by results, because they know they can't deliver crime reduction. Theirs is the important but distinct task of dispensing justice. Court disposals are fire-and-forget, based on a philosophy of just deserts rather than calibrated for strategic crime reduction. Beyond the realms of formalised religion, perhaps no great human institution in any Western democracy is quite so powerful, and yet unaccountable for cost-effectiveness or measured outcomes. Policy-makers can be as tough or tender to offenders as they like but, for the most part, they will be responding to a public mood or private preference rather than making a predictable difference to public safety. There are ways to use the courts more scientifically, but at very best their impact on crime rates will be tangential. Yet the idea that crime and punishment go together is so ingrained in our psyche that detecting and convicting offenders sometimes seems to be the only tool in the toolbox.

This has huge implications for policing. Detection has become one of its most important roles, so much so that politicians and commentators often seek to judge police almost exclusively on detection rates. Later in the book we will see how and why the first police chiefs fought so hard to keep detection out of the equation. For the moment, consider some consequences of confusing catching villains with forestalling villainy.

The first and the most worrying is that it has diverted the police from preventing society's problems to sorting out the mess. We so take this for granted that we don't even expect the police to cut crime. At one stage in the 1990s chief constables were required to meet over a hundred so-called key performance indices but not one of them measured actual reductions in victimisation. The corollary is that they have surprisingly little knowledge about the reasons crime fluctuates, and have access to very few evidence-based means of crime prevention. There are some notable exceptions, but the demands we have placed on the service to improve detection rates have increasingly turned officers into procurers for the courts. And their world gets more bureaucratic each year. Long gone are the days when a word from a copper would suffice to have someone sent down. The law has become increasingly complicated; more people know their rights, and proving guilt beyond reasonable doubt is now a much higher bar than it was in previous generations. It is now a colossal task to prepare a case for trial, and trials that once took minutes or hours now take days or weeks.

So the police become increasingly trapped in servicing the lawyers. And since the end-game is to go to trial, they are far more concerned with offenders than with victims. This has led to frequent and vocal complaints that police let victims down. Campaigners, notably Victim Support, have helped to redress the balance, but fundamentally the problem is a consequence of our whole approach to crime. In many respects the police and courts are facing the wrong way.

There are many other ramifications of this emphasis on detection, not least that it has clouded the picture we have of crime. Since our principal expectation of police is to catch and convict criminals, it follows that people only tend to report things they think the police can do something about. Partly as a result of this, at least half of all crime across all levels of severity, from bike theft to savage injury, is not recorded. To make things worse there are oceans of crime almost entirely uncharted by police because it's not clear their remit extends there, such as internet scams or consumer rip-offs which can cause awful grief but which tend to be downplayed as trading standards matters. All in all, the police know surprisingly little about crime and what they do know can be perilously misleading.

The detection rate agenda also means police privilege the sort of intelligence that helps them prosecute offenders at the expense of information that exposes vulnerabilities in crime targets. This in turn means we are late in recognising and designing out the products and policies which enable and provoke crime. Meanwhile the tidal flows of crime are dictated by gravitational forces far beyond the control of conventional policing. The reckless manufacturing of high-value cars or mobile phones with no inbuilt security was tackled only when the products had spawned crime epidemics. Now, as crime migrates from physical to virtual, the police are ill placed to prevent the next pandemic. As fraud becomes pervasive, most forces have no fraud squads let alone decisive understanding or control of crime which has no clear physical location. They certainly cannot be said to have their hands on the levers that will dictate the next crime surge. The emphasis on criminals means we suffer more crime.

Yet the dogma is so entrenched that we describe a crime as solved when we have found someone to blame.

Almost all experts have lazily accepted the agenda. For journalists, crime is a dramatic story of dastardly deeds rather than a set of presumptions to be challenged. Academics too have swallowed the view that crime is caused by criminals. As we shall see, criminology is so obsessed by criminality that it has contributed almost nothing to our knowledge of how to cut crime.

In recent years some police have begun to grasp this, albeit half-heartedly, and there have been ingenious efforts to tackle underlying causes rather than manifestations. But so-called problem-oriented policing is more talked about than embedded in the culture, largely because most voters and politicians have never heard of it, don't know what it is, and so the pressure on borough commanders and police chiefs is to stick with chasing crooks.

Finally, by seeing crooks as the big issue we tend to not to notice how important immediacy is in crime. We favour solutions which are remote, such as bad parenting in years gone past, rather than the absence of security at the scene of the crime. When we learn that crime rates have been cut by a procedural or technical innovation, we tend to dismiss it as a sticking plaster rather than a cure. The truth is it is more like vaccination, keeping a disease at bay rather than hoping to kill each infective agent one cell at a time.

What we need is a wholesale shift to preventive medicine.

TAKING THE MEDICINE

If pooh-poohing the traditional approach to crime sounds radical it is not. The fork in the path from belief and assumption to reassessing the evidence has been taken many times in other fields of human endeavour and has always been the road to progress, often leading to developments that seem miraculous. It is why we know the earth is round and not the centre of the universe. It is how we learned to put lightning conductors on church steeples rather than pray to be spared the wrath of God. It was why, after all mankind's attempts to copy birds, the Wright brothers stopped flapping and invented powered flight. In crime too, we need to stop flapping.

Above all, we need to learn from medicine.

For millennia people supposed that sickness was a punishment for misdeeds, and even when human anatomy was fairly
well understood, illness was ascribed to an imbalance of energy
or humours. Until 200 years ago, deeply rooted theories about
disease restricted the average European to the life expectancy
of the Stone Age; and woe betide anyone who could afford
a doctor, since the cure invariably involved inducing vomiting, draining blood or forcing wounds open to stimulate
pus. Almost certainly physicians killed more patients than
they cured. But once scientific reasoning began to prove that
spirits could not be cast out, nor bad humours improved by
blood-letting, the results have been spectacular, with such huge
improvements in life expectancy that healthcare systems now
can't keep up with ageing populations.

It was a long and bumpy ride from remedies based on suppo-
sition to evidence-based medicine built on science, and even now
the comforting lure of belief ensures the survival at the fringes
of faith-based treatments; but these are mostly for the worried
well. When something goes really wrong we no longer seek out
witch doctors or their new-age incarnations. We turn to scientific medicine.

In crime too, we need to overcome a deeply rooted assumption: the doctrine that crime is mostly caused by badness. Do not
underestimate the ancient mysticism which underpins our attitudes. It is always tempting to invent the undetectable and the
immeasurable to explain what we cannot otherwise explain. We
used to believe that light travelled through the heavens because
space was filled with luminiferous ether, that fire burned
because of phlogiston, or that cholera spread through a miasma.
Likewise, scratch most commentators and you will find they
really believe that crime rates are determined by fluctuations in
some invisible force which essentially boils down to evil.

The reasons they cite for this malaise are invariably ones which conveniently fit their own perspectives on life. As with Galen's medicine, in which sanguinity was caused by the blood, and anger by the spleen, or Eastern equivalents which posited imperceptible meridians, they fit the facts round their theories and see what they want to see. It is well meaning, but it mostly amounts to quackery and juju. Liberals and left-wingers are convinced crime is caused by unfairness and poverty, and social conservatives are equally certain it is down to lack of discipline and failing values. Religious people cite decline of religion, disciplinarians identify lack of discipline, believers in the power of genes blame nature, others blame nurture, promoters of family values cite decline of the family, social reformers prefer social disaffection, and you can fill in your own blanks according to your outlook on life.

In the absence of more convincing explanations, even non-believers are often taken in by these resolutely argued theories. Tony Blair cunningly appealed to softies and disciplinarians alike in his promise to be tough on crime and tough on the causes of crime. It was merely equivocation, of course, and as I know from a private discussion with him, he really had no answers. Nor could he tear himself away from the ancient presumption that it is the quantum of badness out there in our communities that we need to change.

It is time to follow the evidence and to subject hallowed theories to scientific challenge. Just as doctors learned to be sceptical of intuition, anecdote and ideas passed down through generations, we need to set a new agenda when it comes to cutting crime.

2

CRIME WAVE

Opportunity knocks

If prosecution is not the most reliable way to make a big impact on crime, what is? It just so happens that the last half-century has provided the perfect opportunity to check this out. From roughly the early 1960s onwards in Britain there was a rise in recorded crime that became faster and alarmingly steeper each year, provoking in equal measure anger, despair and fatalism, and prompting politicians, pundits, criminologists, sociologists as well as riled and bewildered citizens to denounce our spiritual, moral and social decline. Petty vandalism became a big irritation but the grand crime wave was really led by three major types of acquisitive crime, all of which grew from modest levels into pandemics: shoplifting, burglary and car theft. Other problems, including violence, proliferated in their wake, but these big three were in the vanguard and came to dominate police statistics and everyday concerns.

What none of the social theorists predicted is that all three of these apparently unstoppable contagions would go into reverse, and soon be followed downwards by most other crimes that had plagued the period too.

Plainly we need to explain not merely why these three crime types multiplied with such frightening speed, but why they faded equally emphatically.

Shoplifting

Shoplifting led the trend; so why and how did shop theft become so rampant? Pilfering had always been a problem from stalls and street displays, but stealing from shops themselves exploded after the Second World War, rising from a few thousand reports each year to account for an eighth of all recorded crime, and helping to define an era when morality seemed to be going to the dogs. It coincided with the teenage revolution, the age of rebellious mods and rockers, and with much talk about the breakdown of society. Little wonder people blamed a loss of discipline and order. Maybe that was part of the equation, but something much more obvious, yet rarely recognised, was going on; something that was bound to have a dramatic effect on the relationship between a shopper and a shop. Retailers had discovered they could provoke impulse buying and dramatically cut costs by encouraging self-service. They took down the shop counters.

Tantalised by a vast array of attractions within easy reach, many customers helped themselves in more ways than they should. With no need to ask a shopkeeper for goods, people could rationalise stealing as a victimless crime, 'like punching someone in the dark', as the cartoon tearaway in *The Simpsons* once memorably put it. At a time when women did almost all the shopping for the family, shoplifting became known as the housewife's crime. And when sweets and toys were placed on unsupervised displays on low racks where children's eyes would feast and their hands could reach, the young were vulnerable too. I stole sweets myself as a child – an admission that would one day be splashed front-page in the British tabloids – but it was common for ten- to fifteen-year-olds to shoplift. It almost would have been odd not to, though most shoplifters say they don't know why they did it. This was not a crime of need but of fecund opportunity, which is why even wealthy celebrities were caught at it. One of the saddest cases to make headlines was that of Lady Isobel Barnett, a qualified doctor, a Justice of the Peace and a household name as a television star, who in 1980 stole a tin of tuna and a carton of cream and was so shamed by the publicity that four days after the court case she committed suicide. But even the horror of exposure was not enough to deter other public figures, and a long list of luminaries followed her into the dock, including more recently Antony Worrall Thompson, Winona Ryder, Peaches Geldof, Richard Madeley and Britney Spears. Shopkeepers had created the biggest surge in crime ever known in peacetime, recruiting vastly more people from all social backgrounds into criminality than the mafia could ever dream of.

Yet paradoxically it was good business. Stock 'shrinkage' was a price worth paying. It was not just the supermarkets and department stores; in time even the smallest corner shops put their stock out on display, entrusting customers to present it at the till.

This all provoked a storm of anger about failing morals. Given society's deep-rooted faith in criminal justice, more and more miscreants were reported to the authorities, with police recording a 23-fold rise between 1945 and the turn of the millennium. But blaming the offenders seemed to make no difference to the trend. Losses continued to climb.

Almost no one reproached the shopkeepers themselves, and when anyone dared to do so they were pummelled for blaming the victim. (I once received a furious public rebuke from the British Retail Consortium for suggesting they were the authors of their own misfortune, although industry leaders privately conceded I was right, and the largest ever study of the problem concluded that 'many losses by retailers are due to choices about how to conduct their business'.) Whether or not retailers had caused the problem, the more important question was, did they have a remedy? They could scarcely put the genie back into the bottle. Few stores could make money nowadays with all their stock at the back of the place, their customers at the front, and the shopkeeper standing between them behind a barrier.

But just as water finds its level, so eventually does crime. When the costs of shrinkage became intolerable there was a new business case for crime prevention. Bit by bit, countermeasures were introduced: staff were trained to be vigilant, cash tills were relocated to give better sight-lines down the aisles, window displays were changed to expose vulnerable corners to glancing passers-by, mirrors and CCTV were introduced, store detectives and exit guards were recruited, high-value items were tethered or locked behind glass, dummy goods or packaging were put on display without the costly product inside, and a whole ingenious new industry was spawned to provide lockable cabinets, tell-tale markers, sensors, alarms, spider wraps, security gates, radio-frequency tags and extended families of visible deterrents and hidden electronic article surveillance.

Just as the removal of shop counters had led to a crime epidemic, so restoring a semblance of security alleviated it. Shoplifting still accounts for almost half of all known commercial crime, but surveys suggest it fell 60 per cent in the decade up to 2012. Though losses remain enormous – guessed at £840 million in 2011 – they now represent less than 0.0025 per cent of UK retail sales.

The British Retail Consortium is justifiably proud of the industry's success in cutting crime and trumpets its achievements; and yet the instinct to blame criminals runs deep. Retailers continue to appeal for tougher penalties.

CASH TILLS

If you still need convincing that crime levels owe more to temptation than to badness, reflect on another big lesson from the high street: how shopkeepers largely eliminated an even greater challenge to their industry. For thousands of years, and certainly since cash replaced barter, business owners had problems reconciling their takings with the day's trade. Staff simply couldn't be trusted. A hired manager or shop assistant could sell things cheaply to accomplices, or simply pocket some of the payments. Open cash boxes presented enormous temptation to everyone who used them, and unless the stall owner could catch someone in the act, he might never understand why his profits were so meagre or his business was trading in the red. One of those who suffered was the owner of a grocery and general store in Ohio, one John Patterson. His experience, late in the nineteenth century, would have been familiar to retail proprietors everywhere, and was about to change the world:

> We were obliged to be away from the store most of the time so we employed a superintendent. At the end of three years, although we had sold annually about $50,000 worth of goods on which there was a large margin, we found ourselves worse off than nothing. We were in debt, and we could not account for it.

As luck would have it, another Ohio man had similar problems and thought he had invented a solution. James Ritty, a saloon keeper, patented a machine he called his 'Incorruptible Cashier', which had a crude mechanism that went ka-ching to ring up sales and could add up the total at the end of the day. When Patterson bought two of them his fortunes were transformed.

'We put them in the store, and, in spite of their deficiencies, at the end of twelve months we cleared $6,000.'

He was so impressed he bought the company, or at any rate he bought the rights, and in 1884 started his own business. He called it National Cash Register, which became the legendary NCR. He created a design team to build more robust and thief-proof tills with cash drawers that stayed locked shut except when a sale was in progress, devised aggressive sales techniques and created large-scale flexible manufacturing, so that by the start of the Great War Patterson's 'thief catchers' so dominated commercial life that he had been prosecuted by the US federal government and convicted of criminal conspiracy under antitrust laws. Undaunted, he continued to innovate, and by the 1950s his firm was one of the pioneers of modern computing.

Cash tills were never foolproof, and never will be. Over time, shop workers devised all sorts of wheezes to defeat them. On some machines cashiers could leave the drawer ajar and pilfer from it; or, if in league with a confederate, they could 'sweetheart' or 'under-ring' a sale by not keying in all the items presented at the checkout. They could ring up a transaction but cancel it when the customer had left, or ring up a lower amount and hope the customer wouldn't notice; they could invent a 'refund', or even install a dummy cash register of their own. In the 1980s a British pub chain was so baffled by missing money at one outlet that it installed CCTV to monitor what was going on. Eventually someone spotted that the pub had an extra, illicit, till.

Cash registers did not change human nature but they helped

it to default to honesty. Staff theft now accounts for only 3 or
4 per cent of retail crime. Tills largely eclipsed the problem of
supervising shop assistants, and permitted the development
of retail chains and department stores. Today, British merchants
take £1 billion a day without owners like John Patterson having to
supervise each sale. And modern point-of-sale equipment does
much more than radically curb crime. It can calculate VAT,
audit and even order stock and compile management reports.
Rather than target-hardening, they are business-enhancing.

Burglary

Changing situations rather than people also explains what
happened with burglary. The twentieth century democratised
housebreaking as surely as it emancipated affluence. Once the
consumer age had taken hold we all had something worth stealing. It is true that people used to keep their homes unlocked.
But before we get too nostalgic, think back to the relative dearth
of anything worth taking in the pre-consumer age. Where was
the TV, the hi-fi, the video recorder, the key to the car outside?
There were no credit cards, and most folk had precious little cash.
If you burgled the average home in the 1930s you would come
away with not a lot. For those who did have wealth, they locked
it up, and tended to have servants and gardeners to act as guardians. Most of their precious possessions, like silverware, jewellery,
fur coats and cars, were exclusive to their class, and would have
looked flamboyantly out of place in the hands of the lower orders.

But the essence of mass-market products was that anyone
might own them. That meant a burglar could keep or pass on
the stolen goods without drawing much attention. We will see
in Chapter 4 that wealth is a far greater progenitor of crime than

poverty. This apparent contradiction used to baffle people, but if you chart burglaries from the 1950s until the 1990s and compare it with a graph of Britain's gross domestic product, you will find a compelling match.

Even so, it was little wonder that in the 1960s the finger of blame for rising crime was pointed at moral failings. As the Prime Minister, Harold Macmillan, famously put it, Britain had never had it so good. Accordingly, commentators readily convinced themselves that if life was getting better, people must be getting worse. As always, liberals impugned selfishness while conservatives pointed to indiscipline, inflaming a latent political slanging match between left and right which simmers to this day.

But there was a better explanation, one that would eventually be able to quantify rates of burglary and even the types of goods that would be stolen. In 1976 four Home Office researchers tentatively put forward the idea that crime might be caused by opportunity and, in particular, by lack of security and supervision. They had noticed how steering column locks saved cars from being stolen, and that vandalism on buses rarely happened where drivers or conductors could see what was going on. Of course, like everyone else, they assumed the underlying cause of crime was lack of moral compass, and they warned that better security might simply move criminality elsewhere. Nonetheless they cautiously suggested criminologists might usefully supplement their interest in 'social' crime prevention by at least considering whether 'physical' prevention might have a role to play.

They had stumbled on a great truth, and one far larger than they realised at the time. But three of those authors, Ron Clarke, Pat Mayhew and Mike Hough, became more and more intrigued and shifted their research from criminals to crime, until concern for victims rather than offenders came to dominate their interests and ultimately take over their professional lives.

Their idea caught on with others too. In 1979 two prescient US academics, Marcus Felson helped by Larry Cohen, built on the British insight to publish a credible explanation of how crime and prosperity are linked. Felson called it the 'routine activity theory'. Instead of seeing crime as deviant, he said, we should think of it as a rational reaction to daily life as seen from the perspective of the offender. As the Home Office team had suggested three years earlier, it took not just a motivated offender but an attractive target in the absence of effective controls.

At first this seemed little more than academic rumination. It was denounced by a few criminologists and otherwise ignored. Everyone knew that crime had social, psychological and moral causes, so seeking mechanical linkage with opportunity was simplistic and naive. But more and more data seemed to fit the theory and by 1990 Simon Field, a British civil servant, had turned the idea into a mathematical formula. He calculated that for every 1 per cent increase in the stock of consumer goods, burglary and theft increase by around 2 per cent. Field also factored in demographics: over time, for every 1 per cent increase in the number of youths aged fifteen to twenty, burglary and theft would increase by roughly 1 per cent.

Field's Law proved pretty accurate. In the US the recorded rate of burglary doubled between 1960 and 1975 and then doubled again to 1990. The same thing happened a few years later in Britain and in most other industrial countries. Being burgled became part of life. And finally it inspired an effective response.

Even from me. One night in the early 1980s I woke up in darkness to find a stranger peering round the door. 'I'm a police officer,' he said unconvincingly. 'Get dressed, there's been a break-in.' I slammed on the lights, leapt out of bed, ran out to the hall in pursuit, and found myself, brightly lit at the head of the stairs, peering down at my open front door and out into the street. A

TV and video recorder were lying abandoned on the carpet. After that I changed the locks and bought an intruder alarm.

Lots of others did the same. For the first time, we, the ordinary people, behaved as the aristocracy had always done with valuables. We locked things up and, since we didn't have servants, we fitted alarms. There are no reliable figures about the sale of deadlocks, window guards, shutters and the like, but we can get an indication from the proliferation of intruder alarms from police reports. Such a thriving industry developed that by 1995 a quarter of all emergency calls made to police in Britain were prompted by burglar alarms. Most of these were false alarms, a huge distraction which has lessons in itself, but here was solid evidence that home-owners had at last been taking security precautions that were commensurate with their growing wealth.

As burglary peaked and then declined, Field's Law had to be revised; but the insight still corresponded to the facts. It had always envisaged that if a target is inaccessible, or property is properly protected, a crime will not occur. Felson had even used the word 'rational' about crime, in contrast to the theories about deviance and delinquency. So while traditional criminologists were at a loss to explain the steep fall in crime (so much so that many people denied for years that it was happening), those who saw the power of opportunity were vindicated. Sadly, almost no one took much notice.

Nonetheless the rate of reported burglaries, which had doubled in Britain between 1981 and 1993, halved in the next decade and continued to plunge at an increasing pace. The change was registered not just in police statistics but in insurance measures and large-scale studies of people's everyday experience. In 1995 the British Crime Survey reckoned there were 1,770,000 domestic burglaries in England and Wales; ten years later there were 733,000, a drop of almost 60 per cent. Significantly, this was accompanied by a rise in the proportion of failed burglaries, where a would-be intruder failed to gain entry. The equivalent US Department of Justice survey, the National Crime Victimization Survey (NCVS), recorded burglary victimisation rates falling from 11 per cent of households in 1973 to under 3 per cent of households three decades later. Similar falls were recorded in all industrialised countries from the late 1980s onwards.

There was a bleak and stubborn corollary to this success. As the middle classes bought their way out of victimisation, burglary became increasingly concentrated on the poor. But generally burglary declined. By 2000, the European Commission could report that: 'There is a remarkably sharp decrease of domestic burglary in many EU Member States. One of the main reasons for this spectacular fall is probably the influence of increased preventive behaviour among the population.'

We now take it for granted that there are national and inter-national security standards for doors and windows, for a whole range of locks and for burglar-proofing of new-build homes, and we scarcely notice the vast array of security gadgets on sale in the shops, or even the (uncounted) millions of CCTV units people are installing. Not all of this is welcome. The smartest precautions make dwellings feel like homes, not fortresses, but the penalty for having disposable wealth is that, if unguarded, it is indeed disposable.

BURGLAR ALARMS

Unless you had a watchman, animals were the only alarms until the early 1700s, when an English promoter called Tildesley thought to string a wire between a door and a set of chimes. His idea caught on and quickly spread to the colonies, where it was enlisted as perhaps the world's first mechanical bank alarm. In Plymouth, Massachusetts, a wire was rigged from the handle of the safe to the cashier's house next door.

By the 1820s the age of electricity had dawned and in 1852 an inventor near Boston called Albert Augustus Pope created an alarm which essentially set the standard for every system that followed. He fitted doors and windows with magnetic contacts and metal foil, all connected by a pair of insulated wires leading to a battery and a bell. A near neighbour, perhaps an associate or a rival, called G. F. Milliken soon came up with a more sophisticated version, and in 1857 Pope's patent was bought by Edwin Holmes, who improved it further and took it to market in New York, linking up with Alexander Graham Bell to pioneer centrally monitored alarms.

By the 1970s, transistors and integrated circuits allowed motion sensors to be added, and by the end of the twentieth century DIY alarm kits could be bought for £100, while professionally installed systems came with video options, wireless capabilities and inbuilt intelligence which could identify triggers, suppress false alarms and self-diagnose internal problems.

I do not for a moment say that security precautions are the only factor that has been at work. More focused policing no doubt had a role, and perhaps imprisonment had an impact too. That, though, is very much open to question.

Much has been made of the fact that from 1980 or thereabouts, embattled by crime, the US ratcheted up its punitive policies. Many people were adamant that this was the route to salvation, and for a while it looked like they were right. In two decades, America built dozens of new penitentiaries and tripled its prison population. The contrast with Britain was stark. In England and Wales the number of prison places increased by 50 per cent, but that was barely one-sixth of the pace in America and substantially less than the equivalent growth in crime. While the proportion of burglars imprisoned in America rose, the proportion imprisoned in Britain fell by a substantial margin. And while in 1981 the US burglary rate was slightly higher than in the UK, by 1996 the English burglary rate was more than double America's. On the face of it this was an intellectual coup for social conservatives: prison works, they said.

Had the story ended in 1991 or 1992, even the most resolute liberal would have been confounded. But, as we have seen, UK burglary rates soon fell too. And they did so without any substantial change in Britain's prison-building programme. All across Europe, whatever a country's penal policies, the trend was similar. With hindsight it is clear that on both sides of the pond there had to be some factor other than imprisonment at work, and whatever it was, it had been happening in America some five years in advance of Britain and Europe.

Of course it might well have been partly demographic and it could have been a social factor, but two things are for sure: burglary rates declined as investment in home security increased; and America was in the lead. Just as post-war fear of crime had gripped the US first, so US spending on protecting homes from burglary was ahead of the European curve. By the 1970s American householders were busily fitting intrusion detection, locks and reinforced doors, and the proportion of homes with alarms increased ten-fold between 1975 and 1985, after which US burglary began to level off and fall. The UK's home-security market boomed about ten years later and domestic burglary began to fall from its peak in 1993. Sometimes falls in crime could be matched to specific improvements in security. In the Netherlands, new building regulations led to a 50 per cent drop in burglaries of new homes compared to older ones.

Equally intriguing, there was a stark exception to the general trend of falling burglary victimisation. An international survey in 2005 found Danes had unusually few worries about burglary and consequently invested little in domestic security. By 2010 they were twice as likely to be burgled as their English, Dutch or German counterparts.

This is not definitive proof that security works better than anything else, but it does make a strong case. Nor is it to say that imprisoning burglars is wrong, especially for habitual offenders. Burglary often robs people of peace of mind as well as their possessions, removing their sense of being at ease in their own home. Justice may demand a harsh response. But the evidence suggests that, if we want to make a big difference to burglary rates, prevention is better than secure accommodation for offenders.

Car crime

Very early one morning in September 1927, a postal worker in Essex noticed something by the side of a country road and found a dead policeman. PC George Gutteridge had been shot four times in the face. The crime was eventually linked to the theft of a doctor's Morris Cowley motor car from Billericay, some ten miles away; it seemed that PC Gutteridge had stopped the driver and had started taking notes when he was murdered. The stolen vehicle was eventually discovered in south London together with dried blood and an empty cartridge case, and detectives soon suspected two local London car thieves. In a raid on their garage they recovered a Webley revolver whose breech block perfectly matched a scar on the ammunition. It was one of the first crimes solved by ballistic science and the outcome for the killers was described by the *Sunday Dispatch* as 'hanged by a microscope'.

What made things easier for the detectives was that vehicle crime was still rare in the inter-war years. There were only a million private cars in Britain in 1927, compared to more than 27 million today, so anyone coming home with a new motor would certainly attract attention. In any case, not many people could drive.

Car numbers declined in the Second World War, growing slowly in the 1950s and reaching 10 million in 1970, or one for every two households. That turned out to be the tipping point. Car theft suddenly boomed. Around a thousand cars a year were reported stolen in the 1920s, reaching 10,000 by 1958 and 20,000 in 1968; and then, suddenly, in 1969 thefts rocketed six-fold.

Political and social theorists might want to tell us that something must have happened in that time to breed more deviance and badness: less authority, less self-control, perhaps; or more unfairness and therefore less compliance. But the numbers add up to a different story, one that fits much better with Marcus Felson's description of crime as a largely rational reaction. Half the homes in Britain now had hundreds or thousands of pounds' worth of property sitting out on the street unguarded. It was temptation on an ostentatious scale. For young men, in particular, it was a grand seduction.

It was also staggeringly easy. My first car, a Mini, had almost no security at all. Admittedly there was a lock, but so flimsy you could force it with one hand. Failing that, the sliding window could easily be prised open and the door would unlock from inside. To start the car without a key, you simply touched two wires together behind the centre console and you were off.

It was known as twocking – taking without the owner's consent. By 1980 there were 15 million registered cars and a third of a million recorded thefts; by 1990 there were 20 million cars and half a million thefts. To put that another way, the annual risk of a vehicle being stolen was one in a thousand when PC

Gutteridge was killed, and one in thirty when twocking reached its peak in 1993.

Then, like burglary, the problem started to decline. Why?

This is where social theories hit another problem. Community divisions like income inequality were growing under Margaret Thatcher and John Major, not diminishing as liberal theory would require for crime to fall. Right-wing beliefs also faced a contradiction. The proportion of car thieves going to prison was falling fast. There had been no return to hanging, birching or religious observance, and more and more children were born out of wedlock. Yet car theft tumbled. Within ten years recorded numbers halved, and by 2011 twocking had dipped below 100,000, the lowest figure since 1968.

In the US, too, car stealing fell at the same rate, but, in contrast to what happened with burglary, the timing of the change matched that in Britain. By 2011 auto thefts had receded to the levels last recorded in 1967.

So what was happening on both sides of the Atlantic?

For once politicians were involved in wholesale and dramatically successful crime reduction – and oddly, they have never had much credit. In Germany in the 1960s the federal government forced manufacturers to fit steering wheel locks, after which car theft began to stabilise. The US followed suit a decade later with similar results. Another decade on, Margaret Thatcher came to power in Britain as car crime was reaching outrageous levels, becoming the biggest category of crime and representing almost a quarter of all recorded offences. To make things worse, joyriding by teenagers in stolen cars was beginning to make embarrassing headlines across the world. In exasperation, and egged on by her Home Secretary, Kenneth Baker, the Prime Minister summoned the motor manufacturers to Downing Street and demanded that they sort the problem out.

As it happens, the executives were open to the idea that they could. After decades of shrugging off responsibility for road deaths – saying it was all the drivers' faults – the industry was scrambling to make cars safer. Car safety testing was becoming well established both in Europe and in the United States, and the UK government had set targets to get road fatalities down. Leaders like Peter Batchelor, who ran GM's Vauxhall brand, readily saw crime's parallel with safety: one could go on blaming the thieves, or, as with vehicle safety, they could do something about it.

Car-makers began to mend the vulnerabilities in their products – and being multinational businesses, their solutions proved international too. Immobilisers, intruder alarms, central locking, sophisticated keys, tougher door and boot designs, better identification markings for critical components, stronger window rims and laminated glazing were introduced, and all of them had an immediate effect – especially immobilisers, which prevented hot-wiring of the ignition. To protect vehicles from break-ins, the manufacturers began to fit deadlocks to doors and glove compartments and to build in stealable components like radios. Third-party suppliers came up with vehicle tracking devices and a growing range of options to protect older cars, including clamps for steering wheels and pedals.

Though Mrs Thatcher's intervention marked a tipping point, there were profound commercial pressures too. Consumer journals led by *What Car?* magazine began rating security alongside its reviews of comfort, road holding and acceleration. The vehicle leasing industry started to issue league tables of the most stolen cars, and the UK government published its own car theft index, naming and shaming the worst top ten by make and model. In 1992, insurance companies began demanding rigorous security standards known as Thatcham, after the Berkshire village which houses the insurance industry's research centre.

The mid-1990s were watershed years, with offences levelling off and starting to tumble. In little over a decade, car crime plummeted in England and Wales by around two-thirds. The biggest falls were in joyriding, no doubt because the amateur car thief was more easily thwarted, but a 50 per cent drop of permanent losses showed professional thieves were often foiled as well. The government was so emboldened that in 1998 it set up a vehicle action task force chaired by a senior executive from Ford and gave it an aggressive target of cutting vehicle crime by a further 30 per cent within five years.

New vehicle security was not the only cause of this success. In Britain, as elsewhere, the police, local authorities and government launched campaigns to remind people not to leave possessions unattended. There were highly publicised crackdowns on car thieves which made drivers more security aware. Safer car park schemes were launched with new guidelines for car park design. New controls were introduced for vehicle scrap merchants and licence plate suppliers.

Could social, economic and demographic factors have been responsible for this dramatic turnaround? Of course; but similar changes would need to have taken place throughout the industrialised world. In any case they could not explain an especially remarkable feature of this crime revolution.

Instead of the newest, most desirable, cars being most targeted for theft, it became the older ones. There developed a dramatic disparity in a vehicle's susceptibility to crime according to its date of manufacture. In the year 2006, when the Home Office last published its annual car theft index, fewer than 3 per cent of new cars were reported stolen, compared with 30 per cent of those built in 1989. A similar phenomenon has happened everywhere. Sweden has a real-time vehicle crime database which you can filter for age of manufacture; the old cars, the defenceless ones, fill the screen.

The eclipse of opportunist crime will never stop all offending. Determined thieves found ways of stealing car keys, including poking fishing rods through letterboxes, and there was a reported rise in taking keys by intimidation or by force, but the victimisation rates represent a tiny fraction of those at the peak of the great auto theft bonanza.

As Ron Clarke, Pat Mayhew, Mike Hough and Marcus Felson had predicted, crime flourished when easy targets were available and shrank when they were not.

It needs to be said again that synchronicity does not prove cause. It could just be a fluke that rising opportunity matched rising crime and it could be coincidence that cutting opportunity matched cuts in crime. But no other explanation tallies with the facts. And none other works in every Western country regardless of its political leanings or its judicial policies.

Crime requires more than a predisposition to offend. It will flourish when we make it easy and shrivel when we make it hard.

3

VIOLENCE

*I think it's one of the scars in our culture that we have
too high an opinion of ourselves. We align ourselves
with the angels instead of the higher primates.*
– Angela Carter

If opportunity makes the thief, what about motives for other
crimes? What about wild and destructive offences which seem
to have no purpose at all? What about violence, anger, revenge,
jealousy, visceral excitement, lust or simple bloody-mindedness?
Surely offending through this stuff is the preserve of criminals;
whatever the provocation, ordinary folks just don't do that sort
of thing.

Actually, they do. And Chapter 7 will demonstrate how even
viciousness can be shockingly normal. Wherever you are on the
spectrum between angel and psychopath, the way you express
yourself is hugely dependent on what you encounter in your daily
life. Let's spin through a few, counterintuitive, examples.

First, an offence that tends to sicken people, one where we take it
for granted there is something wrong with the offender, and where
the term 'deviant' really comes into its own: child pornography.

Then consider a crime that shamed Britain in the eyes of the
world and involved gangs and seemingly mindless aggression:
football hooliganism.

Of course, there are many crimes that straddle the border between theft and violence, so let's look at mugging.

And finally, let's see how circumstance affects the big one: murder.

Child pornography

Human sexuality is far more versatile than polite conversation usually admits. Since sex is something our species uniquely does in private – most of the time, at any rate – other people's fetishes easily seem mysterious. One man or woman's alternative lifestyle is another's idea of depravity. Yet we can almost all agree on one thing, and we usually do so with disgust: adult sexual interest in children is not just wrong but perverted.

So can child sex crime be traced back to individual failings, or might there be some other cause?

The trouble is that it is extremely hard to get reliable statistics. Child victims rarely tell. The great scandals that have rocked the Catholic Church are testament to that. And when children do tell, it usually has to be coaxed out of them. Although surveys suggest many adults were abused when they were little, definitions of abuse vary, actual figures for paedophilia are scant, and what numbers we have tend to reflect the amount of effort police, social workers and researchers put into investigating the phenomenon.

Thus, even though we are nowadays acutely aware of the dangers (some say we have overreacted and are overprotective), we have no idea if the problem has grown or retreated. Certainly no one could sensibly argue that adult sex with children is a modern invention.

But there is a new phenomenon of sex crime involving children: a huge surge in child pornography. And, though we can only measure the amount of it quite crudely, it is quite clear that its extent has exploded recently.

There is a long history of erotic literature and drawings involving children, and the invention of photography created a whole new trade in pornographic pictures. But by the 1970s the commercial market was being harried by the authorities and production by the big suppliers, Denmark and Sweden, was driven underground. In 1982 the US General Accounting Office was able to report that federal agencies no longer considered child pornography a high priority.

Yet over the next three decades there was a vast resurgence. Had morals changed? Had an underprivileged underclass discovered a new way of escaping the humdrum? Had some mutation created a new paedophile gene? Who can say? What we can tell is that the new wave of child pornography grew in uncanny parallel with the internet. The web provided the perfect means of exchange: quick and cheap to upload in vast quantities, and easy to access privately and anonymously with the click of a button, even from one's bedroom. Anyone who had ever had dark fantasies about children could now indulge themselves with – so it was believed for many years – no chance of being caught. It is impossible to know how many people access the stuff, but when, in 2004, BT first introduced filters for child porn sites, they recorded a quarter of a million attempts to access blocked material in their first three weeks.

The supply is still substantial. The British-based Internet Watch Foundation has reported a huge decline in criminal sites since active site-blocking measures became routine. Even so, in 2011 they discovered 12,966 URLs that contained child sexual abuse hosted on 1,595 domains worldwide. There was also an increase in the proportion of videos and photos featuring brutality. Police and other authorities have often found personal computers with thousands of pornographic images of children, sometimes scrupulously catalogued.

The web not only made obscenity accessible, it did something more insidious. It lent child porn an air of normality. If all this material was available, then presumably lots of people must be viewing it, so individuals could excuse themselves for looking, and could rationalise the fact that many (though not all) images must have involved mistreatment or actual child assault.

Thereby the web created a new market. In the old days you had to be committed to seek out child pornography through the furtive cottage industry. But the internet sucked people in. And, intriguingly, it did so even if they had little interest to begin with. We know this from an ingenious experiment by two British researchers, Christina Demetriou and Andrew Silke. The pair of them set up an internet sting called the Cyber Magpie. Their website attracted people with terms like 'freeware', or 'free soft-ware', and when surfers got there they were offered links not just to shareware but to soft and hard pornography. By tracking the key words some 800 visitors had used to find the site, the inves-tigators were able to show that only twenty-six had previously been looking for pornography – but temptation is a powerful thing, even to those without much prior motivation. Having seen the opportunity, almost 500 clicked on the option for hard porn. Soft porn was second favourite, while freeware, the thing that everyone had been looking for, got fewest clicks of all. Freed from inhibition, people take paths they never had intended.

Commercial pornographers are well aware of this. The Internet Watch Foundation notes that a regular feature of the industry is that innocent domains are hijacked so as to increase the likelihood of online users stumbling across child sex material, presumably in the hope of them becoming titillated and then intrigued.

Perhaps the internet is a portal to hell, or simply proof of human curiosity. Either way, while the Cyber Magpie links were bogus, elsewhere on the web an inquisitive visitor might be confronted with all sorts of forbidden fruit, as tempting as the apple was for Eve. We are all just clicks away from a whole range of sexual images: of women, men, bondage, sadism, fetishism, and sometimes naked children too.

CHILD ATTRACTION

Of course, access to lewd pictures does not on its own explain how children's bodies, especially prepubescent ones, can come to be sexually arousing. But maybe that needs little explanation. Whatever our own taboos, sexual attraction to children has been quite normal in many cultures. Pederasty (love of boys) was a common feature of ancient Greece and remained so in many parts of the world until quite recent times. By the nineteenth century in England, when the age of consent for a girl was twelve or thirteen, predation on children was so rampant that Victorians had all sorts of euphemisms like 'ruination' and 'corruption', and Parliament finally enacted a string of legislation to try to deal with it. The more people looked, the more they discovered, so that while in 1800 around a quarter of sex cases brought to court involved a victim aged under thirteen, sample records show the proportion rose to half by 1830 and three-quarters by 1900. In colonial days, the fact that settlers disapproved of sex involving children did not mean that they never indulged. While the Child Marriage Restraint Act, imposed by Britain on India in 1929, set a minimum age of fourteen, several accounts by maritime voyagers relate how Western sailors readily had union with children when sex was offered. And today what we regard as a terrible crime others see as normal. I vividly remember how a Maasai tribesman in East Africa was reluctant to introduce me to his new bride

because he knew that as a tourist I was likely to be shocked
that she was twelve. In rural parts of Zambia it is not uncom-
mon for children to start having sex from the age of five, and
in several countries girls are married off at the age of seven,
often to much older men.

So the internet was new but the attraction it presented was not,
and it ensnared many people who otherwise would have had
no chance to experience anything like it. It was a classic case of
circumstance creating crime and thereby creating criminals.

No other explanation seems plausible. Perhaps in theory web
access might simply have coincided with an increase in sexual
deviation caused by changes in social sensibilities or some other
corrupting influence on personal morality. But there is no sign of
any changes in attitudes to child sex abuse other than growing
awareness of the problem. The outrage it provokes suggests social
values are as uncompromising as they have ever been.

Bear in mind the people caught for downloading images tend
to appear normal in most other respects. US studies of offenders
all point to the same conclusions: few had previous sex convictions and as a whole they were much more educationally and
socio-economically diverse than people convicted of child moles-
tation. When British psychologists compared internet offenders
with contact abusers, they found surfers tended to be under-
assertive rather than manipulative, and kept to fantasy because
they could readily empathise with victims. The fact that many
abusers are into kiddie-porn does not mean pornography addicts
are into abuse.

But even if all those child-sex-hungry people were out there
anyway, already calibrated to be aroused by little bodies, it was the
internet that gave substance to their propensities. If we want to

curb the trade in explicit images there have been far more effective ways of reducing downloads than changing people's sexual predilections. We shall see how the problem has been tackled in Chapter 20.

Football violence

The fact that circumstances help determine how people behave does not deny the importance of personal morality. But it does suggest most remedies to crime are closer to the action than are aspirations for moral revival or social reform. And it does imply that policing needs to be more strategic, aimed at prevention rather than counting the rates of arrest. Detection is only one weapon in an extensive armoury and, ideally, when used it should be calculated not piecemeal, disrupting trust between conspirators, targeting key enablers and removing prolific offenders. So let's see an example of how a series of clever interventions worked. The challenge was a form of violence for which Britain, and England in particular, became notorious.

Football violence is an example of what is sometimes called 'expressive crime', like joyriding, graffiti and 'happy-slapping', where the motive is 'sensation gathering' and where there is no economic benefit to the offender. Old-fashioned criminologists, who think situational crime prevention is 'sociologically deracinated' (yes, really) and only works with 'shallow end' acquisitive crimes, have argued that these 'culture of now' offences are the result of an increasingly selfish consumer society and are immune to situational interventions. Far from it. There is a new breed of crime researchers – I call them crime scientists – who see past all this (see Chapter 15). In a forceful rebuttal, one of them, Graham Farrell, has pointed out that expressive crimes all have their own rewards just like any other voluntary act: the fun of joyriding, the thrill of violence, the gratification of pornography or the self-publicising buzz of graffiti ('there is no little irony in the fact that graffiti artists use signature tags to retain their informal intellectual ownership'). This is why systematically obliterating graffiti is effective. This is why joyriding has been thwarted by steering column locks and immobilisers. And this is how football violence was tamed.

A GOOD KICKING

Football was associated with hooliganism from its beginnings in the thirteenth century, so much so that by 1314 the Mayor of London commanded 'upon pain of imprisonment, that such games shall not be practiced henceforth within this city'. Soccer bloodshed, riots and prohibitions were a sporadic feature of every subsequent century. In 1909 the pitch at Hampden Park in Glasgow was destroyed by 6,000 rampaging fans; in the 1950s football supporters wrecked several trains. But violence became more common in the 1960s as more fans travelled to away matches, and it often spilled into the streets. In 1968 a new Public Order Act allowed for offenders to be banned from football grounds, but disorder grew in the 1970s and '80s, and became more organised with gangs of football hooligans like Chelsea's Headhunters, Manchester United's Red Amy, Millwall's Bushwackers and West Ham's Inter City Firm. Racism was rife, fights and pitch invasions were commonplace, and though the football authorities put up fences to segregate rival fans, essentially they shrugged their shoulders and blamed the problems on society.

Other countries experienced even greater problems,

especially in Argentina, where between 1925 and 2010 some 250 fans were murdered by gangs called *barras bravas*. International fixtures led to more than 300 deaths in a riot between Argentine and Peruvian fans in 1964, and even sparked a brief war between El Salvador and Honduras in 1969.

But it was the English supporters who became the most notorious. Football violence became known as the English disease. Every major stadium would seethe with aggression and reverberate to wounding chants, foul language and screamed obscenities. Even when supporters were miles away from the match they often acted as though immune from normal stand-ards of behaviour. Such tribalism was officially countenanced and even encouraged. With the arrival of television, football had become very big business indeed and the industry was quite content to be riding on the back of a tiger. Public address announcements were openly one-sided. Visiting fans were belittled, given the worst seats and sometimes excluded from seeing scoreboards or information signs. A great football arena was regarded as one that encourages a sense of confrontation, so the best ones would amplify the noise and the excitement with what's often called the Wembley roar.

The game still struggles with many of these faults. Even so, what followed was a remarkable turnaround. It transformed English fans from being the most reviled to among the most respected in Europe, and it had less to do with changing the nature of the football supporters, or their circumstances at home, than with making the game itself less conducive to aggression.

It took a catastrophe to force a change of heart. In 1985, at the dilapidated Heysel stadium in Brussels, English and Italian crowds gathering for a European Cup match traded insults then missiles, and just before kick-off Liverpool supporters stormed their Juventus rivals. In the resulting stampede thirty-nine people died and 600 more were injured. The British Prime Minister Margaret Thatcher was roused to outrage, and instead of seeking to defend English football she demanded that English clubs should be withdrawn from European competition. Emboldened, the European and world football authorities, UEFA and FIFA, banned England from all international competitions. It was a punishment that ended a golden age for English soccer clubs in European championships and from which they did not recover for twenty years. For the first time football understood that it had the power and responsibility to put its own house in order. The industry could go on insisting that the violence was symptomatic of wider social problems, but that was not the point. The point now was to stop it.

Reform was accelerated four years later when the Hillsborough disaster in Sheffield claimed ninety-six lives – again involving Liverpool FC, and again resulting from inadequate crowd control and stadium design. This time there was no hooliganism but the subsequent Taylor Report led to a substantial rebuilding of major football stands and a big rethink of policing. Clubs were obliged to apply for licences and to demonstrate they had effective control of crowds and, mostly because of changes forced on management by its own fecklessness, English football slowly regained an honourable reputation. Each club pays for policing and hundreds of its own stewards, along with CCTV control rooms, and is responsible for marshalling and controlling its own supporters even at away matches. Clubs can be fined, and in theory could have points deducted or even face bans if there are serious episodes of violence. This is not to downplay the hugely skilful public order capabilities developed by the police, nor the enormous efforts they have made to find and catch the worst of the football hooligans – banning orders have proved very important. It has been a partnership success. But on average there has been only one arrest per match, mostly away from the grounds themselves, and the classic law 'n' order solution, prison, has been at best peripheral. As every English soccer aficionado knows, the most important steps were taken by the football clubs themselves.

There is still a long way to go. The atmosphere at major matches is far from sportsmanlike, with jeers and personal abuse for opposing players, and many fans still indulge en masse in cruel songs and disgusting chants against individuals. There is still an ugly thuggishness by some beyond the stadium, with unprovoked attacks which can cause grievous injury. In a test case Leeds United shrugged off responsibility to contribute to policing outside its grounds in a worrying High Court decision which may prompt other clubs to set the clock back too. There is also a problem of displacement, with vulgarity and violence shifting to railway trains bringing in the fans for major fixtures, and racism is common at some junior-level matches. The remedy is simple: the big clubs should have exemplary expectations of civilised behaviour and should lose championship points whenever their fans misbehave. It is a straightforward self-policing mechanism already adopted in principle by the football authorities. For example, Article 58 of FIFA's disciplinary code allows that points can be deducted for racist abuse or that matches have to be played behind closed doors. Society may have to oblige the clubs to act more decisively, since essentially the football industry still believes it profits from tribal and edgy supporters.

But by 2007 the mantle of soccer's bad boy had passed elsewhere, notably to Italy, which lost its bid to host the 2012 European championships as a penalty for appalling violence and corruption. 'The ugly face that Italian football has shown the world recently', wrote the newspaper *L'Unità*, 'has been duly punished.' Bit by bit, with two steps forward one step back, the industry is cleaning up its act.

Mugging

Violence is not a discrete class of offending. A normally peaceable thief may fight if flight is blocked. There are offenders who bully and cajole but rarely use physical force. And there are those for whom violence is just part of a wider repertoire. All these came together in the 1970s to cause a good deal of public dismay and a great deal of media outrage. At first mugging was almost universally seen to be a symptom of social corruption – as usual, Marxists blamed capitalism and conservatives despaired about failing morals. But with the benefit of hindsight, this was an example of how circumstance collided with personal and social factors to create a perfect storm. The rise of mugging, and its eventual loss of momentum, surely owed at least as much to the temptations of an age as to its temperament.

At a time when mass-market goods were lining shopkeepers' shelves and mass-market cars were lining the pavements, so mass-market products were lining people's pockets. Unprecedented in history was the sheer quantity of stuff to steal from ordinary people in the street.

STAND AND DELIVER

The combination of treasure and isolated places has always invited danger. Highway robbery is as old as travel. Even the current slang for it goes back at least to the eighteenth century. The term mugging was adapted from expressions like 'hitting

someone in the mug', which came from the fashion of deco-
rating tankards with faces, as with Toby jugs.

But to be mugged did not necessarily mean that the victim
was physically assaulted; he could 'be a mug' in the sense of
being in the wrong place and without protection for his money
or his valuables.

In the strange way that criminals sometimes become romanticised, especially when stealing from the rich, real muggers
like Dick Turpin became celebrities, and imaginary ones like
Robin Hood became legends. What is for sure is that the risk
was very real. A Swiss visitor to England in 1726 noted how
street robbers could be merciless to those who tried to defend
themselves, although 'I have been told that some highwaymen
are quite polite and generous.'

Anyone with any wealth was susceptible to what were
known as 'footpad' ambushes in town and to highway robbery
in the countryside. Horseback heists gave way to arterial road
improvements in the eighteenth century and the last recorded
mounted hold-up in England took place in 1831. But, as the
urban middle classes expanded, there were garish tales of
street attacks in the big cities, leading to various scares about
garrotters and other ruffians in the Victorian era and well into
Edwardian times.

The modern epidemic, like the word mugging itself, is often
assumed to have been imported from New York. In fact, the
British and US experiences of street crime were rather different.
New York's was born out of a wholesale breakdown in civic order.
Despite the general economic boom, the 1960s and '70s were bad
for the Big Apple, with fiscal irresponsibility and waves of public
sector strikes compounding the loss of textile manufacturing,

shipping and a naval dockyard. Infrastructure decayed, a million residents moved out of town and racial tensions flared into riots. Strip clubs, pimps and prostitutes colonised Times Square, and throughout Manhattan, Brooklyn and the Bronx there was a collapse of trust in policing and municipal authority. Every sort of crime exploded, and revival of the old word 'mugging' conflated a whole series of them into what sounded like a single offence, from purse snatching to armed hold-ups. The term also had strong racial overtones: the perpetrators were overwhelmingly black. In short, mugging came to epitomise everything that was rotten in Gotham and alarming to the middle classes. It seemed a classic proof that crime is caused by lack of social cohesion and/or lack of discipline.

We will return to the story of New York because the received wisdoms about its stunning recovery from muggings and other crimes – which some people insist Britain should learn from – are partly based on myth. (British pundits, especially conservative ones, have a propensity to look to America rather than elsewhere in the world, as though they are rather in awe of it.)

Britain is not America and London is not New York. Mugging was only noticed as a problem as Britons looked in dismay at what was happening across the pond. With hindsight, there had been a clear upward trend in robberies starting about 1955, and since the early 1960s the Metropolitan Police had kept separate records of 'robbery in the open following sudden attack'. Even so, these only accounted for 3 or 4 per cent of recorded crime and when, in 1973, 'muggings' first made headlines, the scale of the problem lagged far behind the US.

Thus many criminologists tried to dismiss it all as 'moral panic'. But they were victims of their own innumeracy; even their own figures showed the problem was growing at a rate unprecedented in the twentieth century. Also, much to the discomfort of white liberals, in London as in New York the assailants were disproportionately black. (Actually, most were specifically from West Indian backgrounds, rather than from African or southeast Asian ones, though few people drew such distinctions.)

By the 1980s, race had become a core policing issue, with riots in Brixton and what police conceded were 'no-go' areas in other parts of London. By now mugging was seen almost universally as a malaise of disillusionment and social disenchantment. To a large extent that must be right; and yet one aspect in particular didn't fit that simple explanation. The targets for mugging were not chosen randomly as some sort of lashing out against authority. Nor did they conform to the stereotype. The typical victim of reported crimes was male, defenceless and had something worth stealing. In other words, the motives were largely cogent.

It turned out that the worst of the UK's street crime phenomenon lagged almost two decades behind the US, with reported cases doubling in the 1990s when they were sharply declining in America. Seeing London's crime rate rise as New York's fell, it became fashionable for commentators to berate Britain for moral decay and to criticise the police for 'throwing in the sponge'. It failed to occur to these experts that most crime would soon be tumbling in London too. Even so, street theft remained an obstinate challenge.

It was also a largely juvenile business. Of street crimes reported to police, more than two-thirds of typical assailants were teenagers, many aged between eleven and fifteen and some were under ten. Almost a quarter of the victims were also under fifteen, and nearly half were under twenty. In reality most victims and offenders were probably younger still – surveys of schoolchildren suggest crime among young people is largely unreported.

There is nothing new in principle about unsupervised children oppressing their peers. Back in the 1960s when I was in my early teens I was waylaid several times and had my pocket money stolen, and in one case I was intimidated into giving up my prized bag of thick-cut fries as I emerged from the chippie. Such humiliations were never reported to the police, and only rarely to parents. It was known as bullying. Kids were expected to butch up.

But towards the end of the twentieth century British youngsters generally carried more than a few pennies or deep-fried potatoes. From the age of ten or so, boys and girls were likely to have expensive watches, classy jackets, cool trainers and the latest gadgets. They were especially vulnerable on their way home from school, and all the more so after mobile phones became the rage. All the ingredients for trouble had come together: potential offenders and tempting targets in the absence of capable guardians. And as the emboldened bullies grew up they stayed out late at night and bullied adults, with the result that after the turn of the millennium a quarter of victims were in their twenties and some were older still. Here the pickings were richer and when the pubs closed the quarry was often tipsy or drunk.

Once the genie is out of the bottle, it can be hard to get it back in. Violence can become fashionable in its own right, and although street robberies are mostly about acquiring ready cash and status-enhancing consumer goods, muggings became status-enhancing in themselves. Violence, with the adrenalin rush from overpowering victims and the excitement of triumph, trophy and escape, brings out the hunting instinct.

That goes down well in some cultures, and there is no doubt that culture plays a big role. While in some ways British mugging was home-grown, there is one big transatlantic similarity. Even at the peak of street robberies in the mid-2000s only about a quarter of the offenders were white. Perhaps unsurprisingly, different cultures can exist in crime as in anything else, an issue we will explore in Chapter 13.

But cultures are hard to change. Circumstances change all the time.

All of which leaves the question: why, having surged, did mugging start to fade? More specifically, once it had faded, why for a while did it then peak again? There is probably no single answer. Despite targeted police attention, detection rates rarely rose to 10 per cent, and there are no obvious social or economic factors that would explain the general trend or the double rise and dip. But there is a more prosaic possibility. By the turn of the millennium, the market for the proceeds of muggings was becoming sated. Almost every teenager had trainers and a Sony Walkman. After 2001, street robberies began a sharp decline. Then, in 2003, the market for mobile phones exploded – some half a billion were shipped worldwide that year – and the following year they were spreading rapidly to teenagers. Mobile phone crime is a remarkable story in its own right and we will come to it shortly; but at the same time the Apple iPod hit the shops and in 2004 robberies surged again. By 2012 there were 10,000 mobile phone thefts reported to the Metropolitan Police, two-thirds of them taken from children aged between thirteen and sixteen.

We had made fashion victims of our kids.

Murder

And so let's turn to the big one, the quintessential crime, the one that evokes horror and fascination in roughly equal measure. There is so much written about homicide that one might expect people to know a lot about it. But most of what we read or see is invented to feed our appetite for thrills. It is about as real as the killing of Dr Black by Colonel Mustard with lead piping in the drawing room. In Britain we produce far more fiction about murder every year than there are victims. Even the true stuff in the papers is more dramatic than the dismal reality, which is to say that journalistic clichés propel some sorts of murder into the news and ignore the rest. Most killings owe less to conspiracy than to happenstance and rage. Half of them are hot-headed, through quarrel, revenge or loss of temper.

Even so, murder is the ultimate crime and many feel it deserves the ultimate deterrent. It takes a special nastiness to kill. *Or does it?* How much of homicide is down to wicked people, and how much to context? A transatlantic comparison is revealing.

On the face of it, Americans are decidedly unpleasant. In the first decade of the new millennium, they murdered about 15,000 of each other every year, which is more than five fatalities for every 100,000 citizens. The average in England and Wales was 810, a rate of 1.5 per 100,000. In both cases murder rates have dropped significantly, but the good folk in America remain well over three times more homicidal. Why? Are Yanks intrinsically nastier than Brits? Or do they have more opportunities to kill? America's big gun lobbyists are convinced it is the former: 'A gun is a tool – the problem is the criminal,' says the National Rifle Association.

Accordingly, it would be revealing if we could take guns, especially handguns, out of the equation and compare the results. Well, in a way we can.

Two-thirds of US murders are by gunfire. In 2010 around 9,000 people were shot dead in America compared to forty firearm deaths in England and Wales and a handful in Scotland. Those proportions remains consistent year on year. But let's just focus on other killings in which no guns were involved, mostly through stabbings, blunt objects, fists, feet or strangulations. There were 4,220 non-firearm homicides in the US versus 559 in England and Wales and 98 in Scotland. If those figures are adjusted for population differences, Americans are just one-third more murderous than the English and a third less so than the Scots (738 US murders compared to 559 in England and Wales and 1,007 population-adjusted killings in Scotland). Suddenly the Americans appear to be very much more civilised.

The American debate about guns is noisy, with each side guilty of selective reasoning and cherry-picking evidence (see below). The plain fact is Americans have probably balanced their safety and liberty as best they can. The issue is so much a matter of faith, politics, lifestyle and vested interest that if the Second Amendment was repealed, millions of Americans would disobey. Remember Prohibition. But it does seem improbable that if one *could* eliminate firearms Americans would find other ways to murder each other in similar colossal numbers. As the actress Jodie Foster has drily observed, you can kill a person using a gun with less effort than it takes to chew gum.

TRIGGER FACTORS

As US gun proponents point out, firearms crime was comparatively rare in Britain when gun ownership was virtually unrestricted. But such historical analogies are treacherous. Flintlocks are hardly comparable to automatic pistols, and almost as soon as modern handguns were invented they *were* controlled. The only exception was at a time of civil war.

Britons were obliged to keep arms in protection of the realm at least since Henry II's Assize of Arms promulgation of 1181. However, these were mostly cudgels, swords or pikes. The first rudimentary handgun appeared in England around 1375 and the first crude rifles were issued to the Yeomen of the Guard in about 1475, along with bows and arrows. Sporting firearms appeared in the 1530s and quickly provoked the first gun controls. The carrying of 'pocket dags' was forbidden in 1541, and an Act of 1671 disarmed all but the very wealthy. This was soon reversed in reaction to the Catholic struggle for power. In 1689 the Bill of Rights encouraged Protestants to keep arms for self-defence – a hundred years before the Second Amendment to the US Constitution confirmed such rights for Americans.

Relaxed attitudes to guns in Britain persisted through the nineteenth century, until the effects of Samuel Colt's invention of the revolver began to spread to the UK, soon inspiring the Webley. The change from one- or two-shot weapons to the five- or six-shot revolver was the most radical advance in history in civilian firepower. Meanwhile mass production made handguns far more readily available.

From 1903 onwards, successive British governments tried to curb guns, ostensibly because of crime and accidents, though also out of fears of anarchists and revolutionaries, and worries over public order. Firearm suicides fell immediately the controls were introduced, though the effect on homicides is unknown. Concern increased when millions of young men were demobbed after the First World War, and the UK's Firearms Act of 1920 required gun owners to be licensed, though even then an acceptable reason for keeping a gun was as 'protection against thieves and burglars'. Thereafter pistols became a rarity.

There was a further clampdown after the Second World War when Home Guard guns were rounded up and combatants returning from abroad were made to relinquish weapons and were searched for contraband ones. Nonetheless, the recorded rate of homicide rose rapidly in England and Wales, falling back after about ten years (347 in 1947 to a low of 265 in 1961). After the 1960s, when guns were used in crime they were often sawn-off shotguns – cut-down long-barrelled weapons designed for country sports – and then increasingly airguns (these sometimes accounted for 40 per cent of firearm offences) or imitation weapons (about 25 per cent).

Mostly because of airguns and imitation weapons, recorded firearms offences steadily rose in England and Wales to 2003, since when they have fallen year after year back to the level of 1990. By 2011 gun crime in Scotland had fallen to a 32-year low.

Thus, all in all, British history does not make a compelling case for firearm libertarians.

To cite weapons as a cause of murder is not to deny that personal and social factors can be a big part of the equation. Violence tends to affect poorer areas disproportionately and people whose sometimes limited self-control has been further weakened by alcohol or drugs. This is why the homicide rate in Russia is comparable to that in the United States and why murder in Scotland is so prolific. Four out of every five Scots charged with homicide are drunk or drugged at the time of the killing. But even drunks usually need a weapon in order to kill, which in Scotland is mostly a knife. Sharp instruments also account for a third of all killings in England and Wales, which is why the authorities have been so keen to restrict knives and even, as we shall see, to change glassware in pubs. Murder is hardly ever the conspiracy beloved of screenwriters and journalists. It is mostly the result of violence that has gone too far, 'where the difference between life and death depends on the intervention of a bystander, the accuracy of a blow, the weight of a frying pan, the speed of an ambulance or the availability of a trauma centre'. It is dangerous to have *any* weapon at hand when people quarrel, especially when it can be used without much reflection or endeavour.

Thus, even with murder it is not enough for an assailant to have the will, or even the tantrum; he or she also needs the means. Just as with acquisitive crimes, there is more to be done than arresting our way out of trouble when it comes to crimes of passion and downright irrationality. We can remove or restrict the things that enable harm.

4

THE SOCIAL THEORIES OF CRIME 1: POVERTY

Seven sins and seven wonders of the world

Thieves were rare in the Ramtops, where people weren't rich enough to afford them.
– *Mort, A Discworld Novel* by Terry Pratchett

Instinctively, almost everyone thinks poverty, or at least relative poverty, is the prime cause of crime. This is especially true for the liberal left, for whom it has been an article of faith, a belief that has been endorsed by most criminologists notwithstanding the sometimes contradictory assumption that criminals are deviant. If the left is right, as it were, then in theory we have at our disposal a real weapon against crime, albeit involving massive social engineering: if we cut income inequality, we can cut rates of offending. This is one of the justifications claimed for tax-and-spend redistributive policies, but it was always one of the incentives for philanthropic social policies proposed by reformers like Charles Dickens and famously summed up by his American contemporary, Robert Charles Winthrop: 'The poor must be wisely visited and liberally cared for, so that mendicity shall not be tempted into mendacity, nor want exasperated into crime.' Even right-wingers and fiscal conservatives who are viscerally opposed to subsidies at heart share in the assumption that the poor are somehow dangerous. *Fear* of the poor is one of the most powerful reasons that middle-class folk seek to live in middle-class districts and avoid what they see as perilous sink estates.

It seems logical, even romantic, that poor people would rebel at the unfairness of the way the world is organised. The idea conjures up an image of teeming real-life Robin Hoods. In fact, of course, most crime is suffered by the poor and not the wealthy. More surprisingly, perhaps, there is no correlation between a society's experience of crime and its sense of fairness. In a poll of 12,000 people in twenty-three countries, Greece emerged as the country with most grievances against the affluent, with over 90 per cent believing the rich did not deserve their wealth; whereas almost two-thirds of Australians thought they did. Yet Greece has one of the lowest crime rates and Australia one of the highest.

Plainly there is a link between poverty and crime, or at least the sort of blue-collar crime that fills the newspapers and prisons. The police spend most of their crime-fighting careers pursuing people who dwell in social housing, and our prisons are filled with society's losers as a result. But, equally plainly, the relationship between wealth and crime is far from straightforward. In fact, curiously, the link has more to do with affluence than destitution.

Sadly I was not the first to ponder this, since the man who did won a Nobel Prize. Gary Becker, a professor of economics, had the insight in the 1960s, in his case brought on by want of a New York parking space. One day he was late to test a student at Columbia and opted to park illegally, reckoning his chance of getting caught was low enough to make the risk worthwhile. As he walked to the exam it occurred to him that it was odd that economists had not considered this before: crime often makes sense. He wondered whether criminals do probability analysis. In fact that was the first question he asked his unfortunate student in the oral. History does not relate how the scholar fumbled for an answer, but Professor Becker went on to do some serious research. He quickly realised that if you commit a major crime, the police will throw the book at you; but for most offences, the mass transgressions from parking to shoplifting, burglary or car theft, crime can make economic sense.

For Becker, like Marcus Felson whom we met in Chapter 2, our fascination with unusual crime has blinded us to the realities of everyday crime. Even if we are not highly predisposed to be antisocial, if the temptation is big enough and the opportunity is wide open, most of us will transgress. We do not need to start off with criminal intent. On the other hand even a professional villain needs a target and the chance to get away with it.

To put it in another way, crime has a *motive*, something we all recognise when it comes to detection but underrate when we think of prevention.

When it comes to crime, people, or any other factors which are benign on their own, can become potent, even dangerous, when multiplied together. You can think of crime as a formula like $E=MC^2$, or in our case $C=PTO^2$. Crime is the outcome, people are just one of the components that make up the equation, temptation is the mainspring, and opportunity is the enabler and by far the largest factor in dictating how much crime takes place.

It can't be said often enough that people are more or less the same from one generation to the next, and it has proved formidably hard to undo what genetics and parenting have done, or to unscramble the effects of unwise friendships or imperfect cultures. In general, people are the most difficult parts of the crime mechanism to alter, quite apart from the fact that the very process of *trying* to change them creates all sorts of moral conundrums.

Thus, for a moment, let's put human predisposition to one side. Let's check out the other factors that drive the great majority of crime. And let's examine two fundamental assumptions about economics and offending: first, that poverty itself is a cause of crime, and second, that relative poverty is. So that we don't get bogged down in messy details let's also set aside arguments about how to measure trends. We know that historic crime statistics are rarely comparable with modern ones, and that modern ones reflect insurance penetration, police activity and so on, not just changing rates of victimisation. But let's take what we can now regard as an unarguable case: that offending rose steadily and at times substantially from the 1960s to the 1990s. It happened throughout Western Europe and North America, though quaintly each country tended to think that it alone was suffering a special plague. Murder rates, for example, having generally fallen in Britain from 1900 to 1960, then more than doubled to a peak in the mid-1990s. Almost every other measure of offending went up too. What was going on?

Well, for a start there were peaks in the supply of people most likely to commit offences and be victims of them, notably young males. There were two post-war baby booms, with another small spike in the 1960s, which no doubt had a major influence. There were also economic troughs which made people idle and frustrated and may have encouraged some of them to, shall we say, cut corners. But in general this was a time of unparalleled prosperity. Throughout the Western world it was the 'golden age', as economies powered ahead, with the US leading the way in a 'showcase era of capitalism', while Australia had its 'long boom', Germany its 'Wirtschaftswunder', France its 'Trente Glorieuses', Italy, Scandinavia and Japan each had their 'economic miracles' and, as we noted in Chapter 2, Britain had 'never had it so good'. In all these countries, growing affluence was accompanied by falling income inequalities.

Sweden was the most striking example of this paradox. Since the birth of criminology, experts had been assuming crime was the product of poverty. A classical illustration taught to students had been to correlate the price of bread in nineteenth-century Bavaria and the numbers of people arrested for vagrancy and theft: as the price of bread went up, so did the arrest rates. Since most criminologists were socialists or social democrats, they predicted that 'most forms of crime would simply disappear as soon as just, egalitarian society would have been established'. Sweden epitomised the social democrat Utopia, and yet its recorded crime rate rose faster than that in almost any other European nation. Nor was this some statistical aberration: the trend turned out to be equally pronounced when victimisation surveys became available to supplement police statistics.

Thus, crime was a paradox. America had also led the trend and by the swinging 1960s it had got so bad that President Lyndon Johnson set up a National Commission on the Causes and Prevention of Violence, and the experts were mystified.

'Why, we must ask, have urban violent crime rates increased substantially during the past decade when the conditions that are supposed to cause violent crime have not worsened – have, indeed, generally improved?'

One by one, the bewildered authors ticked off the socio-economic markers that might point to trouble, but incomes were up, unemployment was down, more poor and black children were completing high school, and the number of families living in poverty was declining sharply.

So whatever else was causing crime to rise, it was not poverty, at least not in the conventional sense of the word. On the contrary, it was wealth. Wealth brought with it seven great progenitors of rising crime, and the reasons are plain to see, even if most criminologists haven't bothered to look. Higher wages and more credit meant that there was more spending and thus more to steal, more spare time in which to get up to mischief, more late nights carousing, more alcohol and other recreational drug-taking, more social mobility in every sense (and in Britain a collapse of the old class structure), more travel, more anonymity, and more of all the other ambiguous benefits that come with rapidly rising standards of living. Just think through the huge implications...

First, there was simply an unprecedented hoard of treasure and so many new inventions to inspire entirely new temptations. As old offences like sheep stealing, horse theft and highway robbery became extinct, new ones multiplied and our responses lagged behind. As we noted in the last two chapters, the waves of post-war consumer innovations brought with them ripples of attendant crime: shoplifting, car theft, credit-card deception, air-time fraud with mobile phones and crime scams through the internet. Most of this was only made possible because ordinary people had acquired possessions that were unavailable to generations past.

And after the Second World War, this extra temptation was matched by a second factor: a whole new world of opportunity. The lower orders were melting away. Rigid social distinctions which had defined Europe, and especially Great Britain, were dissolving fast. We forget that class had been a huge restraining influence on crime. The great majority of families, the proletariat, rarely had the faintest chance of breaking through the barriers of snobbery. A few adventurers prospered, often by going abroad, but for the most part if we were common people we were stuck. We were locked in by expectation, by lack of education and by lack of time. We were literally working class, we worked long hours and we were breadwinners from an early age. Our ambitions were limited by how far we could walk in half a day, by the requirements of the gentry and obligations to the church, by a wall of snootiness and by the expectations of our family and friends. The local aristocrat might have a fine carriage, or in later years an automobile, but we would never aspire to such a thing. It is not that we thought of ourselves as failures. We were what we were. The destruction of class barriers has unfettered the great mass of the population from serfdom, unleashed enormous energy, intellect, democracy and economic growth. In one sense Karl Marx got things precisely wrong. He thought crime was the result of conflict between the classes, but it was the breakdown of class rigidities that opened the floodgates. It has changed our dreams and made us hope that they really might come as true for us as they have done for many others. It has made us aspire and made us envious. It has meant that stolen goods no longer look out of place, for we can own cars and televisions too. We are all consumers now.

Third, and a key to opportunity, was leisure. One of the by-products of economic success is that we have more time on our hands, and none more so than the young. The employment of children was widespread throughout history and even when labour reforms and mandatory education encroached as the nineteenth century edged into the twentieth, most families could ill afford non-productive members. Long gone are the days when small boys climbed up chimneys or toiled down mines, but when youngsters left school at fourteen (after 1918 in the UK) or fifteen (after 1944), they went straight off to earn income for the household rather than themselves. Free time and pocket money were both precious. In the inter-war years spare time was more of a problem for the well-to-do, and it was often youths from the upper classes who earned a reputation for acting badly, with wild pranks, drunkenness and licentiousness – the British expression 'behaving like a public schoolboy' did not mean behaving well. As the pitilessly direct Conservative sage Lord Tebbit put it: 'When I look at what we denounce as the appalling conduct of "ordinary people" I see the way the rich have always behaved. It's just that they have had the resources to deal with the fallout.' Post-war emancipation of the working classes meant that for the first time in history adolescents as a whole were working less. The teenager came into being as a distinctive phenomenon and, ironically, thereby social progress had the effect of democratising opportunities for mischief. As anyone from the baby boom can testify, teenage leisure was frequently accompanied by aching boredom, and yet also by unprecedented time to go out and forage for fun with friends. The 'night out' became a Friday and Saturday routine, and sometimes an everyday escapade.

Fourth was another sort of freedom that money can buy: the loosening of constraints. The post-war change in social attitudes was perhaps as profound as any in history. Though sometimes written off as a collapse of values, it was more like a refurbishment, stripping out old rigidities, cruelties and hypocrisies, along with a raft of good manners and self-restraint, and replacing them with a new swashbuckling individualism and with a different set of etiquettes. By the standards of any previous generation, and not just in contrast to the austerity of wartime, the baby boomers were emancipated. They had access to new ideas through education and television, often shocking their parents with an independence that until the war would have been considered insolence. The Teddy boy was born, the mods and rockers, and their descendants, and they became an increasingly important consumer group in their own right. As never before they rocked to their own genres of music, their own hairstyles and clothes, they bought motorbikes and scooters and cars, and they gulped down alcohol in growing quantities. They got raunchy, too, with the publication of *Lady Chatterley's Lover* and the launch of the contraceptive pill. By the 1960s they were also beginning to experiment with drugs.

It is hard to imagine the conformity that was required until the 1950s; perhaps harder still to imagine how people of that period would react if teleported into the bewildering range of fashions and the diversely insolent behaviours of today. The fuss that greeted rock 'n' roll, the sensual leer of Elvis Presley, the hair down to the collar that was so shocking about the Beatles, the increasing directness of sexual innuendo, the stirrings of feminism and gay pride, the new age of satire, the migration of TV interviewers like me from deference to sneer, the liberty of both sexes to dress provocatively, to behave loudly, to offend people, to do one's own thing. More and more families became child-centred, with the parents fitting their lives around the desires of their offspring rather than children being expected to adapt to the mores of the adults. Youngsters could speak back with a directness that would have been unthinkable in previous generations, and threats like 'just you wait 'til your father gets home' soon began to sound quaint and ridiculous. There was simply more acceptance of individual differences – which meant correspondingly less conspicuity if people were behaving oddly. The boundaries of being good and being bad were being blurred.

Fifth, the new wealth meant new physical mobility. A century previously, Ruskin had feared that the railways would allow for unbridled social chaos, since 'every fool in Buxton can be in Bakewell in half an hour'. Ruskin would have been aghast at the perambulations of the 1950s and beyond. Travel brings new temptations and opportunities within reach. Apart from which, every stolen car in Widnes could be in Warrington in half an hour.

Sixth, one result of this mobility, combined with less settled urbanisation, was the development of anonymity as a natural phenomenon, and even a right. Distance lends enchantment to misbehaviour, because in distant places we are strangers, and so are our potential victims. With fewer pangs of conscience, less chance of being caught, self-seeking is apt to triumph over self-control. In the village, or the street, where everyone knows you, there is a web of relationships to consider, but when our identity is hidden in a crowd we are less likely to be restrained by those around us.

Seventh, there were fewer people around who were likely to restrain us. The enormous growth in post-war wealth meant wages went up fast and many jobs became unviable. Armies of uniformed authority disappeared; not least bus conductors, railway porters, park keepers and caretakers. Who would keep order on the top deck of the bus now there was nobody in charge, and who would watch out for bullying and theft at unmanned railway stations and many other public spaces newly emptied of informal guardians? New opportunities for bad behaviour blossomed just as so many new temptations were in bloom. This withdrawal of protection also happened in the home. As a result of full employment, along with rising expectations and the wartime experience of women in the workplace, females went out to work in steadily increasing numbers. In the US the proportion of women of working age who had a job roughly doubled between 1945 and 1995, a trend that was echoed in the UK and all of Western Europe. Huge numbers of homes were left unoccupied during the day, which (contrary to popular assumptions) is when most successful burglaries take place. Just when we had unprecedented amounts of consumer goods to steal, we stopped guarding our houses and apartments.

So, seven wonders of the world, the harvest of post-war prosperity. Here was a feast of attractions, seductions, frustrations, provocations, excitements, liberties and opportunities which, for all their manifold blessings, were sometimes perilously similar to the seven deadly sins. It is hardly surprising that more people found themselves supping with the devil.

And when they did, the chance of getting caught diminished year on year. As more and more citizens broke the rules, the further the authorities were stretched in seeking to police them. And with an ever-lower likelihood of being brought to book, more people were tempted to break the rules. It was a vicious circle which left people scrambling to explain a collapse in moral values, dividing their exasperation across the fault-line of those who blamed the individuals and those who blamed society. Where people settled their views defined their politics and personalities – whether they dressed to the left or the right. None of them thought to blame prosperity.

RESPECT

This is not to deny that haves and have-nots behave in different ways. Take acquisitive crime. For rich people it usually makes sense to play by the rules unless a huge amount of money is at stake. For someone poor, a little extra cash can make a lot of difference and there is less to lose in getting caught. Our financial standing also dictates the temptations and opportunities we face in daily life. The middle classes have better access to discreet offending we call white-collar crime, while those lower on the social ladder tend to be restricted to physical theft and contact crimes that stir public anxiety.

And while lack of money is not normally a cause of crime, poverty has a dangerous relative: lack of self-esteem. When others do well and you do not it can lead to a shortage of self-worth. This is why most people involved in violence are low achievers and why 'dissing' someone can be so provocative. If the person you insult has little self-respect to start with, an absurdly trivial slight can wound and can lead to serious aggression. This is especially perilous when tongues and fists have been loosened by alcohol or when an entire community has little prestige and is living on the edge. It may explain why some places have so much black-on-black belligerence. A *Washington Post* journalist who'd grown up in a black ghetto reported:

> They'll kill a nigger for dissin' them. Won't touch a white person, but they'll kill a brother in a heartbeat … It was as if black folks were saying, 'I can't do much to keep white folks from dissin' me, but I damn sure can keep black folks from doing it.'

In the 1970s US television cop show, Detective Lieutenant Kojak, in between sucking a lollipop, would ask as he clamped on the handcuffs, 'Who loves ya, baby?' The unspoken answer was often nobody at all.

Or as William Butler Yeats put it, rather more poetically: 'I, being poor, have only my dreams … / Tread softly because you tread on my dreams.'

Lack of status is another way of saying life is cheap. Rough estates really are sometimes rough and on the whole gentlemen really are gentler than those at the bottom of the social scale. A survey in the English Midlands found people from the most deprived areas were four times more likely to be admitted as assault victims than those from the least deprived ones. In fact, it seems that low self-esteem can be dangerous in itself. It has long been known that poor people die young, and more recently this has been shown to hold true even when factors like smoking and bad diet are factored out of the equation. In other words, rich smokers live longer than poor ones. Much the same is true for other status-conscious mammals.

Among non-human primates like baboons and macaques, those of lower status tend to have more health problems and die younger than their counterparts above them in the hierarchy. US medical researchers have compared indicators of poverty and low self-esteem with outcomes like life expectancy and found that lack of confidence in others was more closely linked to early deaths than income inequality. More intriguingly from our point of view, it was also very closely correlated with violent crime, especially homicide.

So when research suggests that simple lack of money is the problem – for example, homicide has been broadly found to match income inequality across more than thirty countries – it might be that poverty is a symptom not the cause; a circularity in which low status leads to low academic achievement which reduces prospects, breeds defeatism or anger and closes doors to self-improvement. At any rate, when forty years of post-war economic growth were checked against a dozen forms of crime, violence did not diminish as society grew richer. It grew in step with per capita consumption.

This will not be music to the ears of those whose politics insist that want is the mother of crime rather than its cousin. No doubt poverty was pivotal when people really stole out of need, but even in Victorian times, long before the welfare state, most offenders seem to have had sufficient means to support themselves. The last time the hunger excuse was used in Britain was after thugs were chased out of a Michelin-starred restaurant in Notting Hill and one of the culprits explained in mitigation that he had needed food. It turned out he and his equally well-nourished co-defendants lived in housing provided by Kensington & Chelsea Council, in one case worth £2.5 million.

Nor does crime appear to be caused by cuts in welfare. On the contrary, UK social spending rocketed after the Second World War, and accelerated when crime was growing fastest. Health, education and welfare budgets are all many hundreds of times larger than in 1945. In fact welfare payments have risen four times faster than GDP. Oddly, when the proportion spent on social security levelled off in the 1990s, crime turned the corner and began its long decline.

Some economists continue to insist that rising unemployment, or cuts in benefits or wages, are linked with more offending. But at best the evidence is inconsistent. After the banking crash in 2008, Britain experienced the worst financial crisis since at least the 1930s. Unemployment surged from 5 to 8 per cent and almost all pundits and criminologists predicted crime would zoom back up. They were wrong. Almost every category of offending continued its downward profile.

5

THE SOCIAL THEORIES OF CRIME 2: BADNESS

We may pretend that we're basically moral people who make
mistakes, but the whole of history proves otherwise.
– Terry Hands

If the left believes society is at fault, the right blames individuals. But do the totemic beliefs of conservatives withstand evidence any better than those of their political foes? Essentially, social conservative views can be articulated as follows:

> The real problem is the loss of internalised moral principles that prevent people from committing crimes in the first place. Young people who grow up in troubled and dysfunctional households in which moral values are not inculcated, who attend schools where teachers are afraid or unwilling to teach the difference between right or wrong, who live in communities in which the influence of religious faith is negligible, will naturally be drawn towards the self-gratification and situational ethics that predominate in contemporary culture.
> – Norman Dennis and George Erdos, *Civitas*, London, 2005

Undoubtedly there is truth in all those statements. No doubt crime is a dynamic interaction between lots of factors including some or all of the above. But across the world we have witnessed massive growth in crime rates and then equally decisive falls. Can conservative articles of faith explain them?

Let's start in the presence of God. Religion is commonly held to provide and underpin our moral values. For those who believe in rules laid down by a deity it seems self-evident that without those holy commandments there is nothing left but nihilism. Religion has enshrined some of the best aspects of humanity: family values and concern for others, self-discipline and humility; it has inspired the creation of hospitals and schools, quite apart from sublime art and towering cathedrals, temples and mosques; and it has brought many sinners to repent. Adam and Eve were cursed and were banished from Eden because they disobeyed instructions. Fear of eternal retribution must surely have kept many people on the straight and narrow.

There is evidence that anything which reminds us of moral values helps keep us on the straight and narrow. In a neat illustration of this, a group of students at Harvard was asked to write down ten books they had read in school. Another group was asked to write down the Ten Commandments. Later they took part in an experiment in which half of them had an opportunity to cheat on a test of mental arithmetic. Most of the 'book recall' students who were able to bump up their scores did so; none of the Ten Commandments ones did. This included many who could remember few of the commandments and no doubt some who were not religious. It seems that having clear rules avoids the ambiguity that encourages us to indulge in naughtiness-creep.

However, there are nagging problems. For one thing, religion tends to be at least as popular in prison as outside. In England and Wales, twice as many inmates and three times as many sex offenders declare religious faith as claim none, and believers represent almost all flavours of religion including Buddhists,

Christians, Hindus, Jews, Muslims and Sikhs. Atheists and agnostics dominate a few offences, especially motoring ones, and no doubt some of the religiosity in prison is by way of atonement, or to pass the time, or in the hope of impressing the authorities and winning early release. On the other hand, some inmates claim their offending is the work of providence – that life is preordained – or divinity placed a victim in their path. Whatever the cause of all this piety, it is scarcely an unimpeachable advertisement for religious faith.

In any case, as many sceptics and atheists gleefully point out, religion has promoted, enforced or endorsed some of the greatest immoralities in history, including many which we now regard as serious crimes. There was formal ecclesiastical support for slavery, apartheid, racial segregation, torture, profound religious discrimination and sectarianism, and several of the world's great religions still advocate bigamy, treating women as chattels, stonings, amputations and other exquisite means of enlarging human suffering. Religion can lead to self-righteous sanctimony just as it sometimes inspires empathy for fellow human beings. The conquistadores who ravaged the indigenous populations of South America ploughed much of their plunder into extravagant churches and probably prayed quite as fervently as compassionate priests who worked among the natives. 'Manifest Destiny', through which vast numbers of 'uncivilised pagans' died in the New World, was a policy of good, God-fearing settlers. Doubtless many of the most brutal slave traders who raped and flogged their captives were quite as pious as the likes of William Wilberforce, who fought to have slavery abolished.

More recently in Ireland it emerged that priests routinely beat, bullied and sexually abused thousands of children over decades, a disgrace that was covered up by church, police and state authorities at every level, leading to a long-running scandal that brought down a Prime Minister and exposed astonishing depravity and hypocrisy in devout institutions in one of the most religiously fervent nations in Europe. Similarly vile and tragic events involving clergymen have been uncovered in several other countries. These could be written off as reasons for more religious purity, not less; but frequently believers are at war with each other, as with the slaying of abortion doctors in America, one of whom was shot dead while serving as an usher in his local church.

Then, of course, there is the greatest crime of all: mass murder. Atheists can be genocidal too, of course, not least Stalin, Pol Pot and Mao's wife Jiang Qing. But religious intolerance has been one of the most common excuses for ethnic cleansing since the dawn of history. Religion has mixed perniciously with nationalism and fed another powerful human impulse: tribalism. Its malignant influence can sometimes be disguised because it dissolves into other ugly proclivities, and apologists can claim that Nazis and other anti-Semites despised the Jews as a race and not a religion, that Hindus and Sikhs in India or Protestants and Catholics in Northern Ireland have nationalist or economic motives for their internecine wars, not sectarian ones. But all in all it is hard to deny that religion can be a mixed blessing.

What then of the charge that, whether or not through decline of religion, society has lost its moral compass, that teachers are afraid or unwilling to teach the difference between right and wrong, and that a culture of self-gratification has overwhelmed a civilisation based on ethics?

Or, on the contrary, are we now more concerned with right and wrong than ever before in human history?

It is common to look back fondly on the sunshine days of youth and take a curmudgeonly view of how new generations are making an unholy mess of things. As Gustave Flaubert put it: 'Our ignorance of history makes us libel our own times. People have always been like this.' But blaming crime on falling moral-ity has a special appeal to conservatives who have lost out to changing social fashions and want to justify their own positions: *if we had had our way things would have been very different.*

To some extent their concerns about coarsening standards are self-evidently true. Rude language is so often used in films and on TV that most people barely notice it. We are swamped by erotic imagery and sexual innuendo; on trains and buses, boys and men rarely give up their seats any more, even for elderly women. Almost everyone could point to some things that they feel are getting worse.

On the other hand, we are increasingly aware that many aspects of bygone days have been romanticised. Nostalgia isn't what it used to be, and in many ways people are far more caring now. Whether you look at our rising concern for the environ-ment and for animal welfare, our forbearance of racial difference or sexual orientation, our passion for the human rights of others, our interest in gender equality and egalitarianism in general ... on all those measures, and many more besides, it is hard to sustain the view that morality has vanished down a one-way street.

The psychologist Steven Pinker has shown persuasively that the proportion of humanity killed in homicide or battle has consistently declined over the centuries; and when we do go to war our reverence for life is now so great that individual deaths of soldiers tend to make the news. Nowadays, although we point nuclear weapons at each other, even enemy casualties can cause us moral pangs – witness the precipitous abandonment of the first Gulf War in 1991 after public distaste for the carnage on the 'highway of death' as Iraqi combatants withdrew. Or recall the convulsive reactions in the US, and later on a smaller scale in the UK, when coalition soldiers were found to have abused Iraqi prisoners; never in history has so much moral outrage been expended by the victors over claims about misbehaviour by their own troops.

Is it that nowadays TV makes us more aware? Maybe, though let us not patronise earlier generations for their supposed ignorance of what warfare really meant – soldiers returning from the trenches in Flanders; Londoners sheltering from the Blitz; civilian refugees in Poland or in France; communities laid siege to or overrun by advancing armies – people knew very well the suffering war causes. In any case, judging by the value we now place on human life, if the immediacy of war brought into our homes by the media has had any effect on our morals it seems to have improved and not diminished them.

Our concern about death and injury in peacetime has increased too. Workplace accidents were commonplace in the UK in the nineteenth and early twentieth centuries but fell below 1,000 a year in 1967 and were down to 175 in 2010. Concern for workers' welfare has become so great, and so institutionalised, that the very term 'health and safety' has come to conjure up images of nanny-state interference.

Nor is lack of morality shown on the roads, once the biggest cause of death between infancy and middle age. Britons killed roughly 6,000 of each other each year in traffic accidents between the 1920s and the 1970s until a decision was made to set ambitious targets. Deaths fell below 2,000 in 2010. On the whole this was achieved consensually, sometimes requiring considerable restraint – literally in the case of seatbelts – and citizens agreed to relinquish long-established pleasures, such as drink-driving. Hardly signs of a nation's moral degeneration.

It seems just as perverse to claim standards have collapsed when you look at changing social attitudes in general. Until relatively recently people accepted arrant snobbery and virtually insurmountable class divisions. Racism that was institutionalised is now reviled. And if men no longer offer up their seats on trains to women it is partly because women now see themselves as equals rather than the weaker sex; many would be affronted.

We have a long road of moral improvement still to travel. I have little doubt that our descendants will be appalled that we allow Third World privation and starvation, just as we are scandalised that our ancestors permitted the great Irish famine. But, given the intrinsic selfishness and ruthlessness of human nature which we will explore shortly, it is impossible to make a cogent case that through the twentieth century our moral nonchalance grew worse. And in any case, the argument that crime rose because of failing morals palpably fails to explain why, in the 1990s, crime began to plunge.

6

THE SOCIAL THEORIES OF CRIME 3: BASTARDS

There are illegitimate parents, but I don't believe
there are any illegitimate children.
— Rick Warren

Even if public morals have improved and we're not all going to the dogs, it does not mean that everyone is being swept along on the empathetic tide. Could it be that one section of society has been sliding backwards, a murky undercurrent descending into increasingly dysfunctional lifestyles, and that this sub-group caused the surge in post-war crime? It is a popular assumption. It fits an entrenched view of the facts, which is that a small number of lowlife miscreants commit the majority of crime. And it has the virtue of making sense whatever your political persuasion. The left can blame capitalism, with its heartless subjugation of the workers and its abandonment of those who don't meet its requirements. Free enterprise liberals can upbraid a thoughtless culture of exclusion which has deprived poor families of know-how, contacts, cars and credit cards and other prerequisites of getting on in life. Those on the right can rail at the bogey of socialism, with its rash abandonment of hard-working values and its reckless hand-outs which fostered a dismal culture of dependency.

In the 1980s and '90s all these swirling issues came together in a colourful and often charged debate about the *underclass*. The word seems to have originated in the US in the 1970s, at first without insinuating anything pejorative – it just meant people at the bottom of the heap. But it sounded like under*world* and quickly carried echoes of dissoluteness and criminality. No one could measure it, but matter not. Now that there was a word for it, the underclass, whatever it was, seemed to become a tangible fact.

THEM AND US

There is nothing new about an underclass. Until the Reformation it was the duty of every citizen to feed the hungry, welcome the stranger, clothe the naked and minister to the sick in accordance with Christian teaching. But by the sixteenth century, economic and social change had brought about large numbers of homeless and unemployed who were beyond the reach of individual philanthropy, and the Elizabethan Poor Law of 1563 set the tone for the way we think and act today. The destitute were to be registered and sorted into three cat-egories: the *impotent deserving poor* (those who were too sick, too young or too old to work, who were to be given indoor relief in almshouses, poorhouses and the like), the *able-bodied deserving poor* (the unemployed, who were given outdoor relief by the parish or put to work for a wage), and the undeserving or *idle poor* (who were to be whipped through the streets until they saw the error of their ways). It was the idle poor who worried the authorities most. These were the vagabonds – the vagrants and beggars, the pickpockets and highwaymen – and they could be flogged, imprisoned or executed, and for a time branded by burning through the right ear. There was probably a good deal of rough justice; it must have been hard for small communities to distinguish between migrant workers roaming the country hoping for a wage and villains set on stealing chickens or slitting throats.

Nonetheless, the Elizabethan Poor Laws were so effective they survived for almost 300 years. Come the nineteenth century, Thomas Malthus had argued that the poor would breed themselves into starvation, and the French wars followed by the Corn Laws seemed about to prove him right. There was a huge influx to the towns, and parish relief was becoming overwhelmed. So the Poor Law Amendment Act of 1834 tried to cut off welfare to everyone except those who were really desperate. Outdoor relief was officially abolished, which meant it was off to the workhouse for anyone who needed help. At least that was the theory. In fact the Act was mostly threat and bluster. By the 1840s, of the 1,300,000 people who received relief, only 192,000 were in workhouses. Of almost £4 million spent on poor relief, over £3 million went to people in their own homes. The Act was much more benevolent than its reputation, and in practice the idea of the undeserving poor was generally abandoned. This was formalised a hundred years later when Britain's welfare state was formed. In practice *poverty* and *blame* seemed to have been disentangled.

It was not until the 1980s that the two became extensively conjoined again.

It was liberals who first warned about a neglected group outside the mainstream of society, but it was the New Right that made the underclass its own, describing a class of scroungers which was perpetuated by welfare benefits and riddled with drug-taking, dishonesty, truancy, unwillingness to work and casual violence.

One man above all raised the spectre of this threat and promoted a view of crime that is still influential three decades on and has been entrenched in a bestselling book. The story is intriguing because it is a classic example of how political mindset distorts assumptions about crime; and also about how partial statistics can bamboozle.

In 1984, the American libertarian Charles Murray published *Losing Ground*, which excoriated President Kennedy's welfare revolution of the 1960s. He described a twenty-fold increase in federal costs which had transferred a vast amount of wealth from the haves to the have-nots. Yet Murray pointed out that this 'generous revolution' had been accompanied by the biggest ever surge in crime. He put two and two together: hand-outs were sapping the will to work and encouraging barefaced immorality. More ominously, in a throwback to the alarming predictions of Thomas Malthus, Murray warned that this underclass – 'the New Rabble', as he called them – was fast breeding greater trouble for the future.

Five years later the London *Sunday Times* invited Murray to apply his fertile mind to the problems facing the UK, and predictably his diagnosis was the same – though oddly, 'The difference between the United States and Britain is that the United States reached the future first.' I say this is curious because Britain's post-war welfare revolution started earlier and was more decisive than that in the US, which hardly fits Murray's paradigm. Nonetheless he was not to let the facts of history spoil his theory. Though he was vague on statistics he was clear in his message: Britain was heading for a crime rate, and specifically a murder rate, comparable to that in the US – and maybe worse.

He was equally clear that single mothers were to blame. He lamented the loss of shame and stigma about illegitimacy, and scorned the welfare and housing systems which demolished financial disincentives to having children outside marriage. He insisted that, as night follows day, illegitimacy leads to crime. Young and impetuous women who get pregnant become hopeless single mums. The problem is exacerbated when they have sons, because boys are naturally more impulsive than girls and more likely to get into trouble with the law; they need stability, and they need limits imposed by a father. 'Illegitimate births are the leading indicator of an underclass and violent crime is a proxy measure of its development.'

It is conceivable – forgive the pun – that there was some good sense behind Murray's concerns. I confess I share his preference for the nuclear family even if I would hate to return to the cruel stigma of illegitimacy. I like the idea that children should be brought up in loving, stable relationships with a mother and a father, or at least that they should have good role models for each gender. I have always imagined that single parents have a tough time, that girls brought up without mothers miss out on maternal love and guidance, and that boys brought up without fathers are prone to lack masculine cues including boundaries. I have seen first-hand as a journalist how terribly unsuitable some parents can be, and that life at the bottom of the heap is crueller than at the top. I am well aware that within the teeming millions that make up our society there are families drained of initiative or ambition, mostly without formal jobs, drawing benefits, sometimes scavenging in an uncharted economy of stolen goods and bringing up feral children for whom crime is a routine way of making their way through life. No doubt we foment trouble by bottling up poor people in some inner-city estates. I am ready to have my prejudices confirmed. I would instinctively support anything that might help parents be more responsible.

But does illegitimacy cause crime? To prove his point Murray compared graphs. One showed a steep rise in children born to unmarried mothers and another purported to show a matching rise in violent crime. And Britain, he opined, 'used to have hardly any crime at all'. It sounded convincing, especially to those on the right. But even if we took all his figures at face value, there were and remain at least three major problems for the Murray thesis. The first is that the charts didn't actually correspond. Illegitimacy did not begin to rise in the UK until 1960. It then flattened before taking off around 1980. Yet the rush of crime preceded it. The crime graph started climbing in 1950, gathered momentum in 1970, and pitched up steeply again in the late 1980s. Unless the apparent surge in rape, robbery and mugging was caused by unborn foetuses and toddlers, it is hard to see how illegitimacy could have had any impact on crime in the timescale covered by the charts. In fact, contrary to Murray's London predictions, recorded crime began to fall just as the majority of these boys reached their middle-teens.

The second problem is that, even if the figures behind the graphs had a consistent basis, even if the graphs themselves had coincided at the right time, and even if the expected flood of crime had continued to rise throughout the 1990s, the two things could be wholly unrelated. Around this time Saddam Hussein had brushed his teeth one morning and occupied Kuwait, but his dental hygiene was presumably incidental to the invasion. Murray's was a classic of *post hoc ergo propter hoc*, the fallacy of mistaking correlation for causation.

The third problem lay in Murray's conviction that where America leads the world will follow. If he was right, if boys born out of wedlock really are a proxy for a 'New Rabble', then the correlation with crime should be obvious everywhere. It was not. According to European victimisation surveys, crime followed a universal trend, soaring to a peak in the early 1990s and declining thereafter, just as it did in the USA. And the countries with the highest rates of illegitimate births were not the same countries which had the highest rates of crime.

In any case, Murray's illegitimacy graph is a very crude representation of an increasingly complex phenomenon. Babies born to unmarried mothers are not necessarily deprived of a loving father. Cohabitation was a defining characteristic of the closing decades of the last century, so much so that by 2002 nearly 64 per cent of live births outside marriage were jointly registered by parents living at the same address. This does not mean these are always stable families – there is some evidence that unmarried parents are much more likely to break up than married ones, often affecting children who are very young indeed. Nor does this mean that broken homes don't represent a problem. For example, a survey in the late 1990s found more offending by youngsters from single-parent households or stepfamilies than by those living with two natural parents. But curiously, and in contrast to Murray's theory, the risk was starker for girls. And in any case all this has happened at a time of falling crime.

Charles Murray continues to proselytise, describing Western Europe as 'the canary in the coal mine', but the canary is still chirping, far more healthily than when all this commotion started. So while he remains preoccupied with the thought that poor bastards caused the swell of crime, it has occurred to others that a shortage of them might explain its fall.

After all, if feckless girls are the cause of crime by having unprotected sex then one thing should cut crime at a stroke: abortion. The idea that abortion helped reverse the crime wave was popularised by *Freakonomics*, the bestseller by economist Steven Levitt and journalist Stephen Dubner. In a chapter called 'Where have all the criminals gone?' they questioned why in the 1990s US crime levels began to plummet, with homicide diving roughly 40 per cent within the decade. The book is light on detail but Levitt's original research had been meticulous in partnership with John Donohue from Stanford Law School and backed by the granddaddy of economic inquiry into social issues, Gary Becker. By far the biggest answer, it appeared, was *Roe* v. *Wade*.

Abortion had mostly been illegal in the US until the 1960s, when several states began to liberalise the law. Texas wasn't one of them and in 1969 a Dallas mom, Norma McCorvey, reluctantly discovered she was pregnant. She already had two children and didn't want another, so, under the alias Jane Roe, she challenged the Texas state attorney Henry Wade to have the state's prohibition on abortion set aside. In the event her third child was born long before her legal challenge was resolved, but in 1973, in a judgment that has divided America ever since, the Supreme Court deemed abortion to be a fundamental right under the US Constitution. Within a year a fifth of all American pregnancies ended in abortion. By 1980 almost a third of them did.

In their original papers, Donohue and Levitt cite evidence that women who do not want babies are less likely to love and nurture them and that unloved boys are often trouble. They move on to back-of-the-envelope numbers which show that America's drop in crime fits their theory like a glove, before getting down to some serious calculations plotting trends in different types of crime that are expressed by different age groups. And it's hard to fault their caution or their methodology. Fifteen years after abortion went mainstream, crime, especially property crime, had begun to fall. If their abortion thesis proved correct and the impact was as big as they said on the tin, they had emerged with one of the greatest ever insights into crime.

Unsurprisingly they provoked a storm and, as Dubner recalls in *Freakonomics*, the genial Levitt 'was called an ideologue (by conservatives and liberals alike), a eugenicist, a racist, and downright evil ... Conservatives were enraged that abortion could be construed as a crime-fighting tool. Liberals were aghast that poor and black women were singled out. Economists grumbled that Levitt's methodology was not sound...'

Soon academic detractors began to emerge, picking apart several complex assumptions on which Donohue and Levitt had constructed their intellectual palace. Some of the arguments were esoteric and couched in economists' jargon, with talk about zero-inflated negative binomial regressions and whether standard errors were clustered correctly, and so forth. These statistical refutations were followed by challenges to the underlying logic, for example, showing that homicide was falling not just among the young but, equally decisively, among offenders who were too old to have been affected by *Roe* v. *Wade*.

These inconsistencies opened the doors to a larger problem. If abortion radically cuts crime then, as Levitt himself accepted, its effects should be eye-catching wherever abortion laws are changed. So let's look across the pond. The British liberalised their abortion laws in the 1960s, five years earlier than the US, so offending in the UK should have declined five years earlier than in America. Far from it. Take your pick of different measures of crime, but property crime only started to go down in Britain five years *after* things changed in the US, while violent crime and homicide took even longer to level off and then descend.

In short, the drastic and unambiguous findings that millions read and believed in *Freakonomics* are not clear after all.

It's a pity to throw the illegitimate baby out with the *Freakonomics* bathwater because it is only to the good if more economists and those from other disciplines turn their thoughts to analysing crime. But equally, it is a shame that Donohue and Levitt never thought to examine situational answers that were hiding in plain view: the huge growth in temptations and opportunities that had lured people into crime and the huge security correction that rebalanced the equation, helping people to look after themselves and their possessions with more care.

Instead, like many convincing-sounding social doctrines about crime, the abortion theory seems to rest on false assumptions. For a start there is a profound difference between an unwanted pregnancy and an unwanted child. Many parents will attest to this, but so do the adoption rates. As abortions rose in Britain after 1968, adoptions fell, and within a decade had dropped by 75 per cent. Many of those supposedly unwelcome children might have been welcomed after all, even longed for. Adopted children were brought up by couples who had been vetted by local authorities for their suitability as mums and dads. On the other hand, abortion did not affect the one group of youngsters most likely to get into trouble with the law: those brought up in care. After 1968 the numbers remained obstinately the same.

Incidentally, it is not at all clear that bad parenting causes bad offspring. It might often be the other way around. We are all far more than what our parents hope to make of us, so that an impetuous and hyperactive child will be treated differently from a sibling who is calm and pensive. Apart from that, many of our attitudes and behaviours are shaped less by our immediate families, or by teachers, than by our peers. A child's accent is testament to that, especially with migrant families: far more likely to be like that of friends than that of mum or dad.

More significantly, it is a myth that people who go for abortions are disproportionately from what Murray would call the underclass. Just as contraception is used more methodically by people who are well informed and cautious rather than by those who are less educated and impetuous, so it is the richer, better-educated women who are least likely to take unplanned pregnancies to term. In fact, paradoxically, abortion, along with the contraceptive pill, seems to have been part of a culture which *increased* illegitimate births. In the old days girls were more cautious about 'getting knocked up'. A striking attendant of liberal abortion was more liberal attitudes to having sex – in fact abortion reform itself was a product of this new freewheeling ethos – which is why the proportion of children born out of wedlock went on rising. Indeed, it may be that the total number of boys born to unmarried, unstable and unsuitable mothers barely fell at all.

In short, as the tide of crime turned in the 1990s – so much so that in the US, remember, there was a 30 per cent drop in most offences and a 40 per cent drop in homicides – it did so *despite* the fact there were now more teenagers whose mums were just the sort of girls the theorists were so worried about.

In any case, killing foetuses is not likely to figure in crime prevention manuals.

SINGLE MUMS AND CRIME

If one-parent families are a major cause of crime, it should reflect in prison populations. But it doesn't, or at best the evidence is mixed. The most comprehensive UK study was conducted in 1991 at a time when recorded crime was just about reaching its zenith. Almost two-thirds of prisoners in the National Prison Survey had spent most of their time as a child with both parents. Less than a quarter came from one-parent households, which is close to the average make-up of British households.

One of the best predictors of crime may be having no parents to care for one at all. Eight per cent of the prisoners had spent most of their childhood in an institution, and 26 per cent said that at some time in their childhood they had been taken into local authority care. Dozens of other studies have come up with similar findings.

Nor is fostering always the ideal; being looked after is not always the same as being cared for. A massive survey in 2004 found half of all sixteen-year-olds admitted to breaking the law but so-called 'looked after' children confessed to twice as much theft and almost twice as much violence. They were also far more likely to be bullied and to carry a knife to school or be excluded from class.

But of even more concern to us should be boys and young men who are permanently excluded from school. This is a group which turns out to be highly vulnerable to violent crime and suicide. In fact, school exclusion is probably the best predictor of ending up in prison.

Another intriguing theory is that *pollution* was a major source of crime. The notion had been around for quite a time but in 2007 it was promoted as the Big Idea. Again the author was an economist.

Jessica Reyes, like Levitt and Donohue, reasoned that *something* had to account for the rise and fall of young offenders – and on her calculations the culprit was lead in petrol. Leaded fuel in the US was progressively phased out between 1975 and 1990, a change which correlated neatly with the fall in violent crime after 1992. In fact, Professor Reyes claimed more than half of the fall in America's violent crime could be attributed to reductions in atmospheric lead.

It sounded so improbable that it wasn't taken seriously by many for a while and has never made an impact in mainstream scientific journals; but it was credible because we know that lead is toxic and can have irreversible and damaging effects on mental functioning. That was why it was outlawed. On the other hand, could it really have had such a massive impact on behaviour as to cause the biggest crime wave in peacetime history?

Well, not entirely. Jessica Reyes herself acknowledged that there was no match with murders in New York, whose steep decline has captured public imagination. But more importantly, nor did the theory work for acquisitive offences – the thefts which had largely driven crime rates. If lead caused cognitive impairment like assaults and murders, how come it failed to correlate with all the other equally impulsive crimes? Nor was there compelling evidence that offenders, in prison for example, had higher lead levels in their blood than anyone else.

In any case, correlation does not prove cause and there are lots of similar, if less persuasive, contenders for why people go bad, including other heavy metals and junk diets. They might all make contributions. But probably only at the margins.

There is one other aspect of social theories about crime that bears examination. Whatever political traditions they are rooted in, they all assume that crime is caused by criminals. That is to say, they presume crime is abnormal; that most people just aren't like that and only a few people are. In the next chapter we will challenge the first idea and show how, given the right (or the wrong) circumstances, almost all of us can be encouraged to do very bad things indeed.

It is naive to believe in a dichotomy between saints and sinners.

7

CRIME AS NORMAL 1: VIOLENCE

*And it came to pass as they came, when David was returned
from the slaughter of the Philistine, that the women came out of
all cities of Israel, singing and dancing, to meet king Saul, with
tabrets, with joy, and with instruments of musick.*

*And the women answered one another as they played, and said,
Saul hath slain his thousands, and David his ten thousands.*
– 1 Samuel 18:6–7

It is a nice idea that we are nice. We tend to think of humanity as essentially virtuous, and only call people *in*human when they are really bad. But genes, together with millennia of often hostile environments, have shaped *Homo sapiens* into the most successfully aggressive species on the planet. We have so cocooned ourselves from nature it is tempting to assume that being peaceful and honest is the default state of affairs. It is not. Our avarice and aggression have made us top dog in a very dog-eat-dog world. If you don't believe it, look around and you can grasp how emphatically we humans have stamped our own needs upon nature and have nudged rival creatures to the margins. It is possible (though controversial) that our ancestors extermi-nated our own near-relatives, *Homo erectus* and Neanderthals, and in comparatively recent times the Bushmen of South Africa were hunted to extinction. Along with our nearest relatives, the chimpanzees, we are the only animals where gangs of males extend their territory by deliberately exterminating neighbouring males. We have always slain each other in vast numbers including well over 150 million in the last century alone. We kill not just in defensive war but for enrichment, racism, religious zeal, paranoia, twisted ideology or just for fun.

THE BUTCHER'S BILL

Human skeletons recovered from archaeological sites suggest 15 per cent of prehistoric humans died from deliberately inflicted wounds. Life became less brutish and short as societies became more organised and submitted to central authority. Over the millennia our violence has been curbed – so much so that, in proportion to the global population, the twentieth century was perhaps the least bloody in human history.

Even so the tally is spectacular. Discounting local quarrels like Northern Ireland (some 3,000 dead) and skirmishes like the Israel–Arab conflict (which since 1948 has killed about 65,000 people) there were more than a dozen clashes which claimed more than a million lives: the Mexican revolution (1910–20, about a million), the Armenian massacres (1915–23, 1.5 million), the Korean Wars (1950–53, killing about 2.8 million, on top of which North Korea contributed perhaps 3 million corpses more through violence and starvation), Ethiopia (1962–92, resulting in some 1.4 million deaths), the American incursion into Vietnam (1965–73, with 1.7 million dead and 1.8 million more from other phases of the conflict), Nigeria (1966–70, about a million dead), Bangladesh (1971, about 1.25 million), Cambodia (1975–78, where Pol Pot's regime killed 1.65 million), Mozambique (1975–92, about a million killed), Afghanistan (1979–, perhaps 2 million and still counting), the Iraq–Iran war (1980–88, another million or so killed), Sudan (1983–, about 2 million), and the Rwanda and Burundi catastrophe (1994, just under a million murdered, as well as hundreds of thousands killed in previous years). Those are among the relatively small fry. The big ones include the 15 million in the Great War, the 29 million who perished in the Russian civil war and at the hands of Stalin, over 40 million killed in the Chinese civil war or who died in Mao Zedong's revolution, and 55 million or so who lost their lives in the Second World War.

Through most of humankind's existence, peace and tranquillity, rather like the arts, have been extravagancies to be indulged in when more basic needs are satisfied. Which is why the notion that people are essentially peace-loving and empathetic is scarcely a complete description of humanity. Instead it might make more sense to regard us as capable of the whole spectrum of feelings and actions towards others: from furious brutality and insouciant cruelty, through indifference and disregard, to fellow-feeling and valiant self-sacrifice. Given our nature, crime is not remarkable at all.

This conclusion should scarcely be surprising to anyone with a passing knowledge of evolution. Competition for food or sex or anything is intrinsically amoral. What Richard Dawkins dubs the 'selfish gene' involves more than survival of the ruthless. Kindness and cooperation also have Darwinian value, which is what another science writer, Matt Ridley, calls 'the origin of virtue'. Perhaps compassion and benevolence began as an extension of parental instincts; the family became an extended family and then a tribe, acting rather like an organism, all of whose components need to be defended. When it comes to our own self-interests a sense of justice runs deep: every parent knows the cry 'it's just not fair!' But teamwork needs empathy and trust – an expectation that if I take a risk you will share it, or that favours given today will be returned tomorrow. We now formalise a lot of that as law.

As we saw in the last chapter, empathetic morals are improving on the whole. But our instincts for selfishness and our needs for collaboration remain rivals nonetheless. Our civilities can easily break down and this chapter seeks to lay bare just how easily that happens. We will start with the horrors of the Second World War, see how social-science experiments replicated those cruelties in the 1960s and show how what they provoked in the laboratory translates into real life today.

How would we have acted if we were under Hitler's rule between 1933 and 1945? It would be a relief if we could blame the Holocaust on something exclusively German or maybe Austrian; or at any rate some evil that was peculiar to the fascist recruits in central Europe. It is inconvenient that so many people behaved so badly in the Netherlands, Belgium and France, and to some extent almost everywhere that Hitler's armies conquered. Despite the post-war mythology, few people joined the resistance; most tried to put their heads down. It was the same for victims too. There were heroic acts of gallantry and kindness in ghettoes and concentration camps, but survivors recall how people also behaved appallingly: stealing, cheating, denouncing, even killing to get food or clothing, anything to stay alive. The haunting question is, what if? What if the Nazis had succeeded in their aim of world domination; how would our forefathers and mothers have reacted? How would we behave?

The likely answer is: not very well. The Nazis' great enemies, the communists and Slavs, acted much as the fascists did.

Informing against neighbours, indifference and pretence became the common themes. Nobody knows how many people died under Stalin's rule in the Soviet Union, maybe 20 million, but it could only happen because almost everyone swallowed their doubts or their self-loathing and acquiesced. The Japanese were even worse. So many ordinary soldiers were involved in barbarous acts that it beggars belief: torturing prisoners, using them for bayonet practice and abducting tens of thousands of girls and women as sex slaves. In one incident, the Rape of Nanking, over a quarter of a million civilians were shot, tortured to death or buried alive and thousands of women were raped and mutilated. Yet unlike Germany and Russia, Japan denies its past. Its school books airbrush Japanese savagery from history; the memorials at Hiroshima and Nagasaki portray the Japanese as victims.

What causes ordinary people to behave this way? It can't all be dismissed as following orders or acting out of fear. In his epic masterpiece *Berlin: The Downfall 1945*, the historian Antony Beevor describes how advancing Soviet troops raped almost every available female in eastern Germany. Russians say he exaggerated the horror, but nobody has challenged the essential fact: ordinary young men, who presumably were not given to sexual violence at home, humiliated and ravished their way to final victory. In one sense they were doing what many conquerors have done from time immemorial, but it cannot all be written off as reprisal. With only a few officers and political commissars attempting to restrain them, they raped liberated civilians in central Europe and even Soviet women who had been captured and imprisoned by the Germans.

Presumably Soviet soldiers had no particular predisposition to sexual violence; there is no record of mass rape on their advance towards Germany through liberated Russia, and so far as is known there was no epidemic of such assaults when the combatants went home.

History is written by the victors, who conceal and then forget their own misdeeds, but we know that the Allies in the West also frequently behaved as badly as their Nazi or Japanese foes. The brilliant American writer William Wharton confessed, but only in a memoir published after his death, that he and the platoon he commanded after the Normandy invasions were responsible for appalling crimes and that American GIs in general were often 'worse than the Russians'. He vividly describes the brutalising of civilians and the looting of French property, and how German prisoners of war were tortured and shot in the legs before being executed and buried in shallow graves. Some of his compatriots saw themselves as avenging angels, but the callousness privately haunted him in later life: 'When dug up, the buried guilts of youth smell of dirty rags and old blood.'

Of course total war is not a time for scrupulous personal morality. Very few Allies at the time became indignant at British and American bombing of cities, and most cheered the use of nuclear weapons at Hiroshima and Nagasaki. The misgivings tend to come later, at more convenient times.

But our propensities for cruelty never go away; nor does our ability to rationalise or look the other way. Post-war colonial conflicts were sometimes dirty, as any in history. Malaya and Kenya both saw massacres and mutilations including British soldiers amputating penises of prisoners. Rumours of these atrocities were widespread in Africa but suppressed and simply disbelieved in the UK until more than half a century had passed.

If you still think this is merely history, that these people were unlike you or me, were sociopaths or were bullied into it, and that these events have little to teach us about everyday crime in peacetime, then it is time to turn to what must rank as the most famous experiment in social psychology.

It began in 1961 after the notorious Nazi war criminal Adolf

Eichmann had been abducted from Argentina by Mossad agents. The case caused a sensation and the trial was televised in grainy black and white around the world. Eichmann disputed nothing and freely admitted his role in mass deportations to the gas chambers. But, he said from his bulletproof glass dock, 'I never did anything, great or small, without obtaining in advance express instructions from Adolf Hitler or any of my superiors.' He was following orders as anyone else would have done.

The excuse was ridiculed by some, but Stanley Milgram, a psychologist at Yale, wondered how many of us would have gone along with orders too.

Accordingly he placed an ad asking for volunteers, promising $4.50 for an hour of their time. He recruited forty for what he told them was a study of memory and, specifically, the effects of punishment on learning. Each volunteer was paired with another man and asked to choose a slip of paper which would randomly assign him as 'teacher' or 'learner'. In fact the other man was an actor, and both slips of paper read 'teacher', but the actor always claimed his said 'learner'. This fake 'learner' was taken to an adjoining room to be strapped into a chair and wired up with electrodes, mentioning in passing that he had a heart condition. The 'teacher' was to ask him questions and every time the subject got the answer wrong he was to administer what he was told was an electric shock.

The first punishment started with a '15v slight shock' and went up in 15v stages through a bank of thirty switches to an ominous sign reading 'Danger: severe shock', followed by two levers labelled '435v' and '450v' and marked 'XXX'.

Many people hesitated, and most needed firm instructions from the scientist at a desk behind them, but not one person refused to do as he was told. In fact nobody defied orders up to 300v despite cries of pain, banging on the wall, and pleas from next door about the heart complaint. In fact, even with screams followed by silence two-thirds of them (twenty-seven of the forty) pushed the shocks right up to the apparently dangerous and possibly fatal dose of 450v.

Stanley Milgram had proved that even presumably decent and honest Connecticut folk back in the swinging '60s would succumb to social pressure. Normal behaviour outgunned by circumstance. But was that a one-off, or just the product of a compliant age? Sadly, Stanley Milgram really *did* have a cardiac condition and he died in 1984 from a heart attack at the age of fifty-one. But by then he had tried out nineteen variations on his original theme and found, among other things, that women were as obedient as men. Many other experimenters copied his iconic methods, both in the US and around the world, and when, much later, Thomas Blass of the University of Maryland pooled the results, he found that the proportion of people prepared to inflict a fatal dose is remarkably constant, between 61 per cent and 66 per cent. What's more, over a 25-year period he found a zero correlation between the level of obedience and the year of the experiment. In other words, there is no evidence that since the 1960s we have grown any less vulnerable to abandoning our internal ethics when external conditions suggest we should.

Nor are we heartless only when ordered to be cruel. In 1971 another psychologist, Philip Zimbardo, converted part of his university department into a makeshift jail and placed an ad in the local paper for volunteers to find out what it would be like to be in prison. What followed was another classic of social psychology which is known as the Stanford experiment. By the toss of a coin recruits were assigned as guard or prisoner and given consent forms which effectively signed away their freedom for two weeks. Unknown to the volunteers, the local police were part of the experiment. Some time later, out of the blue, they made full-scale public arrests of those who were to be the prisoners.

The guards had been given no formal training but were told to strip-search and wash the inmates, tag them with ID numbers, dress them in prison uniform, and keep control. Within thirty-six hours the prisoners had become so upset and demoralised that one became hysterical and had to be let out. When the others staged a protest and barricaded themselves into their cells, the guards became aggressive and domineering, apparently forgetting they were role-playing. Their behaviour became especially belligerent at night, when they thought they were not being observed, though in fact they were under surveillance all the time. Things became so bad that the experiment had to be halted prematurely.

Even Zimbardo was stunned at how rapidly and seamlessly these apparently decent and moral volunteers had descended into violent bullies. He had demonstrated the extraordinary power of circumstance to foment evil. He describes it as the Lucifer Effect, after God's favourite angel who turned into the Devil.

Zimbardo went on to spend three more decades amassing further evidence and his research is widely quoted and admired; yet his findings were never really influential. Despite the evidence that we humans are all malleable, we prefer to see ourselves as masters of our own destiny. We are charmed by the cosy but increasingly implausible notion that we are governed by free will, and when things go wrong our instinct is to blame individuals as though they have failed a test of decency that we would pass with flying colours.

Three decades after the Stanford experiment, newspapers and TV news around the world showed a hooded man with electric wires attached to him being tortured by US troops in Abu Ghraib jail near Baghdad. It could not have been more repellent had it come from the archives of Saddam Hussein. In time, more and more pictures came to light: naked prisoners smeared in excrement, being dragged on leashes like dogs, forced into sexual acts of submission or being terrified by snarling dogs. Finally it emerged that prisoners had died under Army interrogation.

Eleven soldiers were court-martialled, with one who took the photos, Lynndie England, achieving particular notoriety. The US Army issued instructions that this sort of thing was never to happen again, and that, more or less, was that. Someone had been found to blame. It did not feature in official thinking that serious abuse was probably widespread but not usually disseminated on the web. It did not occur to the military brass that they should have learned anything from history, or from Milgram or Zimbardo, and should have expected it and planned to head it off.

The British didn't see it coming either. They appeared to have clean hands when the scandal broke, but with tragic inevitability they soon had to acknowledge that their own troops had indulged in mistreatment and even murder. With classic buck-passing, the armed forces minister blamed a small minority of soldiers rather than the Army command or his officials, let alone himself. Senior officers tried to block an inquiry which they feared would undermine front-line morale and eventually a civilian prosecutor had to be brought in to bring small fry to book. Once again nothing was learned and no new safeguards were put in place.

It later transpired that British commanders had covered up hundreds of allegations of abuse involving deaths and serious injuries. Senior officers and even medical staff had become as ensnared in the brutality as junior ranks, leaving the British public baffled and angry that Iraqis showed so little appreciation for the sacrifices of British troops.

We always write off violence as an exception. We find individuals who are to blame, after which we regard the case as solved and the issue can be closed.

None of this is to say there is no place for finding fault, apportioning blame or meting out punishments. Nor are human affairs as bleak as this chapter might suggest if read in isolation. But it does mean that instead of demonising offenders we could afford to be less holier-than-thou. And we might be wise to head off trouble in the first place.

8

CRIME AS NORMAL 2: THEFT

Hee that is without sinne among you, let him first cast a stone.
– John 8:7

If violence helps define us, so does the propensity to be dishonest. In this chapter we shall see how most of us cheat and steal and almost all of us can be persuaded to. Yet we rationalise our own behaviours while we denounce the sins of others. We have constructed a fantasy world in which we the goodies must be protected by the police and the courts from a minority of potential baddies.

In reality most of us break the law. A third of British males born in the 1950s had acquired a criminal conviction by the time they were middle-aged (see Chapter 13). If you think that sounds fantastic, several follow-up studies have shown similar results. Taken at face value, that means it is more usual for a man to be sentenced for a crime than to be a smoker. And what about the other two-thirds? Have they never been criminals? Or could it be that they never got caught and convicted?

By definition we can never get the answer from court records, but we can get an approximation by asking people to confide about crimes they committed and got away with. And the answer turns out to be remarkably consistent. Provided we can remain anonymous, most of us admit to criminal acts. This excludes most trivial and motoring offences and it includes quite a lot of violence.

Reader's Digest has had quite a bit of fun with surveys in this field, and in 2003 it asked 4,000 people from nineteen European countries how they would cope with various temptations. Almost half the Britons would evade income tax, two-thirds would dodge a fare or install illegal software, almost as many would steal office stationery and over a quarter would filch a hotel towel. For 'would' one might reasonably substitute 'had'. In a separate study most people admitted to fraud and theft they had actually committed. Over three-quarters said they had accepted too much change in a shop, a third had fiddled their expenses, and over a quarter had shoplifted. In another survey almost half of 14–21-year-olds questioned in the UK said they had committed a criminal offence within the last year. (Swiss and Dutch kids confessed to even more.)

You may dismiss most of this offending as small fry but, if you do, the fact that you are not scandalised means we have already crossed the Rubicon. Fiddling taxes, dodging fares, cheating on expenses, pirating intellectual property or even a bit of shoplifting might be socially acceptable to some people, but none of us would feel so forgiving if we were tax or train inspectors, employers, inventors, artists or retailers.

Perhaps the best illustration of double-think is our attitude to motoring offences. A generation ago, drink-driving was socially acceptable, even a bit of a joke. Yet by the end of the 1970s drunken motorists caused three times as many deaths as murderers. And, now that drink-driving is out of favour, speeding is regarded as a trivial offence. Speed cameras were vilified and had to be painted yellow so that people could see them and slow down, and hundreds were scrapped in what one newspaper described as 'a victory for motorists and fair play'. Yet not a single road fatality is caused by lack of momentum. Even after 2011, when Britain's roads were at their safest since records began in 1926, motoring still created three times more victims than homicide. For anyone concerned with consequences – bereaved families for example – the priority might reasonably be road safety ahead of murder.

The fact that we think motoring offences are trivial, or that white-collar stealing is less unacceptable than physical theft, does not mean that they have fewer repercussions.

Take avoiding tax, where it sometimes seems hypocrisy runs rife. Most people concede they would pay less tax if they could, and there is a thriving industry of tax advisers to stretch the rules and perhaps an even larger black economy in which cleaners, gardeners, tutors, builders and other traders are paid cash. In fact, the extent of middle-class cheating – something that doesn't even feature in official crime statistics – might well dwarf the social costs of offences that do. Not all of it is necessarily against the law, providing you regard the law as a mere technicality to be got round.

This distinction exposes self-delusion, or at least a lack of intellectual rigour, in the business world. The corporate sector has often claimed that it is for governments to make the laws and it is not for companies to add limits which disadvantage sharehold-ers. This is a sort of Nuremberg defence: so long as I obey the rules I don't need to think for myself. Free enterprise leaders who usually call for less official interference are effectively handing that most prized freedom, their own and their corporate ethics, over to the state. This is more than just ironic. It is a reminder of widespread moral bankruptcy. Even many of the biggest firms which have embraced the fad for CSR (corporate social respon-sibility) diligently seek loopholes to avoid paying tax, including shifting profits round the world for largely artificial reasons. As it happens, business is progressing from rules-based to principles-based accounting; the Treasury would be billions richer every year if they also moved to principles-based ethics.

Thousands of wealthy families in Britain, perhaps the majority, have even fewer scruples and use tax fiddles which are only just the right side of criminality. People who claim to be decent law-abiding citizens, many of whom no doubt denounce welfare scroungers, are siphoning money on an industrial scale, and depriving security, health, infrastructure and welfare as surely as if they were thieves. According to the Treasury, the basic rate of income tax could be cut by at least 2p if everyone 'simply paid up what they owed'.

In 2012 a reporter for *The Times*, posing as a highly paid IT consultant, had no problem finding lawyers and accountants eager to hide his money from the Revenue. One genial tax-dodging expert promised to cut his tax bill from 45 per cent to 1 per cent. 'We can't explain on paper what we do,' he said. 'It's a game of cat and mouse.' Among that firm's 1,100 clients was the comedian Jimmy Carr, who sheltered over £3 million a year from tax and was able to rationalise his own amorality while ridiculing tax scams by others.

McKinsey and Company's former chief economist reckons the world's super-rich alone have squirrelled away £13 trillion, which is the size of the US and Japanese economies combined. That is straight cash deposited in tax havens and excludes undeclared assets like property, private jets and yachts. Some experts challenge such a colossal figure, and others say concealing cash isn't proof of tax evasion, but no one doubts that governments around the world are being fiddled on an epic scale.

Fraud is a decisive demonstration of the vast role played by temptation and opportunity in crime, as opposed to need. If character is what you are when nobody is looking, the real character of markets is emancipated when economies are surging; everyone is making money, and no one looks too closely at the deals. The enticements are colossal. Only when the tide goes out do people see the rocks and all the chicanery flapping out to dry on the sand. Michael Snyder, chairman of the City of London's policy committee, describes the huge temptations for fraud in the financial capital as 'a billion-dollar problem rooted in a trillion-dollar success'. The opportunities for cooking the books in commerce are legion: overstating revenues, violating trading rules, price-fixing and market rigging, misleading clients, money laundering, insider trading and hiding losses. Financial instruments can be so complicated that it is hard to explain them, let alone audit them. And bendable enforcement seems to lead to flexible morals. A report from the Chartered Institute of Building, the trade body of the construction industry, found that 75 per cent of British construction professionals thought bribery to obtain a contract was not corrupt, and that falsifying accounts or invoices is acceptable and commonplace. Such dishonesty has been tacitly backed by governments, not least with the UK's 'biggest sale of anything to anyone', the Al Yamamah contract to supply Saudi Arabia with sophisticated weapons.

So white-collar crime, far from being the fault of the odd rogue trader, has been deeply rooted in many of our most trusted institutions. Finance houses employed analysts who inflated valuations so their banks could make lucrative trades. Great institutions like Citicorp and Credit Suisse First Boston pretended to give unbiased advice while being up to their necks in deals they recommended and, like Goldman Sachs, 'ripping their clients off' and deriding them as 'muppets'. British banks rigged inter-bank lending rates and 'mis-sold' pensions. Other major firms swindled their investors. Huge corporations like WorldCom were out-and-out frauds. Many other great names tumbled because of criminal conspiracies, including Enron, Enterasys, ImClone and

Tyco. One of the world's biggest auditors, Andersen, was found to have conspired to cheat the very shareholders it was paid to protect, and one of the biggest banks, HSBC, helped launder billions of dollars on behalf of drug cartels, rogue regimes such as North Korea, and even al Qaeda.

Many of the deceptions and conspiracies involved huge numbers of partners, managers and employees: tens of thousands of people were engaged in exploits they must have known were wrong, not least in shredding incriminating evidence. In the case of Enron, hundreds of staff knowingly conspired to blackout and thus blackmail the state of California; and virtually all the major Wall Street institutions raked in some of the profits while they looked the other way.

And these are just the palpable scandals, the crimes which failed because they were rumbled. Many might not have been discovered had investors not tried to withdraw their cash and found it had gone to money heaven. White-collar crime rarely leaves broken glass in its wake, so that for every big company that goes rotten and for every headline-grabbing conman like Robert Maxwell or Conrad Black, Nick Leeson or Bernard Madoff, much (and maybe most) skulduggery is never detected at all.

Yet some of it is titanic, especially in the public sector, where chains of ghost transactions called carousel frauds cost the Exchequer a fortune and, according to the European Commission, they probably drain the EU of well over €50 billion, more than the entire budget for the common agricultural policy. At least the Commissioners admit they have a problem; the private sector usually conceals it. The accounting firm BDO Stoy Hayward conducted an annual survey which suggests only 15 per cent of businesses report their losses to the police. In other words, because of the embarrassment we rarely get to hear about these things.

And for every big fraud there are thousands of little ones. Not much has changed since, two-and-a-half centuries ago, Adam Smith, the father of economics, noted that self-interest is the engine of industry: 'It is not from the benevolence of the butcher, the brewer, or the baker that we expect our dinner, but from their regard to their own interest.' Little wonder that merchants had to be regulated to stop them substituting meat, watering the beer, adulterating bread, tampering with scales, falsifying descriptions and generally ripping off their customers. And little wonder that trading standards officers are still overwhelmed and consumer protection has become an industry in its own right.

Since human nature is involved, no one is immune from cutting corners – not even heroes who risk their lives for their country. In 2008 an audit in the British Army found soldiers were treating expenses as a 'cash machine'. According to the chief of staff, dishonesty was so widespread that 'every single sample they have looked at this year has turned up examples of fraud'. Nor, as experience has taught, can we rule out the stars who epitomise sportsmanship. Never mind the 'bungs' in football, the betting scams in cricket, the rip-offs in horseracing or the cheating in cycle racing, the endemic nature of the problem can be judged from the fact that the Olympic Games involve thousands of random blood and urine samples and require dope-tests on all top five athletes in every competition.

There again, we rarely think of our trusted advisers as criminals, but that may be because the code of silence is as strong in the professions as it is in the criminal underworld. Telling tales is discouraged and whistleblowing needs almost reckless courage. Accordingly, we will never know how many financial consultants have put their commission ahead of good advice, how many doctors have claimed for fake patients or procedures, or how many lawyers have rifled client accounts. What we do know is

that the law had to be changed to protect clients from investment advisers; that ambulance-chasing lawyers are a menace and
that each year dozens of solicitors are struck off or entire firms
are censured for bending the rules; that university dons have been
caught on camera cheating on marks to improve the college pass
rate; and that estate agents have rigged markets, gone for fast
commission rather than best price, removed rival sale boards, and
even on occasions supplied fake documents. And we all know the
venality of the bonus culture. As the veteran City commentator
Neil Collins observed, 'Performance rewards are manipulated to
get the number you first thought of.'

The Canadian criminologist Thomas Gabor may exaggerate
a little in the title of his book *Everybody Does It*, but he is spot
on that:

> Dividing all of humanity into two camps – the decent and the
> villainous – is at odds with the facts ... almost everybody violates
> criminal or other laws on occasion. Crime ... is more like the
> common cold – an affliction to which no one is completely
> immune but to which everyone is not equally susceptible ...
> This all-or-nothing dichotomy is an antiquated view.

So what about you and me? Are our little fiddles as excusable
as we like to think? We regard it as mean and reprehensible if
a cat burglar climbs through an open window and steals money
from the administrator's desk in a hospice, but do we think
through the consequences of concealing a foreign purchase from
customs at the airport? Financially it has a similar effect. In 2002
the National Audit Office estimated that smuggling and unpaid
VAT by British citizens was costing £17.1 billion a year.

And have you, or has someone in your family, never bought
fake Gucci handbags or imitation big-brand trainers, underwear

and T-shirts? Then what about illegal downloads? Around half of young people surveyed are relaxed about stealing software or music and don't believe it should be punished.

For all our moralising about other people, these small offences make us collude in a vast criminal conspiracy. The World Trade Organization and the OECD both reckon 5–7 per cent of global trade is made up of counterfeit goods and pirated intellectual property. That's around a trillion dollars, bigger than the GDP of Australia, Saudi Arabia or all but fifteen of the world's economies. And along with the phony Viagra, gold watches that rust and DVDs recorded from the back row of a cinema, there are sub-standard baby powders, cigarettes high in arsenic, antibiotics and contraceptive pills with no active ingredients, unsafe car parts and even forged aircraft components.

DIRTY DEALING AT THE TOP

To exemplify human nature, maybe we should look at the institution we elect to represent us, the House of Commons – and it turns out MPs are rather like the rest of us. In 2008, details began to emerge that several of them had abused allowances. The chairman of the Conservative Party and the Home Secretary were among those embarrassed by the leaks, and given the politically explosive nature of the story, someone thought to steal a complete list of parliamentary expense claims and tout it to national newspapers for £150,000. Since it was plainly stolen property, at least two editors turned it down and, interestingly, it was bought by the *Daily Telegraph*, a paper which takes a noticeably tough line on other people's crimes. But that is another story. If ever the dividends justified criminal means, this was it: the scoop was sensational. Ministers as well as backbenchers across every party, large and small, were caught up in what *The Times* described it as 'Parliament's darkest day'. MPs had had ample scams to choose from: buying, improving, furnishing and even renting out unnecessary second homes; evading tax; submitting any number of claims below £250 which did not require receipts; and claiming costs such as food even when Parliament was in recess.

Half a dozen ministers lost their posts, and 180 MPs, more than a quarter of the Commons membership, repaid between them some half a million pounds. The Prime Minister was among them. More than two dozen stood down, were forced out or were taken to court. Half a dozen went to prison.

How had it happened? Despite the public's *schadenfreude*, the episode suggests that, in yielding to temptation, MPs are remarkably normal. Veteran parliamentarians had grown into a system where expenses were regarded as part of the remuneration package. Younger ones seemed caught in the headlights, often simply doing what their elders did or what officials and party whips had told them to do. And in spite of what became a lust for blame, the real culprit was readily identified. The expenses protocol itself was the real scandal; an invitation to defraud. The Speaker of the Commons, who defended it, was hounded out of office, the first time that had happened in three centuries.

Perhaps the more interesting question is: why were we surprised? Presumably because we honestly believe that we are not vulnerable to temptation and so are free to feel opprobrium for anyone who does. But that apart, we had had ample warning. An anonymous survey of MPs a decade earlier found that a sizeable minority conceded they would cheat if no one asked them to pay for a bottle of wine or a train fare. In any case, Parliament has long hosted scandals, with peerages and other honours being sold for party favours, fiddled expenses, illegal donations and backhanders such as 'cash for questions'. Sleaze helped sweep the Conservatives from power in 1997 and came to dog Labour just as badly.

Two leading government figures (Cabinet minister Jonathan Aitken and party treasurer/chairman Jeffrey Archer) were both sent down for perjury and, but for a twist of fate, they might have been joined in prison by the Prime Minister. In October 1992 a satirical magazine called *Scallywag* had claimed that for five years before he got to No. 10, John Major had had an affair. Mr Major furiously denied it and warned that accusations of adultery amounted to a serious attack on his reputation.

When the allegation was repeated (by the *New Statesman*, as well as *Scallywag*, both naming the wrong woman), he issued a writ. The Prime Minister won apologies and £27,000 in damages, and *Scallywag* went bust. It was ten years before the truth emerged. In October 2002, John Major's former colleague Edwina Currie published her memoirs and sensationally announced that John Major had indeed had an affair for several years – with her. Only John Major can answer what he would have done in the 1990s had the magazines not capitulated to his threats. Had the issue gone to court he would undoubtedly have been asked if he had ever been unfaithful to his wife. Would he have thrown in the towel and resigned; or would he too have committed perjury to save his skin?

At least he didn't try to have his former lover murdered. In the 1970s, Jeremy Thorpe, leader of Britain's third party, the Liberals, was involved in a plot to kill off stories of a homosexual affair – a relationship that was said to have happened in the early 1960s when such acts were illegal and were open to blackmail. In 1975 Norman Scott, a former stable boy, was waylaid by a gunman who killed a large dog Scott had borrowed for protection, and apparently tried to shoot Scott himself but the gun failed to go off. In a sensational trial Thorpe was acquitted of conspiracy to murder, but whatever the truth of the matter it ended his career.

Interestingly, the Tory grandee Lord Tebbit, known as the Chingford Skinhead and a 'semi-house-trained polecat' for his uncompromisingly tough views, showed great understanding when it came to fellow politicians: 'Members of the House of Commons are neither subhuman nor superhuman. They are as prone as the rest of us to give in to temptation.' Indeed they are.

We even cheat when we have little need to. The psychologist-cum-economist Dan Ariely tested this on privileged students at Ivy League universities. He set them a multiple-choice test, asked them to mark their own efforts, and got them to transfer their answers to a score sheet. Now the cunning bit. Some score sheets gave the right answers, some listed only the questions. And while some students had to hand in the original test paper, others didn't. In other words, one group couldn't cheat, the rest could, and some could be sure their cheating would never be discovered. Ariely describes the results:

> When given the opportunity many honest people will cheat. In fact, rather than finding that a few bad apples weighted the averages, we discovered that the majority of people cheated, and they cheated just a bit ... The second, and more counter-intuitive result, was even more impressive: once tempted to cheat the participants didn't seem to be as influenced by the risk of being caught as one might think.

As I say, these were not hot-headed, poorly educated and socially deprived misfits; they were smart economics undergraduates at

Princeton, MIT, UCLA and Yale. They were people unusually well equipped to calculate risks and for whom being caught should have been a big deterrent. On the other hand, even those who kept back their original test papers, and so could never have been caught burnishing their scores, only bumped them up a bit.

This 'just a bit' cheating fascinated Ariely, and in his bestselling book he explores how we all rationalise bending the rules. He tempted students by leaving cans of Coke in communal fridges to see how long they would last – all were stolen within seventy-two hours – but when he left plates of dollar bills, the money was untouched. In other experiments he found that businesspeople would steal stationery but not cash and would buy presents for their family on the company account at faraway airports but not at their home airport. 'None of this makes sense,' he wrote, 'but when the medium of exchange is nonmonetary, our ability to rationalize increases by leaps and bounds.'

Given a bell curve of human behaviour, almost all of us will rationalise, but some of us will rationalise a good deal more than others. There is no way to measure these things, but I would be surprised if there were not proportionately as many people cooking books from middle-class backgrounds as families on the fiddle on social security, or as many unscrupulous deals done by workers in white collars as by their counterparts in blue. It's generally the poor wot gets the blame, and well-heeled folk with their roomy apartments might be incandescent if a stereotypical crook with scar and swag-bag stole their handbag or their wallet. Yet, in its own way, Middle England seems perfectly capable of cutting corners, and the rich and even super-rich are not exempt.

All of which is a further challenge for the mainstream political philosophies. Seen in the round, crime simply cannot be explained as a response to unfairness and inequality. But nor can it be blamed on the feckless lower classes. We all have ethics, and each of us has different limits, but sainthood is not the default position of humanity and for most of us our morals are for sale if the price is right.

9

STATISTICS

*False facts are highly injurious to science
because they often endure so long.*
– Charles Darwin

If crime is a normal part of the human repertoire, *why is the crime rate so low?* The question sounds perverse given that crime statistics have caused public consternation and political paranoia. But the answer is instructive. All crime statistics vastly underrate actual victimisation. And among the flakiest of all are the figures most people think are most reliable: those that come from the police.

It is essential to grasp how untrustworthy their records are – and how misleading they can be – to understand why the police get so distracted and why the courts are so feeble at controlling crime. But we also need to find a better metric, because if we can't measure crime properly we can't tell if it's going up or down, we can't calibrate our responses, and we can't know if our solutions are making things better or worse.

It all once seemed so simple: if you want to know the crime, ask a policeman. The police are the experts and there is something comfortably definite about police statistics, not least that they can be traced back to actual victims. When the figures are published as tables or graphs they seem so tangible they must be real. Despite long-standing criticisms most policy-makers and commentators still take them at face value. The government even insisted that police statistics should be plotted on street maps and posted online so that, in theory, citizens can judge how safe they are. (I was privileged to be in at the pilot stage of one of these, in the English West Midlands, which showed a huge and obviously dangerous hotspot. It turned out to be the police station where suspects were searched for drugs or stolen property.)

There are three glaring problems in trusting police experience of how big or bad things are, and they all go back to a fundamental problem: crime, by definition, is illicit. As a general rule, people who break the law try not to draw attention to themselves. Sometimes their misdeeds are conspicuous, like a smash-and-grab raid in the high street, but mostly crime is surreptitious, intimate or even virtual. Every now and then someone will confess to a whole string of offences that were unknown to the police, but as a general rule, bullies, fraudsters, drink drivers, drug dealers, music pirates and rapists try to keep their crimes a dirty secret.

Accordingly, we expect the police to go and find crime for themselves. But officers rarely come across a crime in progress and, oddly, when they are proactive they actually distort the picture. A swoop on clubs will expose drug problems; a search for knives will uncover weapons. One area may have had a blitz on burglary, another on domestic violence or uninsured drivers. The arrival of a new chief constable or borough commander can have a huge impact on how the police operate, whom they target and what they prosecute. Some chiefs will turn a blind eye to street prostitution, others will clamp down on it. Often this gives rise to the perverse effect that better policing is rewarded with higher crime rates: if the police persuade more victims of rape to come forward, their tally of sexual offences will surge. Curiously, we can also get 'more crime' if those in government demand it.

Officers have often been given targets, such as two arrests per month, and charges are inflated (from, say, drunkenness to harassment – which counts as violence) to meet the quota. The Police Federation, which represents the rank and file in Britain, has justifiably called it 'ludicrous'.

Similarly disturbing crime waves happen when charities or statutory agencies launch an initiative, or when the media mount a big investigation. Who knew child sex abuse was common until ChildLine came along?

But we the public are by far the biggest source of police intelligence. In other words, police crime figures are largely what we as witnesses, victims and occasional informants choose to tell them. Which is surprisingly little. Even if we see a crime actually taking place. According to a poll for the Audit Commission, almost two-thirds of us would walk on by. We can't be bothered, don't want to get involved or don't think the police would do anything anyway. The reality may be worse than that survey suggests. Avon and Somerset Police set up a small experiment in which a plain-clothes officer blatantly brandished bolt cutters to steal bikes, and though at least fifty people clearly saw what he was doing, not one person intervened or rang 999. The video went online and proved extremely popular.

That leaves the great bulk of recorded crime figures in the hands of victims. And, again, a big majority of us have reasons to keep quiet. When people are asked about crime they've suffered and whether or not they asked for help, it turns out that only 44 per cent of personal crimes are reported to the police. Even that reporting rate is a big improvement, caused partly by the spread of mobile phones. And it doesn't count many of at least 9 million business crimes a year, most of which we only hear about through surveys, or commercial frauds which companies and managers would rather not make public.

Why do we suffer so in silence? The answer is fear, guilt and cynicism. In many ordinary crimes, and some extraordinary ones too, private citizens want to stay clear of the authorities. This is often the case in pub brawls, fights at parties, clashes in the street, domestic violence and a lot of sexual assaults which are too embarrassing to talk about. I saw this for myself when auditing crime in Oxford over two weeks for the BBC. On a typical Friday night at the John Radcliffe Hospital we filmed twelve people wounded badly enough to come to A&E, all male, all the result of alcohol, one with a bottle wound just beneath the eye, one with a double-fractured jaw, and one in a coma. But the police recorded only seven violent crimes that night, including some not hurt badly enough to have needed medical attention. Even more surprising, there was little correlation between the severity of the injury and the likelihood of telling the police.

A pioneering emergency surgeon – we shall meet him later – has systematically checked hospital records over many years and is blunt: 'Police figures are almost hopeless when it comes to measuring violent crime.'

Then there are crimes people tend not to make a formal fuss about. Sometimes the victims perceive what is technically a crime to be normal, as with childhood bullying and theft among school kids. This is even true with full-blown rape, which you might think needs few definitions, but, as we shall see later, it is not just perpetrators who deny it happened; half of all women who have been attacked in a manner that fulfils the legal description do not consider themselves to have been raped. Many victims blame themselves and some are very vulnerable. One of the worst aspects of concealed crime is often dismissed as antisocial behaviour and is targeted at people with disabilities, causing huge distress and sometimes serious harm.

More often it's simply not worth the effort of telling the police, as when an uninsured bicycle is stolen. In fact, some official theft rates do more to measure changes in insurance penetration than trends in stealing. One of the reasons that street crime appeared to rise steeply in the late 1990s was that mobile phone companies were promoting handset insurance. On the other hand, people are cautious if they *are* insured and don't want to jeopardise their no-claims bonus, as where a car is vandalised or broken into.

Apologists for the official figures sometimes demur from such pettifogging and claim that at least the more serious crimes will be recorded. Not so: under-reporting is rife in stabbings or even shootings, so much so that British police chiefs want the medical profession to break patient confidentiality and report patients treated for knife or gunshot wounds.

Even murder is surprisingly hard to count. First it has to be discovered. Britain's biggest peacetime killer, the family physician Harold Shipman, probably killed 218 patients over a span of thirty years, but none was regarded as homicide until shortly before his arrest in 1998. There are thousands of missing persons and no one knows if they are dead or alive unless a body turns up. Even with a corpse, pathologists and coroners may disagree on whether death was natural, accidental, suicide or at the hands of others; and scientific advances can suggest different causes from one year to the next. The statistical effects of all this are not trivial. Prosecutors can have a big effect too. Most years in England and Wales about 100 cases that are initially recorded as homicide become 'no longer recorded' as homicide because of reclassification. On the other hand, other defendants have the book thrown at them, as when reckless misadventure was reclassified as homicide after fifty-eight Chinese nationals suffocated while being smuggled into Britain in 2000, or when twenty-one cockle-pickers drowned in Morecambe Bay four years later.

Since in Britain murder is relatively rare, multiple deaths

like these, or the fifty-two killed in the 7/7 bomb attacks, can massively distort the figures, warping short-term trends. Long-term trends are even more difficult because of gaps in the records, especially from the age before computers, when information was kept locally on cards or paper.

Which opens another can of worms.

A third of all crime reported to the police is not recorded as a crime.

A great deal depends on whether an officer considers that an offence has taken place and, if so, whether it gets put down in the logs, when it is recorded and how it is categorised. Traditionally the police have a great deal of discretion. Retired officers will sometimes readily concede that, in years gone past, many quite unpleasant crimes were not taken very seriously: people who were racially abused, young men 'having a scrap', and even serious bodily harm if inflicted by a husband on his wife. Apart from anything else, turning a blind eye could save a lot of work.

There will always be a lot of wriggle room. When is a young man with a screwdriver equipped for burglary; when is a small amount of drugs not worth bothering about; when is a discarded handbag indicative of a mugging; when is it best to turn a blind eye in the hope of gaining some intelligence; when is a drunken brawl best dealt with by calming people down; when if some-one reports a disturbance should one finish one's paperwork or rush round and intervene? Not infrequently these ambiguities are manipulated cynically, with offences being shuffled from one category to another to reflect better on police performance. As one officer famously put it, the books are frequently 'cooked in ways that would make Gordon Ramsay proud'.

In recent years Home Office counting rules have greatly improved consistency. Even so, in 2000 the Police Inspectorate found error rates ranging from 15 to 65 per cent and in 2013 the

Office of National Statistics was still sufficiently concerned about big discrepancies that it warned police may be tinkering with figures to try to fulfil targets.

MOVING THE GOALPOSTS

Even if all crime were reported and consistently recorded, police statistics can be terribly misleading. Lawyers, legislators and officials keep changing the rules. Karl Marx came across the problem somewhat before I did, correctly noting in 1859 that an apparently huge decrease in London crime could 'be exclusively attributed to some technical changes in British jurisdiction'.

The most blatant example of moving the goalposts was between 1931 and 1932 when indictable offences in London more than *doubled* because of a decision to re-categorise 'suspected stolen' items as 'thefts known to the police'. More recently, changes in counting rules led to an apparent and terrifying surge in violent crime in 1998 and then again in 2002. It started as a noble idea to get more uniformity and be more victim-focused but resulted in completely redefining violent crime. From that point on, *half of all police-recorded violence against the person involved no injury.*

In 2008 violence was reclassified again and this time many less serious offences were bumped up to big ones. For example, grievous bodily harm now included cases where no one was badly hurt. Inevitably the *Daily Mail* reported 'violent crime up 22 per cent'.

It is not just journalists who get confused. Many political advisers and university researchers are also taken in, which can lead to silly ideas and unproductive policy. People often get irate at those who refuse to take police statistics at face value. 'We all know what they mean,' they say. It is as though challenging the figures is somehow to be soft on crime. But we don't know what they mean, and nor do the police.

International comparisons of police statistics are even more unreliable. Different countries have different laws, different customs and very different reporting rates. On the face of it, Australia has seventeen kidnaps per 100,000 while Columbia has only 0.6. Swedes suffer sixty-three sex crimes for only two per 100,000 in India.

Some people actually believe this stuff.

Evidently they don't read the warning on the crime statistics tin. The Home Office has long warned that 'police-recorded crime figures do not provide the most accurate measure of crime', and for years the FBI was so cautious it sounded almost tongue-in-cheek: police data 'may throw some light on problems of crime'. Yet however shallow, however defective, however inconsistent the figures, they have almost always been treated as far more meaningful than they are. Police responses, policy-makers' strategies and public opinion navigated according to a tally which sometimes reflects the real world and sometimes doesn't.

It is not as though we didn't have a better mousetrap. Back in 1973 when crime was racing up the political agenda, the US Census Bureau started asking people for their actual *experience* of crime. For the first time they could get consistent data from year to year and from state to state. It was explosive stuff and immediately confirmed how incomplete police statistics were. The UK was already beginning to track crime as part of a General Household Survey, but from 1982 it followed the US lead with dedicated victimisation polls called the British Crime Survey or

BCS. Other countries soon followed suit and over eighty now use a common methodology. That means we can now compare crime across borders as well as time.

THE BIG PICTURE

There is a lot wrong with the British Crime Survey. For a start, its name. The BCS only audits England and Wales – Scotland started its own SCS – and by the time they finally rebadged it (as the Crime Survey for England and Wales) the term BCS had become ingrained. So, confusingly, historical reports have to be called BCS and new ones, CSEW. If Wales goes its own way it may have to be rebranded yet again. It is also expensive. Since barely a quarter of the population suffers any sort of crime in any year you have to talk to a lot of citizens before you come up with a representative sample of, say, attempted burglary victims, let alone people who have suffered major trauma. That requires almost 50,000 face-to-face questionnaires, and not everyone will give up forty-five minutes for intrusive questions. It means researchers must doggedly go back to find the hard-to-get-at people, especially where victimisation is at its worst, and get them to trust in the anonymity of the process. It's not like an opinion poll; it's a mini-census that costs £100 per interview.

Even so it leaves a lot of gaps. Most obviously, it leaves out business crime, which has had to have a separate survey of its own. It is also hopelessly unreliable on rare crimes – one would have to interview almost a million people to get representative data on homicide. For a long time it missed out on under-sixteens too, fearing parents might object, but that has now been sorted. Past surveys also neglected homeless people and those in communal dwellings like student halls of residence, old people's homes or hostels. An increasingly significant problem is that it largely ignores internet crime, but then so does almost everyone. And it almost certainly undercounts the most vulnerable in society who are victimised repeatedly and whose complaints are arbitrarily capped at five. Finally, being national, it has limited value in describing local crime.

Yet for all that, it has a huge advantage. Respondents may misremember or lie, but there is no reason to assume that memories or candour will change much from one year to the next. In other words, these big victimisation surveys have a power to describe *trends*.

So why did surveys like the BCS/CSEW take so long to catch on with the politicians, press and public? The answer is, they didn't come up with the right answers. Governments wanted to look competent, but since victim surveys uncovered far more crime than was realised hitherto they made the problem look even worse: the BCS revealed 8 million crimes a year compared to 3 million recorded by the police. Perhaps unsurprisingly, the early reports were met with a 'conspiracy of silence'. One of the pioneers, Jan van Dijk, describes how his home country, the Netherlands, reacted with dismay in 1989 when the first international survey put it top of the league table for several property crimes, including burglary. The findings were lambasted for weeks by Dutch politicians, the media and criminologists.

On the other hand, crime surveys came to be disparaged by curmudgeons, including most journalists, because from 1995 they started to show crime was coming down. In fact in ten years, BCS crime fell 44 per cent, representing 8.5 million fewer crimes each year. Critics believed that this was just not credible and preferred police statistics which were far less encouraging and sometimes – on vandalism for example – continued in the opposite direction.

Thus it was that the British media continued to report that crime was climbing long after it had peaked and, incredibly, they went on with their rising crime agenda throughout a decade and a half of steep decline.

That is a story in itself.

10

MEDIA

*Your connection with any newspaper would be a disgrace and
a degradation. I would rather sell gin to poor people
and poison them that way.*
– Sir Walter Scott, 1829

Sexual intercourse began in 1963, according to Philip Larkin; according to popular wisdom, some time around then so did the modern crime wave. It seems almost universally accepted that crime was rare until the early 1960s and has got steadily worse ever since. In the 1990s, when the apparently unstoppable tide did finally recede, most people in Britain would not believe it – and many still don't. When the BCS asked people about fear of crime more than a decade after the big retreat began, almost two-thirds thought crime was continually rising, half of whom thought it was going up steeply. Unsurprisingly, readers of tabloids were around twice as likely to worry as readers of broadsheets. People have gradually become more sanguine since but only slightly. This misperception is more than just a matter of curiosity; most of us hugely overestimate our own chances of being a victim and it undermines intelligent debate. It also obscures one of the most important lessons in all the long history of human interaction. Society can let crime get out of hand, but it has remarkably effective ways of bringing it back under control.

Yet so deep was the sense of cynicism, hopelessness and anger that it was heresy to tell the truth.[†]

How come we were so comprehensively misinformed?

A BRIEF HISTORY OF CRIME

It is tempting to take a romantic view of Merrie Englande, imagining an idyll of rustic harmony. But as more historical archives are analysed, the more it seems that violence was once a much larger part of life than it is now. Historical records show the homicide rates in thirteenth-century England were about twice as high as those in the sixteenth and seventeenth centuries, and those of the sixteenth and seventeenth centuries were some five to ten times higher than those today.

This pugnacious description of England as a whole is supported by local evidence, not least from the county of Kent. The trail of documents from Tudor times up to the present offers strong support for the thesis that the four centuries after 1560 score the decisive decline in the incidence of homicide in England. The secular trend is unmistakably downward: from an average annual rate of 4.6 per 100,000 people in the sixteenth century, to a meagre 0.7 per 100,000 in the decade ending 1980.

Not that most people noticed the improvement. As the Kent researcher observed: 'Every era from the fifteenth century to our own day has produced witnesses eager to

---

† For many years politicians and police chiefs were so trapped in the headlights of public disquiet that one of the government's foremost responses to crime was a strategy to cut the fear of it. A Home Office working party chaired by Michael Grade reported in 1989, highlighting irrational fears even though crime was then continuing to surge. A toolkit was created to help local councils drive down fear of crime and an initiative was launched to improve the image of criminal justice. Few official reports noted that anxieties about crime often mingled with exasperation and anger.

testify to the unprecedented violence and criminality of their own generation.' In other words, every generation has been sure things used to be much better in some far-off time of innocence, even if writers cannot quite agree when the 'golden age' actually took place. A trawl through recent British newspapers generally locates it in the Victorian age, in the Edwardian period up to 1914, in the inter-war years or, at any rate, not now.

What is clear is that recorded crime rose slowly from 1900 to 1930, then accelerated to the 1950s, after which there was a fearful lurch upwards which continued for forty years. The scale of change was phenomenal. Whatever the weaknesses of police statistics, it was far too powerful to be merely an artefact of better reporting and record-keeping. Known offences in England and Wales rose almost seventy-fold, from 80,000 in 1900 to a peak of 5.5 million in 1995. The most reliably recorded crime, murder, went up too, roughly tripling in four decades after 1960. The upsurge was corroborated by other data, not least after victimisation surveys got under way. Crime increasingly became one of the most talked-about vicissitudes of daily life.

Fearing a punitive backlash some liberals and left-wingers tried valiantly to write off public disquiet as a 'moral panic'. In the 1960s a prominent psychiatrist who treated young offenders assured us that 'throughout the last half of the nineteenth century the proportion of the population incarcerated in English prisons was considerably higher than it is now'. In fact recorded crime rates in the late nineteenth century were relatively tiny, while the prison population was proportionally about the same.

In the 1980s, sociologist Geoffrey Pearson almost went so far as to blame the middle classes for hysteria. His book, *Hooligan,*

A History of Respectable Fears, is still sometimes quoted today as proof that crime is nothing new; but all it really proves is that newspapers have always catered to excitement about crime and have rarely been guilty of context.

Even so the book is an intriguing chronicle of what our forebears used to read over the breakfast table. Juvenile delinquency was a big thing in the 1850s, soon followed by concerns about garrotters in the street, cads on the omnibus, roughs in the Underground and hooligans everywhere. The Victorian prose may sound quaint but all the journalistic themes would be familiar today. According to *The Times* in 1862, 'our streets are actually not as safe as they were in the days of our grandfathers', and there was often a presumption that crime was 'of foreign importation'. *The Spectator* warned that roads in London 'are as unsafe as Naples'. What's more, there used to be a nicer breed of criminal: *The Observer* grieved at how the '"gentlemanly" highway-man' had 'degenerated into a coarse, brutal ruffian'. There were repeated calls for the arming of the police, and *Punch* cartoons showed police struggling with masked bandits, or ladies being escorted home by a platoon of officers wielding cudgels, guns and sabres.

In the 1920s and '30s, the worry was over razor gangs, inspiring Graham Greene's *Brighton Rock* with its violent anti-hero Pinkie. The post-war menace was underworld gangs, flick-knife-wielding Teddy boys, mods and rockers who battled at the seaside, and so it went on … skinheads, football hooligans, punks, hoodies … along with the enduring themes of blame: the breakdown of family life, excessive affluence and freedom for the working classes, the corrupting influence of popular entertainment, insufficient floggings or hangings and, of course, whichever party was in government.

If ever there was a tranquil age, content and unfazed

by rampant criminality, it is impossible to discern it from a century and a half of headlines or editorials.

If crime sells papers even when offending rates are relatively low, one could hardly be surprised that it made headlines when crime soared. This was a genuinely worrying phenomenon. Especially to anyone who has worked with victims. And it went on for so long it's little wonder that people came to see ever-rising crime as a force of nature. When circumstances changed one might expect that attitudes could trail a bit behind reality. On the other hand, when the river stopped and then started flowing in the opposite direction, the media had a really good story; if one was inclined to believe in the public and democratic value of the press, you might expect journalists would seize on the crime drop with honest reporting and brave investigations.

After all, crime did not just dip; it plunged.

Almost all the downward trends were masked at first by figures recorded by police, but as we have seen, property crime began to tumble around 1995 and violent crime subsided five years later. In fact hospital attendance for wounding fell every year from 2001 onwards. Police statistics caught up eventually. Homicide seemed to have peaked in 2002, and the police recorded the first minor fall in violence against the person in 2005. After that the police statistics fell ever faster in line with the British Crime Survey. The speed of crime's decline had come to mirror the ferocity of its ascent. In fact, according to the BCS the fall was steeper than the rise, dropping 44 per cent within ten years.

So the fact that most people think otherwise has to be an issue for the media. After all, the belief in rising crime can't be because of personal experience, since that is what is measured by the

British Crime Survey and shows the biggest falls of all. Nor can it be explained by our informal dialogue with friends and neighbours, because their experiences too are charted by the BCS. In fact, the British Crime Survey tells us quite clearly where our misconceptions come from. People consistently think communities elsewhere suffer more crime than they do. And since almost everyone feels the same, we can only be voicing what we have read about or seen on the TV.

All polls which ask the 'how bad is crime?' question yield the same discrepancy. In fact, things get even odder. People are often unaware of local crime risks. Those most vulnerable, notably young males, feel more secure than those at slight risk, like the elderly. And people often have a diffuse anxiety – being home alone or going out in the dark – rather than specific worries. Their local concerns tend to be noisy neighbours, litter, dog fouling, speeding or illegal parking. But their political apprehensions, and often anger about crime, reflect the news.

And just look at the news they were getting.

'A NATION STALKED BY FEAR: Rape up 27 per cent, Violent crime up 22 per cent, Drug offences up 16 per cent.'

This was from Britain's top-selling newspaper, *The Sun*, eight years after crime had started to fall, but I could have chosen any national paper at any time that crime rates have been reported. It typifies a sort of honest mendacity in which none of the singular facts is untrue but they result in a larger lie. A fairer précis might have read: 'CRIME RATE DOWN AGAIN: Burglaries down, Robberies down, Risk of being a victim at lowest for twenty years. Some worrying trends.'

And I don't just mean the tabloids. It was equally true of the posh papers and the broadcasters too, including the BBC, where I was a lone voice in saying there was no cause for nightmares.

Regardless of how far or fast crime figures plummeted, the

media's stories were relentlessly about growing crime, and there were very few exceptions. They could always find something to frighten us with. When burglary and car crime figures plunged, attention turned to violence; and when violence fell the spotlight switched back to property crime. In 2009, on the day new figures emerged showing homicide dropping to its lowest level in twenty years, *The Times* ran: 'Recession blamed for rise in property crime.'

According to *The Sun* it was: 'CRIMECRUNCH UK: Shoplifting and bag snatches rocket; Burglaries rise … first time in 6 yrs; Child cruelty is soaring in recession.'

The *Daily Mail*'s story was: 'RISE OF THE ONLINE CREDIT CARD SHARPS: Annual crime figures reveal fraud soaring to £610m … Serious knife crime attacks rocket by 50 per cent.'

Only *The Guardian* was different: 'Murder rate lowest in 20 years as crime figures show little knock-on effect from recession.'

Not that *The Guardian* was always so restrained. For example, in 2006, again long after acquisitive crime had fallen off a cliff and when violence was now clearly dropping too, here is an ordinary crime story on an ordinary day in a highbrow paper.

Sawn-off shotguns are still the weapon of choice for the more serious armed criminal and can now be bought illegally for between £50 and £200, according to Home Office research … The cheapness of illegal guns in Britain is uncovered in research by Plymouth University academics … Even though those interviewed were in prison, many still viewed gun crime as a 'viable career option' enabling them to overcome their deprived backgrounds to secure wealth and status. One man from Greater Manchester claimed he had earned £52,000 in a week from gun crime. The study shows that though Nottingham is dubbed Britain's gun crime capital, guns are far more available in Manchester, Liverpool, Birmingham and London … The researchers, Gavin Hales, Chris Lewis and Daniel Silverstone, said that increasingly firearms had become a normal part of the systematic violence found in the street-level criminal economy.

The researchers on the other hand, who, incidentally, were at Portsmouth, not Plymouth, summed up their findings in a manner that went unreported:

Illegal guns are not easy to obtain for most people. The study dispels the urban myth of walking into a pub and buying an illegal gun for £50. The illegal guns are generally only available to a small minority of well-connected criminals and these weapons are often shared around. Even in the communities most seriously affected by gun crime, the vast majority of people have nothing to do with guns or crime.

Journalism is about narrative and narrative is about marshalling the facts to fit the story. It is very natural to want to elbow any context if it doesn't help the theme. And I can tell you from long personal experience that journalists are under intense pressures to 'stand a story up'. But reporters are rarely just cynical manipulators. They usually believe their own accounts of the world. As someone once remarked, 'scrutinising the British press for sinister motives in its coverage of crime may be a waste of subtlety'.

Gun crime is a case in point. Early in 2007 three teenagers were shot dead in different parts of London and three other shootings left one man dead and two others injured. Newspapers and bulletins went into overdrive about a 'war zone' where guns were just a fact of life. But homicides involving firearms had almost *halved* in the previous five years, from a peak of ninety-five to fifty. This inconvenient truth was comprehensively ignored, not least by the public-service BBC. It was left to the website *Spiked* to point out that: 'In America there is an average gun-killing rate of 3.97 per 100,000 of the population; in Canada it is 0.59; in Switzerland it is 0.51; in Sweden it is 0.37; in England and Wales it is 0.14.'

In fact, because UK gun laws are drawn so widely, half of all firearms offences in England and Wales were kids playing with airguns and paintballs (10,437 out of 21,521 recorded gun crimes, seven of which had caused serious injury in 2006), and another third involved imitations such as toy guns, pellet guns or just sticks concealed under a coat. Even the presumed real weapons were rarely discharged.

Many fellow journalists will think I am being pernickety and complacent: any death from shooting is a tragedy and fifty in a year was a terrible toll. But that does not justify distortion. A friend of mine, a professor from Newark, New Jersey who was visiting London at the time, was bewildered by the media hype. That year 100 people died from gunfire in his fairly small home city. Incidentally, given that murder attracts more publicity than most crimes, you might be surprised to know that by far the most common victims of homicide in Britain are babies. Infants suffer one-and-a-half times as many killings as the next most vulnerable group, young adults. This is not the picture that is usually portrayed.

A year or two later guns were old news so far as the media were concerned. In 2008 the headlines were dominated by knives, almost to the exclusion of any other category of violent offence. Yet at that time the BCS showed knife crime was stable. Police figures in London – where the problem was said to be worst – recorded a 15 per cent year-on-year drop.

Nonetheless the media tail wagged the police dog. As a result of the publicity the Met announced that knife crime would replace anti-terrorism as the number-one priority.

Maybe we get the media we deserve. Journalists, to a great

extent, are playing to the gallery. News is entertainment with a straight face, a soap opera designed to keep us in our seats. That means that while news is our biggest window on the world, the glass is partly silvered – it is something of a mirror. In crime coverage, as in reporting other stories, there is a natural tendency to reflect back to us the images we want to watch and read and buy. If Tories tend to take the *Telegraph*, if liberals prefer *The Guardian* and if women buy the *Mail*, each paper has every incentive to massage those prejudices rather than confront them; and in Britain the newspaper business has long been the most competitive on earth. Some columnists and producers have privileged independence, but they are exceptions to the rule.

The American media commentator Michael Wolff expressed it with typical flourish: 'Fleet Street is to journalism – journalism as an act of civic responsibility, that is – as military music is to music. Fleet Street is in the audience business rather than the news business, or it is an open rivalry between both impulses.'

Being in the audience business, journalists themselves often fail to see the wood for the trees. Day-to-day crime tends to be reported as a series of isolated dramas, only linked to hype an issue such as gun or gang culture. And each juicy crime can go a long way: the horror of what happened, the police investigation (with endless opportunities for armchair criticism and wild conjecture), background about suspects, maybe a long trial, sometimes an appeal and, in especially infamous cases, an anniversary reprise. Little wonder crime seems relentless.

Broadcasters are no exception, as one of the BBC's main newscasters, Martyn Lewis, discovered to his cost in the 1990s when he cautioned that bulletins concentrate too much on bad news – a statement of the obvious, perhaps, but one that was met with derision from many of his colleagues. And oddly, the requirement on broadcasters to be balanced often has perverse effects when evidence comes up against belief, as I can vouch from many years of personal experience. For example, in 2007 I was asked by the BBC *Today* programme to explain the latest falls in crime. The package was carefully pre-scripted, checked (not least with a Fellow of the Royal Society and of the Royal Statistical Society and the Professor of Public Understanding of Risk at Cambridge University) and pre-recorded the night before the show. But after I went home a producer panicked. He thought it might prove controversial to say crime was declining – so in pursuit of BBC neutrality he phoned round to get a rebuttal. Given that no self-respecting statistician would oblige he found a leader writer on the *Telegraph* who opined that of course crime was getting worse because 'people feel it is going up'. Subsequently newspapers piled in, with a sneering editorial in the *Mail*: 'Perhaps [Nick Ross] would have us tell folk to leave their doors unbolted, cars unlocked and tell Grandmother she can walk home alone after dark.'

And the news pages found a Tory front-bench spokesman to buttress the newspaper's own self-interested perspective: 'We all know Nick Ross is meant to be a great national treasure but he's doing exactly what Labour ministers do, he's being very selective with his statistics.'

After which he quoted some very selective statistics.

Perhaps one should take these things lightly. As Max Hastings, one of the most revered British journalists, observes: 'Journalists often generate synthetic indignation. Indeed, the ability to do so is almost indispensable to media success.'

But I do sometimes wonder how those critics, notably Alasdair Palmer of the *Telegraph* and the shadow minister David Ruffley, excuse their ignorance now that they must surely recognise that they were wrong. Perhaps the only reason they took umbrage is that Labour was then in power; as soon as the Conservatives got in, the party faithful quickly changed their tune. Meanwhile, Labour sneakily measured the turning point in crime from 1997, the year they came to government. Everyone was at it. Even civil servants were criticised by their own information watchdog for politicising data.

In any case it suited politicians, just as much as journalists, to argue about the figures because, frankly, it disguised the truth that, whatever was happening, they had little idea *why* it was happening.

11

FALLACIES

Remember son, many a good story has
been ruined by over-verification.
– James Gordon Bennett, publisher of the
New York Herald

Promoting unwarranted fear may have been the worst product of media gluttony for crime. But cliché journalism sustains many other misleading notions too. Crime reporters are not expected to be intellectuals and in some way this whole book is a challenge to everyday reporting of crime. We've already encountered the curmudgeon's myth that crime is always rising, the deviancy delusion that offenders are abnormal, the glasshouse fantasy that crime is what *other* people do, the rising standards fallacy (which can see reporting rates rise as problems fall) and the criminal justice dependency with its exaggerated assumptions about what courts can achieve. We will encounter more as we travel on. In the next chapter, for example, we will spin through some howlers to do with sex. But before that, let's tick off a few of the other common misconceptions that are relayed, amplified and rarely questioned by a communications industry that claims to be a bulwark of informed democracy.

The conspiracy theory

Who can resist a good conspiracy theory? Whether it's flying saucers or a Bermuda triangle, or that NASA faked the moon landings, JFK was killed by the Mafia (or perhaps by the CIA), 9/11 was organised by Mossad, Princess Di was murdered, the Holocaust wasn't a holocaust, Shakespeare wasn't really Shakespeare or Elvis Presley faked his own death, our collective appetite for plots and scheming is quite as fascinating as the convoluted theories apparently rational people like to believe in. The human condition recoils from the mundane untidiness of reality.

William of Ockham, the fourteenth-century philosopher from Surrey, was rightly sceptical of our taste for embellishing simple explanations with Byzantine intrigues. His advice to keep it simple, stupid is a reliable guide to crime, but one that journalists and their readers much prefer to ignore.

Jack the Ripper is the most notorious example. The detective in charge at the time thought the killer was deranged, a deduction of which Ockham would surely approve, but ever since we've been bombarded with theories, mostly baseless and some inane, accusing the Duke of Clarence, the artist Walter Sickert, an unknown midwife dubbed Jill the Ripper, and – truly an Alice in Wonderland fantasy – the author Lewis Carroll.

Something similar happened after the murder of my colleague Jill Dando.

In 1999 Jill's shooting caused a sensation. At the time she was the most famous and perhaps the most popular presenter on factual TV; given her role on *Crimewatch* the media leapt to the idea that her murder was in response to one of her appeals. Within hours I was the centre of a media furore and was trying to calm the speculation down. The immediate facts made a contract killing improbable but in any case the revenge motive would have been entirely without precedent in modern mainland Britain. There was no history of reprisals against police or prosecution lawyers, trial barristers, judges or anyone else involved in detection or the criminal justice process. So why would an embittered mobster take his anger out on someone who simply voiced an appeal? A gangland conspiracy was hardly the most likely scenario.

For what it is worth, I had anecdotal reason for scepticism too. I was even more identified with *Crimewatch* than was Jill and yet when I visited jails there was never animosity from prisoners; if anything, I was treated with rueful affability, at best as a celebrity, at worst as an industry colleague from a rival firm.

As more evidence emerged, the conspiracy theory on Jill's death became even more unsustainable. The killer had hung around with no disguise at the wrong address – it was chance she turned up. He had no getaway vehicle and so had to walk away down a long straight street with no turn-offs. He didn't have a real gun or ammunition but home-made versions of both. He held the weapon in contact with his victim's head, which would have showered him with tell-tale forensic evidence. (The FBI told me this alone would have been unprecedented for a contract killing.) Jill had her key in the lock but instead of pushing her inside, he attacked and left her on the doorstep. And so it went on. All in all it was about as amateurish and clumsy as a shooting can be.

So I became alarmed when the inquiry seemed to be taking the conspiracy theory seriously. I wrote privately to the head of the investigation pointing out that when celebrities are shot, like John Lennon, the killer invariably turned out to be a loner (by which we often mean a joiner whose attempts at socialising fail):

> Probability takes on a new meaning when you are regularly on popular TV. One of the features is that we are known to a lot of weirdos, far more than most people interact with, because

our circle of acquaintances is measured not in hundreds but in millions. Moreover, they are sometimes more than acquaintances. They may regard us as friends or even lovers. Viewers sometimes think they know us intimately. We do, after all, come into their lives and often share not just their living rooms but bedrooms too. In fact the prospect of Jill being 'acquainted' with someone suffering with an extremely rare psychopathic condition – provided a person with such a condition exists in the UK – is close to 100 per cent.

It turned out that Britain's top profiler at the National Crime Faculty agreed with me, but nobody took much notice. It was a frustrating as well as an upsetting time for me and for Jill's other colleagues on the programme. Yet, when police inquiries drew a blank, causing this first conspiracy theory to fade, I could not have imagined that another intrigue would replace it, one that was not just unconvincing but risible.

According to this new hypothesis, the author of Jill's murder was Slobodan Milošević, or at any rate her shooting was organised on his behalf by his supporters. The reason was that a few weeks before Jill's death she had fronted an appeal for victims of the civil war in former Yugoslavia and there was conjecture that the Serbs had taken umbrage. Then when a Serb TV station was hit by a NATO air strike on Belgrade, a plot was hatched to kill her.

However improbable it seems, this Balkans theory made front-page news and became one of the most popular and persistent explanations for Jill's death. Two years later the Serb assassination plot would eventually be placed for formal consideration before a jury at the Old Bailey.

I won't go into details of why, on a purely practical level, the Yugoslav connection was always far-fetched; all you need to know is how the theory came about, because that reveals all the evidence there ever was to underpin it.

Jill's agent was Allasonne Lewis, a close confidante of Jill's and the last person Jill spoke to on the morning of her death. As you might suppose, Ally was terribly upset and desperate to understand why it had happened. Perhaps more than anyone, Allasonne knew how Jill combined her private life with her broadcasting career, but could think of no one with the slightest motive. Eventually she did vaguely remember something: a note that came with fan mail complaining that Jill's Kosovo appeal had failed to show how much Serbs were suffering too. There was nothing particular about the letter: no green ink, not even the vaguest threat, nothing inappropriate or untoward, and having mentioned it briefly to Jill, Allasonne had thrown it away. But now, 'clutching at straws', it was something she mentioned when she was seen by the police. When word of it reached the press, it quickly became headline news, and convinced even Ally's boss, my former agent Jon Roseman. He later wrote, 'I've always believed there is a Serbian link to Jill's murder.'

So there you have it. An unremarkable letter and – with no verification whatsoever – a leading theory about why one of Britain's most celebrated television personalities was murdered.

For the record, Allasonne now thinks the idea is ludicrous. So does the senior investigating officer, and so do all Jill's colleagues who have been on the inside track of the inquiry. Conspiracies happen, of course. War is a good motive, governments manage to keep dirty secrets for years and intelligence operatives have not always been averse to assassinations. But history is not controlled by losers and with the fall of the Milošević regime there were hundreds of witnesses anxious to testify against his murderous tactics, thousands of documents were recovered, vast numbers of phone-taps were undertaken, and Milošević himself went on trial at The Hague. Not a whisper of evidence, not a scrap emerged mentioning an English TV presenter or suggesting why a regime fighting desperately for survival at home would launch a risky, high-profile and entirely unnecessary assassination of a celebrity unknown to most Yugoslavs a thousand miles away.

Yet crime and conspiracy theories go together as readily as Bonnie and Clyde. We love 'em.

The Moriarty fallacy

Cousin to the conspiracy theory is what I call the Moriarty fallacy: the tendency to exaggerate the cleverness of offenders. Classically, journalists who fall into the Moriarty trap presume that if a crime is hard to solve it must be because the crook was ingenious, not that he is elusive precisely because of his lack of planning and/or consistency. This promotion of criminals to evil prodigies is equally convenient for detectives, who sometimes sound like PR agents for villainy, assuring us that the scoundrels they seek are 'professional', 'ingenious' or 'highly organised' and their crimes are 'well planned' and 'meticulously carried out'.

You'll find the fallacy appearing in almost any major crime. When British holidaymakers and a French cyclist were shot dead in France in 2012, provoking global headlines, the story was instantly promoted to Moriarty level. 'Was Alpine family killer a professional *hitman*?' ran the headlines, and according to *The Times* the victims were assassinated with 'chilling precision'. Except that no, they weren't. No fewer than twenty-five bullets were fired, one child was shot in the shoulder and then beaten to the ground and another child managed to hide.

People reach for this inflation even when major elements of the crimes are plainly opportunist. Once in rehearsal for *Crimewatch* an officer confidently told me that precious rock 'n' roll memorabilia had been stolen to order and, had I not checked with the victim (a well-known rock musician), this intelligence might have featured in our appeal. Except it wasn't intelligent; the owner pointed out that rolls of electric cable had been stolen while the most valuable instrument had been left behind. Another detective told me a robbery had been 'highly sophisticated' on the grounds that the thugs had communicated with each other using walkie-talkies, something my children used to do when they were little. And so it goes on.

Of course there *are* crimes which need a bit of planning, and it would hardly be surprising if there were sometimes reconnoitres and rehearsals, but such things hardly require cunning or sophistication. There *are* some truly clever crimes, but they are much more likely to be complicated frauds than robberies or murders. Most crime is mundane. Which leads us to...

The dramatic fallacy

Forget the cops and robber movies, most crime is dull. Coppers weren't called PC Plod for nothing. It may take courage to commit a crime – in fact bravado is one of its attractions (see below) – but most offending is low-grade and most police work involves repetitive routine: briefings, walking the beat, driving around, standing outside a football ground or nightclub, waiting in court or sitting in offices and filling in forms. Fly-on-the-wall documentaries have to be edited massively to create an active narrative, let alone a sense of drama. Most detective work entails slogging through research that is rarely more exciting than any other administrative chore. Even the blues-and-twos, the 999 emergency responses, are usually far more noise than substance, a bit of macho excitement in the race to another incident where nothing much is happening or where the action is long over. If ever there really is a skirmish or some other drama then patrol cars from miles around will tend to congregate. Arrests are generally mundane too: mostly for small-time offences with suspects who are generally compliant, even sheepish, often involving long waits for transport or for processing back at the nick, and always entailing a lot of form-filling.

Policing can be fulfilling, interesting and comradely. It can bestow a sense of responsibility, nobility and power. But upholding the law is not a good career for those who seek heart-pounding thrills.

On the other hand, breaking the law, though almost always undramatic, can cause quite an adrenalin kick for those who take part…

The cowardice canard

It is sometimes hard to tell the truth, and you don't always get praised for doing so. Like telling children that Father Christmas doesn't exist. Or like conceding that some offences require audacity, even daring. Take the judge who admitted he would be scared of committing the sort of crimes a culprit had carried out. Despite his honour's reputation for toughness in a Teesside court he told one drug-user before him: 'It takes a huge amount of courage, as far as I can see, for somebody to burgle somebody's house. I wouldn't have the nerve.' He was reprimanded by the Office for Judicial Complaints and rebuked by the Prime Minister.

Yet clearly most crime is not for the faint-hearted. On the contrary, the fact that it often takes bravado is, sadly, one of its attractions. Young offenders sometimes use crime as a dare – and say the buzz can be addictive. As one recidivist burglar put it: 'Gambling comes close, but it isn't the same.' Even soldiers who have shown valour in fighting for their country can get sucked in. Troops who have seen combat and are then discharged are one-and-a-half times as likely to acquire a criminal record for violence as veterans who have not fought in a war. These are hardly cowards.

On the other hand, crime is rarely profitable...

The 'crime pays' delusion

We are all attracted to the story of the successful crook with a mansion and large car, but for the overwhelming majority of blue-collar criminals crime is a rotten way to make a living. Despite this, almost every crime story takes the most generous interpretation of the value of anything stolen. The classic goes something like: 'thieves got away with £15,000 of jewellery', when the resale value is very much less and the criminal may be lucky to pocket a few hundred pounds. Every now and then a spectacular robbery succeeds, but usually does more for popular culture than it benefits most of those involved. Stolen property is hot property and most thieves make little money.

Art thefts in particular make little economic sense. After all, where can you sell a Rembrandt? Reports that priceless works must have been 'stolen to order' are almost entirely Hollywood-inspired inventions. While on rare occasions big ransoms have been paid, the cash is usually laundered through several middlemen who pocket most of it. In the great majority of cases there is no money offered and the works are frequently abandoned. According to Robert Wittman, founder of the FBI's art crime team:

> Nine times out of ten, when individuals commit a robbery like that, it's done by individuals or criminal organisations which have the ability to do a burglary, but they don't usually have the ability to sell paintings. What the thieves don't understand is

that the value of artwork comes from authenticity, provenance and legal title. In the twenty-five years I have investigated these robberies, I have never heard of anyone actually monetising these very valuable paintings.

The drugs trade is thought to be one of the most lucrative fields in crime but when, in 2000, economists Steven Levitt and Sudhir Venkatesh did the first detailed study of how much US gang members actually take home, they found that life was far from glamorous for dealers even during the big crack epidemic. While a successful franchise owner could pocket a fortune and a local ringleader might make far beyond what he could earn legitimately, the average foot soldiers – even if they were skimming quite a bit of the profits for themselves – were taking enormous risks for little more than the average wage.

It is true that some crimes can cause a disproportionate amount of damage – metal theft, for example, where massive costs can result from damaging historic buildings or disrupting railway signals – but typically those involved earn less than they could have done in formal employment. When a '£500,000' sundial was famously stolen from the Henry Moore Foundation Gardens, it was recovered from a scrap merchant who had bought it for £46.

The them and us fallacy

It is easy to believe that a large proportion of crime is committed by a very small number of people. Only the name has changed, from the 'criminal classes' of old to the 'persistent and prolific offenders' of today. And it's official. In 2001 a ministerial paper even claimed to know how few culprits there are and how much crime they do: 'We must get to grips with the 100,000 most persistent criminals who are estimated to commit half of all crime.'

So where does the evidence come from that a very small section of society is responsible for a huge proportion of our crimes, leaving the rest of us leading virtually blameless lives? A Home Office study had trawled through the database of all offenders born between 1953 and 1978. It excluded most motoring offences like speeding and focused on the sorts of things most people consider worrisome crimes. And it yielded the remarkable finding that we came across in Chapter 8: a third of all men born in 1953 had acquired at least one conviction four decades later by the time the study ended.

It was such a surprising figure that you might have thought it would make headlines. But rather than noting how remarkably widespread criminal offending was, the Home Office officials chose to emphasise the opposite.

Why? The answer may be that the result was – and still is – politically unacceptable. When I mention the one-in-three conviction figure to politicians they tend to react as though I am deluded. London's mayor, Boris Johnson, told me I must be making it up. We all prefer to think crime is caused by a discrete class of criminals (part of the so-called fundamental attribution error we discussed in Chapter 1). Whatever the reason, rather than acknowledge how widespread offending is, officials highlighted the following:

There are about a million active offenders in the general population at any one time. Of these, some 100,000 will accumulate more than three convictions during their criminal careers. This sub-group represents the most persistent offenders who are responsible for a disproportionate amount of crime. Although they represent only 10 per cent of active offenders they accumulate at least 50 per cent of all serious convictions.

This was then morphed into that dramatic claim about 100,000 baddies causing half of all our problems.

Successive ministers have stuck with the mantra, many opinion-leaders believe it and journalists often repeat it, that the country is held to ransom by a tiny cohort of stubborn criminals. One might wonder why, if the troublemakers are so identifiable, and fewer than one for every police officer, governments haven't sorted the problem out.

The truth lies in the original research paper rather than in subsequent interpretations. It tells us only about crimes that come before the courts, which, for reasons of police priorities, are biased to blue-collar offences. It tells us that it is relatively normal for men to pick up at least one criminal conviction by the time they are middle-aged, and that women are much less likely to be in trouble with the law. It tells us people who get caught usually stop offending when they are still young, or at any rate stop being found out. It tells us that some people get hopelessly ensnared by the criminal justice system and go back before the courts again and again. And it tells us that about 100,000 people at any one time will accumulate more than three convictions during the course of their criminal careers.

Among these are the PPOs, those persistent and prolific offenders. And it is true that they do cause a lot of mayhem. But this is not a fixed group of 100,000 incorrigible villains. There is a lot of churn. Some stop quickly, some persist – and it is very hard to predict who will do which – but like the rest of us they almost all grow out of causing harm.

Undoubtedly there is a minority that needs special attention – through help rather than more sanctions. As we saw in Chapter 6, warning klaxons should go off for kids who are permanently excluded from school and whose trajectory through life is likely to be dismal, short and violent; and there is a wider problem of people who are socially dysfunctional and persistently finish up in prison. That is a rather different issue that deserves a whole book on its own. But crime is not as deviant as people tend to think.

And most of us are not as secure on the straight and narrow as we care to believe.

Once bitten twice shy

Crime, like lightning, can strike twice. In fact, just as lightning defies presumptions – like travelling up not down – offenders also behave in ways that don't seem logical. In particular, they often return to the scenes of their crimes, which on the face of it is crazy unless they are especially reckless; at very least they might be recognised. But going back makes sense. One reason is that some targets are just too juicy to resist. Shop theft is a good example. More importantly, once an offender knows the terrain he has a big advantage. The risks become lower and the rewards more certain. Then he tells his friends.

People spotted the phenomenon back in the 1970s and '80s but it took two crime scientists, Ken Pease and Graham Farrell, to put repeat victimisation on the crime prevention map when they were working for the Home Office in the early 1990s. All it took was statistical analysis: seeing patterns instead of individual crimes. We now know repeat victimisation is one of the best predictors of crime – and of violence not just theft. It is a fallacy to think that if there are a thousand crimes there are a thousand victims. While most people experience no crime in a year, about 10 per cent are victimised three times or more. As in the old Christmas-cracker joke, which Pease and Farrell quoted, 'One person is being burgled every twenty-four seconds in this country – and she's getting sick of it.'

We now know a lot about how, where and when repeats occur. The greatest risk is to the immediate target. This is most obvious in domestic violence but it's true of car crime or break-ins too. In burglary, for example, the thief now also knows the layout of the street and of the house next door. So the danger radiates, eventually degrading over distance and over time. The insight has allowed victims to be warned, security to be beefed up, police to allocate resources more effectively and suspects to be narrowed down.

So if you are ever victimised, take precautions, at least where it happened and for several months thereafter. History can repeat itself.

The blunder fallacy

Each year in England and Wales around sixty murders, serious assaults, rapes, kidnaps and armed robberies are carried out by people who are on licence or probation of one form or another. It seems the authorities have blundered and it provokes a sense of outrage. But is outrage, or even criticism, justified? Let's look at the maths. Those sixty cases come from a pool of some 50,000 violent and sex offenders who are under supervision at any time. So only 0.12 per cent of the worst offences can be pinned on ex-prisoners who are thought to be the most likely to reoffend. Identifying the right 0.12 per cent as opposed to the other 99.88 per cent would be beyond the discriminatory powers of almost any test in medicine.

In fact, medicine has just this problem when it deals with crime. The media demanded 'Why were they let loose?' when it emerged that people with known psychiatric conditions commit a murder every week. But even if mental health professionals could reasonably predict such terrible events – which is extremely difficult – it would scarcely help. There are perhaps 160,000 UK cases of psychosis at any moment, of which maybe fifty will be killers. Let us imagine someone develops a test which is 90 per cent accurate in flagging who the most risky of them are. This is as accurate as many tests for cancer. But 10 per cent of patients would show up as dangerous. Which fifty persons among those

16,000 present a risk? Should we lock up all 16,000 just in case? And what of the 10 per cent chance that the really dangerous patient is among the 144,000 who have been cleared? Should we lock them up too?

Even a really sensitive forecasting tool is pretty well hopeless when it is trying to forecast exceptional events.

The agenda illusion

One of the most thought-provoking of crime scientists, Marcus Felson, has been intrigued by how crime attracts so many abiding myths, canards and downright sensationalism, many of which delusions are shared by the police. Perhaps what exercises Felson most, and should keep us all perpetually on the lookout, is what he calls 'the agenda illusion'. By this he means people's tendency to exploit crime to push their own world view. It is the anchor that drags most crime theory along the bottom of the political mudflats. Felson points out that often you only need know someone's political or religious outlooks to guess who or what will be blamed for crime and what will be touted as the salvation. The ideological cart comes before the pulling power of evidence. He suggests:

> Those who really want to learn about crime should observe the following advice:
>
> - Learn everything you can about crime for its own sake rather than to satisfy ulterior motives;
> - Set your agenda aside while learning about crime.

That's good advice but hard to follow, and agendas other than religion and left–right politics have proved especially hard to set aside. Let's turn next to one of them: sex.

12

SEX

Sugar and spice and all things nice
That's what little girls are made of…

Despite a century of feminism, and perhaps partly because of it, women are still mostly portrayed in crime as weak. It is eighty years since cinema audiences first thrilled to King Kong abducting the hapless blonde Ann Darrow atop the Empire State Building; her only defence was her beauty. Yet the stereotype of a vulnerable female prevails. Even now when women feature in crime stories they are typically depicted as victims not perpetrators. And their demise is especially newsworthy if, like Miss Darrow, they are young and decorous and ideally middle class.

How much of what we are led to believe is authentic and how much is superficial and deceptive? It is certainly true that women appear to commit less crime than men. Around the world, with remarkable consistency, women are about a fifth as likely as men to be arrested, and usually for less serious offences. But are they really sugar and spice or is it a cultural restraint; is there a glass floor as well as a glass ceiling? Many women are subject to domestic violence; but is it really as one-sided as it seems? Why, all things considered, do women suffer far less deliberate injury than men with only a third of the risk of being murdered? And who is to blame for rape? It is plainly objectionable to reproach a victim for her own misfortune; so why do so many women do it? Then what about those tales of date-rape drugs? It is common knowledge spiked drinks are a potent menace; but is it a modern myth? Is prostitution mostly victimisation; or emancipation? Sex trafficking is said to be a growing problem; but how much is voluntary rather than duress? And why, if equality is a goal, do women get much shorter sentences than men for similar offences? Or, paradoxically, if they cross a Rubicon of sex crime, why are they reviled much more than men? These are important questions that any sceptic ought to pose. Yet while challenges to orthodoxy were once scorned because of sexism, they now risk the wrath of feminists.

The established view of old was that females commit less crime because theirs is the fairer sex. In 1895 the 'father' of criminology (an aptly patriarchal sobriquet), Cesare Lombroso, confidently asserted in *The Female Offender* that women are low on the scale of evolution, with smaller brains than men, and are therefore passive, well adapted to a dull and unsuccessful life, and are less capable than men of guile. He noted sternly that female criminals are ugly, hairy and have big hands; in fact, they are strikingly like men.

And that, by and large, was criminology's only major insight about women for nearly three-quarters of a century, though there were a few intriguing observations along the way. When researchers failed to find much ugliness, excess hair or lumpiness in fallen women, Sigmund Freud proposed that when women turned from innate passivity to crime it was because they were envious of penises. Sex also featured in a barmy way twenty-five years on, when in 1950 an American sociologist, Otto Pollak, opined that women are just as much involved in crime but generally don't get caught because – wait for it – they are used to deceit on the grounds that they fake orgasm. Mark you, girls could be forgiven, poor dears, because they had to cope with all those hormones. He added for good measure that when women were found out, men tended to be chivalrous and let them off.

Given this history of patronising nonsense it is surprising how restrained early feminism was. Freda Adler, the first notable feminist on the criminology scene, rejected the thought that females are the weaker sex, innately programmed for nurturing, biologically predisposed to being good. In *Sisters in Crime: The Rise of the New Female Criminal*, she seemed determined to prove that women are intrinsically as nasty as men. Her 'Liberation Theory of Female Criminality' insisted that women's passivity merely reflects their centuries of subjugation and predicted that as women's lib advanced, women's venal and homicidal tendencies would be seen to rival those of men. Just as more women would be doctors and lawyers, so 'a similar number of determined women' would become burglars and gangsters. Well, that was 1976 and it hasn't happened yet. There are signs that the gender gap is closing – we'll see those in a moment – but women's criminal emancipation has a very long way to go.

In fact, the gender gap may have been much narrower once than it is today. A liberal American lawyer, together with a feminist sociologist, trawled through Old Bailey records from the eighteenth and nineteenth centuries. They reported that for the first 100 years or so almost half the defendants were female, three or four times the proportion we see now. Nor were theirs just stereotypical 'women's crimes' like prostitution, infanticide or witchcraft, but often involved substantial theft and violence including multiple murders. The authors described modern failure to acknowledge female crime as 'a monumental blunder'. Certainly a lot of women went to jail. In 1900 almost a fifth of all prisoners were female, compared to one-twentieth today.

Several historians concur and a similar pattern emerges in

other countries too. It seems that conviction of women declined for about a hundred years from the 1850s to the 1950s, and then began to grow again, especially among the young.

By 2005 a survey of 30,000 primary and secondary school pupils in England and Wales revealed a third of girls indulged in vandalism, just the same as boys, and stole almost as much as well (with 25 per cent of girls admitting to theft compared to 29 per cent of boys), though boys were still twice as likely to truant and were four times more likely to carry a knife. Most other findings tended to confirm the dark side of female emancipation. A small but long-term study on the south coast of England compared schoolchildren's behaviour in 1985 with that in 2005 and according to one of the authors:

> The good news, and perhaps unexpected, is that the 2005 youngsters we studied have less problematic behaviour than those in the 1985 cohort. The bad news, however, is that twenty years ago boys drugged, drank, smoked, truanted, stole, vandalised and fought more than girls. Today it is very different. Girls now significantly smoke and binge-drink more than boys. They truant, steal and fight at similar rates to boys but engage in under-aged sex earlier than boys.

Arrest rates corroborated the trend. In the US the FBI reported a significant rise in bank raids led by women and in 2007, for the first time since the war, more women were detained for violence in England and Wales than for shoplifting. But let's not get carried away. Women still commit only one murder for every nine perpetrated by men and they remain conspicuously absent from most big-league crime outrages. Only one in sixty of America's mass shootings like Columbine, Virginia Tec or Newton was committed by a woman. And if there is a long-term trend towards more gender-neutral criminality, it seems to have stalled. As crime rates tumbled, girls and women began to lead the downward trend. Arrest rates for women began to drop twice as fast as those for men, and supervision orders for girls dropped much faster than those for boys.

So what are the lessons; and how do they help us cut victimisation rates? First, on the evidence so far Freda Adler was wrong to think if women could only cast off cultural chains they would become just like the boys. Anyone who has had children will know that boys and girls really are quite different: boys usually prefer more rough-and-tumble and taking risks, behaviours which translate easily into antisocial acts. Clever experiments with children have shown that this is instinctive, not culturally superimposed, and the evolutionary psychologist Anne Campbell has convincingly proposed why prehistoric females forged their own successful strategy for survival, allowing them to live long enough to suckle and raise infants, leaving men to fight for higher if riskier rewards. In this Darwinian view, women steal less for the same reason they tend to earn less: they are as competitive as men but with different priorities. And it does seem to be true that while girls may not have superior morality they do have different tactics. Thus a woman who would not take part in a robbery might provide a false alibi, hide the weapons and spend the ill-gotten gains. Even with the recent upsurge in ladette culture, the only offences where women have typically outnumbered men have been in killing their own babies, prostitution and evading TV licence payments.

On the other hand Professor Adler was right that we need to watch where we're going. What's bad for the gander can also be bad for the goose.

We can see this – if we look properly – where we are so often told we should least expect it: domestic violence.

In 1989 the *Canadian Journal of Behavioural Science* published the results of a survey that was celebrated as a classic exposé of the problem of 'battered wives'. It was taken up as proof of typical male perfidy, and a parliamentary report made almost 500 recommendations to change attitudes in the police and other agencies. But two years later the *Journal* acknowledged a different side to the story: the data had been re-analysed and appeared to have been censored. While 10.8 per cent of the men surveyed had pushed, grabbed or thrown objects at their spouses, 12.4 per cent of women had done so too; and though 2.5 per cent of men used serious violence, so did 4.7 per cent of women. Marilyn Kwong, who exposed the expurgation, examined eight other studies too, and found the pattern was universal.

Feminism did a vital job putting domestic violence on the agenda – the police now take it seriously and in some force areas it represents one in six emergency responses. But the very success of feminism and its flattery by mainstream authority caused the politics of dissent to become institutionalised. The politics soon came to define the problem, and for decades professional interventions assumed that men were always the aggressors and if women were violent it must have been in self-defence.

However, as so often happens when dogma powers research, evidence got fixed around the theory. One researcher complains that we have been bamboozled by 'nothing less than the rejection and devaluing of the scientific method, in favour of politically acceptable interpretations of discursive material'. Despite all this, officials continue to use exaggerated claims, and many agencies, including the police, help propagate the propaganda. It is widely claimed that one in every four women is subject to domestic violence though, depending on the source, the figure might include feeling afraid, mild psychological abuse as well as minor physical assault, and any of this at *some stage in their lives*.

It would be more surprising if three-quarters of women went through their lifespan without ever once fearing some form of mental or physical attack, however inconsequential.

Many such reports also ignored the thought that women can be violent to men. Erin Pizzey, the feminist who founded one of the world's first women's refuges, has been trying ever since to set the record straight:

> I will never forget one woman, who was staying in my refuge, telling me, in chilling tones, 'knives are a great leveller'. That is the reality of domestic violence. It is far less clear-cut than the ideologues like to pretend, with their neat division between female victims and male oppressors. The truth is that much of the violence takes place in squalid, tortured relationships, often involving drink and drugs, where both partners are guilty of verbal and physical assault. In the refuge I opened in 1971, for example, of the first 100 women through the door, sixty-two admitted that they had also perpetrated violence against their partners.

Eventually more and more testimony emerged to challenge the feminist agenda but it failed to resonate with mainstream criminology or with the media. As early as the 1980s, large-scale US research began to endorse Erin Pizzey's view: women often initiated violence and could give as bad as they got. In Britain a big Home Office survey in 1995 found that 4.2 per cent of men said they had been physically assaulted or injured by their partner within the last year – precisely the same figure as for women. A subsequent trawl through over eighty studies, mostly from America, came up with a similar verdict: there was little difference between men's and women's perpetration rates. Even so the terms 'domestic violence' and 'wife battering' continued to be used interchangeably. Again and again successive BCS and other surveys showed how strikingly the prevailing view was incomplete, yet still none of this made much impact on popular or political consciousness. When fifteen years of British findings were put together in 2012, they told an essentially consistent story: between 30 and 40 per cent of those assaulted were men and they suffered a quarter of all the attacks. Although in many cases neither men nor women reported injury or emotional effects, about one in ten in both genders had suffered bleeding or broken bones and 3 per cent of men and 2 per cent of women had attempted suicide.

Not that most men would confess how they were injured. Females are twice as likely as male partners to confide in a professional, five times more likely to tell a doctor or a nurse and three times as likely to go to the police.

Bear with me on this because the women-as-victims view is so entrenched the evidence does need spelling out. And if anyone could still be unconvinced, the same pattern emerged more or less by accident from a landmark health investigation in New Zealand. In the early 1970s about a thousand children born in Dunedin's Queen Mary Hospital were chosen for regular checks on their well-being as they grew up. The idea was to see if there were paediatric indicators of what would happen in later life. When the cohort reached the age of twenty-one, the researchers became interested in the relationships that were being formed, and were intrigued to find that violence between couples was quite common. What was even more surprising, and was cross-checked by interviewing partners separately, is that the women generally hit out first and 'engaged in serious woman-to-man domestic abuse that was not explained by self-defence'. The researchers point out that because women are usually physically less powerful they tended to come off worse but 'naively' believed that if they hit their partner he would not hit back.

The Dunedin study shows, along with other studies, that women's overall rates of partner violence perpetration are similar to those of men. This is not an isolated finding. Many studies have found that substantial numbers of women self-report abusive behaviours toward male partners, and epidemiological studies show that although males are more likely than females to engage in almost every type of violence, the single exception is family violence.

The fact that males as well as females are victims does not diminish the horror of domestic abuse, especially when it is repeated, severe and one-sided. Women do tend to come off worst, and a small proportion of them suffer relentlessly, staying out of low self-esteem or fear, out of stoicism or because, as more than one has told me, they find themselves 'attracted to the rugged ones'. But we should not underestimate the extent of mutual aggression that takes place within the hurly-burly of mundane human discord.

Nor should we forget the extent of emotional bullying, where the wounds don't show, or the effect on children, with the demonstrable likelihood that they will grow up to be violent themselves. Mothers as well as fathers must take much of the blame.

Incidentally, feminists, criminologists and journalists have paid scant attention to violence in same-sex relationships. Claire Turner, who founded a British support group after her female partner tried to strangle her, said:

You end up thinking that society will not think it serious enough because it was another woman who perpetrated the abuse. I did not report it. I really believed that women were great and incapable of being anything but nice to each other. But you come to realise that anybody in society has the potential to behave badly.

The good news is that the government has finally acknowledged the problem of female violence and has funded men's support groups similar to those that have long been there for women. The much better news is that on all measures domestic violence has fallen as dramatically as any other crime: according to the BCS it fell 70 per cent between 1995 and 2010.

So let's now turn to the other crime with which women are almost exclusively identified as victims: rape. Here too we need to challenge assumptions while avoiding the flying fur which purports to be rational debate.

Rape is one of the most violating crimes. Victims tend to feel dirty, embarrassed, wracked with revulsion and self-blame. And, since it almost always involves a male assailant, rape is one of the defining issues for radical feminism. But have the red mists of politics and emotion clouded reality here too?

Again we owe much to advances brought about by feminist campaigning. For centuries women were belittled and held responsible if they let themselves be 'ruined'. Until quite recently it was perfectly acceptable for sons to sow wild oats while daughters' purity had to be protected – and in some cultures that remains the case. Until at least the 1970s and '80s the institutions of the state were steeped in prejudice. There was tactless conde-scension from judges and, as a seminal TV documentary showed with shocking candour in the 1980s, police officers sometimes treated rape complaints with crass insensitivity. There was a widely held assumption that victims had probably been asking for it or at least had rashly encouraged it. Conviction rates were said to be a risible 10 per cent.

Reforms in court procedure and changing public attitudes brought improvements to the way rape victims were treated in the 1990s. Several police forces set up dedicated sex crime facilities, with officers selected and trained for sensitivity;

complainants were allowed anonymity when giving evidence in court; judges began to frown on cross-examinations which implied promiscuity. When that failed to raise conviction rates, England's Solicitor General announced packages of targets and 'guidelines' for judges and juries which would shift the presumption of innocence towards a presumption of guilt. Yet conviction rates appeared to fall. The figure of 6 per cent was widely quoted in the media.

As so often, the politicians and the media misunderstood the problem. In this case they were suckers for politicised advice powered by a desire to push rape higher up the political agenda. On cool analysis it is not that prosecutions fail; they just don't happen. So far as we can tell, roughly 4 per cent of women are raped at some point in their lives, some repeatedly, and about 0.6 per cent of women (and 0.1 per cent of men) are victims of rapes and other serious sexual assaults each year. Yet despite the fact that reporting rates have soared, fewer than 20 per cent go to the police. When they do, about a sixth of rape complaints are rejected (rightly or wrongly) by police as implausible, a third are abandoned for lack of evidence, and a third are dropped because the complainant withdraws. Bear in mind that some of the allegations are made weeks or even years after the event took place and the average rape case takes nearly two years to get to trial. Officers have sometimes pressured women to abandon complaints – if they have no crime it improves their detection rates – but there is no evidence that police fail to prioritise sex offences in general. In fact the detection rates for sex crimes are comparable with many other crimes including robbery, burglary and fraud. For rape specifically the conviction rate is around 33 per cent with a further 23 per cent of those accused found guilty of lesser charges such as sexual assault. The real issue is that hardly any rapes ever get before a jury in the first place.

Is that such a bad thing? The implicit assumption is that any woman who chooses not to pursue a claim is being let down by the state or is acting irrationally. But could it be that she is right? What if she feels partly responsible for what happened? What if she realises there is no evidence other than her word against his? What if her life is bound up with that of her assailant? What if she feels humiliated as well as violated? Should she be expected to disclose all this in public and then put her life on hold for the greater good? Do we want a justice system that overrides the victims' sense of what is in their own best interests, or one that, in order to accommodate them, ceases to be just? Indeed, before we complain about the failure to get more convictions it might be sensible to ask women themselves whether a formal prosecution process is always the most rational way to deal with rape.

Not that logic ever has an easy time with sex crime.

In November 2005 Amnesty International published poll findings which suggested one in three people believe that women who are drunk or who are flirtatious are at least partly responsible if they are raped, and a quarter feel the same about rape victims who dress provocatively. There was little gender difference in the findings, and the poll was widely publicised as reflecting widespread misconceptions. Amnesty's UK director described these attitudes as 'shocking' and several women's groups were reported to be outraged by the 'prejudice'. Vera Baird QC, who headed the Fawcett Society's Commission on Women and the Criminal Justice System, said, 'The attitudes in this survey are glib and outdated. They implicitly mean the guy can't help himself.'

Of course she was right that 'no means no', which is fine as a finger-wagging exercise, but being justifiably indignant is not the same as being prudent or pragmatic. In any other crime we take account of provocation and contributory factors. Even in murder. Why not with sex? Even to raise the question tempts claims of sexism. But a key theme of this book is that we can aggravate crime by tempting fate and curb it by playing safe. We have come to acknowledge it is foolish to leave laptops on the back seat of the car. We would laugh at a bank that stored sacks of cash by the front door. We would be aghast if an airport badly skimped on its security. No amount of incitement can excuse rape, or any other crime, but it is inane to confuse explanation with justification, let alone vindication.

Yet for some it is heresy to suggest that victims should ever be held responsible at all.

There was a further outcry when Britain's Criminal Injuries Compensation Authority cut recompense to rape victims who had 'contributed' to their plight through 'excessive' drinking. The decision had to be reversed, provoking front-page news and a thunderous editorial in *The Guardian*: 'Notions of provocation have no place in sexual violence.' Yet for any other crime, compensation can be reduced according to 'the conduct of the applicant before, during or after the incident'. Incidentally, nobody seems to have noticed the irony that on the very same day the Foreign Office blamed excessive drinking for a rise in arrests of Britons overseas, an announcement which also made front-page news but which was received as a welcome warning.

THE LONG VIEW

Plainly the old mantra that all men are rapists isn't true. Nor is the even older myth put about by mothers to make their daughters behave demurely: that men cannot help themselves. In fact our forebears might be astonished at how safe women are today given what throughout history would have been regarded as incitement.

Not even in the licentious days of the Charles II Restoration in the seventeenth century was it acceptable for women to dress as provocatively as they have done in Western culture since the 1960s. Equally they would be baffled that girls are mostly unescorted and often stay out late and get profoundly drunk. Getting legless isn't new – think of Hogarth's classic satire, *Gin Lane* – but nowadays it is perfectly acceptable for respectable teenage girls and women in their twenties to dress as street prostitutes might have done in times past and to roam our cities, foraging bars and clubs for a good time, sometimes behaving loudly and lewdly, and occasionally vomiting and collapsing into drunken stupors.

Yet so-called stranger rapes, the sort most often reported by the newspapers, make up a small proportion of rapes that women divulge through surveys. Some assaults occur after short acquaintance ('I met him in a bar') but most are carried out by someone the victim knows, often within families.

In 2011 Ken Clarke, then Justice Secretary, was called upon to resign by the Leader of the Opposition for using the words 'serious rape'. The transcript of the interview makes it clear that Clarke meant aggravated rape but it is sacrilege to suggest that there can be any gradation: rape is rape. Yet the real experts, the victims, know otherwise. As we saw in Chapter 9, half of all women who have had penetrative sex unwillingly do not think they were raped and this proportion rises strongly when the assault involves a boyfriend, or if the woman is drunk or high on drugs: they led him on, they went too far, it wasn't forcible, they didn't make themselves clear … For them rape isn't always rape and, however upsetting, they feel it is a long way removed from being systematically violated or snatched off the street.

One of the sadder aspects of sex offences goes beyond the physical defilement and past the violation of peace of mind: it is the tendency to self-blame. But it does no service to victims, or to crime prevention, if we have to pussyfoot around political conventions rather than tell the truth.

Which brings us to another vexatious issue: drug rape.

One Saturday afternoon three weeks before Christmas, two young Lithuanian women went out for a drink in a west London pub and got talking with a group of men. One of the girls went home; the other woke up in an unfamiliar room with a stranger having sex with her. She assumed she had been drugged, was understandably distressed, and the police, quite properly, took her claim seriously. We appealed about it on *Crimewatch* in September 2005.

Hers was the sort of case which gets a lot of publicity. It is known as DFSA, or drug-facilitated sexual assault. But had she really been drugged? What about thousands of other women who made similar assumptions? The answer is probably no.

That same year the Forensic Science Service published a study into DFSA – the largest of its kind. Over three years samples were taken from over a thousand women who had complained of being sexually assaulted after being given drugs surreptitiously. The FSS checked their blood and urine with a battery of sophisticated tests – and found most of the women were drunk. In 98 per cent of cases there was no evidence of drugs other than self-administered alcohol, cannabis or cocaine.

This is in line with other studies in both the UK and the US, one of which was trenchant in its conclusions: 'Detailed examination of the testing results does not support the contention that any single drug, apart from alcohol, can be particularly identified as a "date rape" drug.'

Yet science has not got in the way of scaremongering. The media were so credulous that several TV soaps as well as BBC news and newspapers warned about the growing menace, creating a household name for an obscure pre-anaesthetic sedative called Rohypnol. Fears about Rohypnol's use in rape became so widespread that some bars stocked up with special beer mats that are supposed to give a tell-tale sign if they come into contact with the stuff, and the original makers, Roche, reformulated their pills so they turn dark drinks cloudy, light ones blue and dissolve into visible clumps. Yet there was always an implausibility about widespread drug-facilitated rape. Every assailant would need to control the dosage of a dangerous medication to allow extraction of his chosen victim from her social setting without complaint from her or from her friends. (In the one proven case of drinks spiking in Britain, in which a doorman was sent to prison for tipping the anaesthetic GHB into a woman's drink, the victim collapsed and had to be rushed to hospital.) Perhaps it was little wonder that the Forensic Science Service could find 'no evidence that Rohypnol has been used in the UK for this type of crime'.

Critics suggest evidence was missed because samples were not taken early enough, and the media repeatedly reinforce the impression that Rohypnol is almost undetectable. Not so: some of the studies were on samples taken within hours and in any case some of the metabolites of hypnotic drugs can be detected for days or even weeks.

Perhaps the drug rape story has such a grip on our collective imagination because it fits so well with the time-honoured horror story: the insensible woman at the mercy of the wicked male. And no doubt women who say their drinks were spiked mostly believe it. The man who took advantage was undoubtedly to blame for most of it, even if he too was high on drink or drugs. Certainly it is easier to blame him for your amnesia so far as friends and family are concerned. But police should be sceptical even if the media are not.

We should not forget, of course, that women can sometimes turn sex to their own advantage, which occasionally has other implications for crime.

Prostitution might or might not be the world's oldest profession – as Ronald Reagan said, *politics* bears a striking resemblance. But even in these days of sexual liberation it continues to be secretive and frequently reviled, as was homosexuality a generation back – with clients as reluctant to admit to paying for sex as prostitutes often are to providing it.

But there are starkly different versions of the trade and every now and then there is a scandal or a tragedy which provokes an argument about which is better, or less bad. The middle-class variety tends to be tolerated: the courtesans who operate from flats, the escort agencies which ostensibly provide chaperones but usually make little secret of what's actually on offer, and the high-street massage parlours where eroticism and 'personal services' masquerade among the therapeutic and spa treatments. Small working-class brothels were more or less endured for many years until a scare about human trafficking, since when they've faced periodic crackdowns from local authorities and police – as we shall see in just a moment. But most of the fuss is generated by the open-air sex workers: the traditional street prostitutes. Contact with health workers suggests the overwhelming majority are dysfunctional and at risk of multiple health problems, so the response of the authorities tends to be ambivalent, torn between protecting their safety and protecting community sensibilities. But what concerns us here is how vulnerable they are to violence. Street prostitutes are twelve times more likely to be murdered than other women. And one spectacular tragedy had a big effect on public attitudes.

Late in 2006, five sex workers were strangled and dumped around the Suffolk town of Ipswich. Instead of the traditional reaction to a dead prostitute – 'and then the silly girl went and got herself murdered' as one magistrate famously remarked – the Ipswich killings evoked national soul-searching. There was an almost self-conscious exoneration of the girls' line of work. In the media circus that accompanies any mass murder they were portrayed as real people with hopes and failures, as daughters and sisters and deserving of compassion and entirely worthy of the massive police inquiry their deaths inspired. If there were criticisms they were levelled at the authorities: prostitution should be legalised, we were told. Safe houses should be provided. Girls with drug problems should be given free prescriptions to keep them off the streets. Or we could copy New Zealand, Australia and some European countries which have licensed bordellos so that girls can work together and be regulated.

The question is: would it make much difference? Perhaps more liberal laws could bring mainstream prostitution out of the black economy and have the better-organised sex workers paying income tax. But no one needs a change in the law to go for STI check-ups (for what used to be called VD). And liberalisation will not resolve the problem that stirred the introspection: it will not diminish the vulnerability of women like those who were murdered in Ipswich.

Street girls are not your average 'escort' or 'masseuse', nor the student who finds a lucrative way of paying her way through college, the hard-working female who prefers having sex to sitting at a factory bench, or the self-employed businesswoman who has a call-girl venture rather than going into hairdressing. Street walkers are at the bottom of the heap. They are often heavily drug addicted and prepared to accept degradation, and danger, to get their fix. They are frequently self-destructive – why else would they self-inject heroin or smoke crack cocaine? It would be hard for a law reform to tempt them into a more wholesome lifestyle. Allowing brazen importuning in certain streets or districts is unlikely to lessen the danger that punters will drive off with them and beat them up. Supplying a safe house where they can take their punters will not appeal to all of them and will not create a refuge unless someone staffs it with a guardian. Putting up CCTV cameras may well drive away their customers and simply displace the problem. The proven way to prevent street prostitution is relentlessly visible policing, removing the prostitutes and deterring the kerb-crawling johns. Even then, it will never eliminate the problem of damaged girls – and incidentally sometimes equally damaged boys who work the streets – some of whom will find their way back to business as soon as they can.

Typically, given the yo-yo fashions of politics, calls to liberalise the law were soon followed by plans to make things far more punitive. As memories of the Ipswich murders faded, a new horror seized the headlines: it seemed that hundreds, maybe thousands, of naive girls from Eastern Europe, Africa and the Far East had been smuggled into Britain and, through violence and intimidation, forced to work in brothels and massage parlours. Not surprisingly, headlines about the return of the white slave trade caused alarm, especially when government spokesmen were widely quoted saying that of 80,000 working girls in Britain, 'the majority are working under control from traffickers, pimps or brothel owners'.

The Home Secretary leapt into action and an extraordinary law was introduced. Instead of targeting the pimps who were supposedly persecuting the girls, Section 14 of the Policing and Crime Act 2009 targeted the clients. It placed the onus on them to prove their innocence; it also made it almost impossible for them to do so. From 2009 onwards any man who paid for sex would have to make sure that the woman was not 'controlled for another's gain'. Police chiefs and the chairman of the Criminal

Bar Council warned this might be unenforceable, but as far as Parliament is concerned a moral panic is a moral panic and demands firm action whether or not it will work.

The larger question is: was there such a problem to begin with?

Where had the statistics for prostitutes come from, and how could anyone know that most of them were sex slaves? 'The government figures are completely fabricated,' said one sex worker, 'they just make them up.' That wasn't far off the truth. Because of stigmatisation and the furtive nature of the industry, the only number available, 80,000, had been extrapolated from a small survey compiled twenty years previously by a health outreach worker tackling HIV and AIDS in Birmingham. She described the constant quotation of the figure as 'bizarre'.

As for the alarming idea that most of the women were trapped by violent pimps – a figure of 80 per cent was cited by a former minister – that really does seem to have been invented.

Nonetheless the Met set up a dedicated Human Exploitation and Organised Crime Unit called SCD9 and police around the country set up Operation Acumen to investigate the crisis and try to tackle it. Their estimate was that 30,000 women were working as escorts or from flats and brothels, of whom almost 12,000 were vulnerable to violence or debt-bond and of whom 2,600 were definitely trafficked.

How did they know? They asked the women themselves. Or at any rate they asked about 250 of them and generalised from the results. Excluding forty British women from the sample, that left 210 who came from abroad, of whom fewer than twenty indicated they were not working entirely of their own volition. Leaving aside the statistical stretching that this exercise required, how meaningful are the results? The researchers reasoned that their trafficking figure might be an underestimate because some of the women would be too frightened to divulge. True. But what about the other possibility? If you were raided by police while working in a brothel, if you were an illegal immigrant, if you may have to go to court and if your mother might find out, what would you say when asked if you were duped or under duress? It would hardly be surprising to say yes. To paraphrase one of Britain's most famous call-girls, you would say that, wouldn't you – especially if that is what everyone half-expected. And even more especially if you knew that not one illegal immigrant who has claimed to be exploited has been deported.

Perhaps the proof of the pudding is what happened next. Despite big, some said heavy-handed, police raids on sex establishments, there were very few unambiguous cases of women who had been forced into sexual servitude. One series of 822 raids found only eleven victims who asked for police help. Two intelligence-led sweeps involving fifty-five forces found 250 people who might have been trafficked, though many were in domestic service. When a London borough had a big clampdown on brothels, only one out of hundreds of women interviewed claimed to have been trafficked – and bear in mind there is no agreement on what 'sex trafficking' or even 'coercion' is. There were more proactive raids in the run-up to the Olympics but the predicted surge in victims failed to materialise – just as it had in South Africa during the 2010 World Cup, when not one of 40,000 expected sex slaves was encountered.

In fact the most reliable figure we have for people brought to Britain on false pretences and exploited for sexual purposes is approximately 250 a year. This is half the number of people 'conclusively' recognised as 'victims of trafficking' by the national reporting scheme coordinated by the police. The other 250 or so recognised victims are thought to be exploited for labour or domestic servitude.

Undoubtedly this is not the whole story. All sex crimes are

hard to get at, and advocates like the Poppy Project, which works with trafficked women, point out there may be a much larger and heart-breaking problem of people in horrible conditions hidden away in private houses or closed immigrant communities. But it is a far remove from the headlines and the parliamentary bally-hoo that gripped everyone's imagination.

Let's go back to Hilary Kinnell, the woman who first tried to quantify prostitution in modern Britain and whose estimate of 80,000 became the bedrock for all that has happened since. She has become utterly cheesed off. She protests her original figure was no more than a guess and that the trafficking scare that followed was based on wild exaggeration, elision and invention. It's worth hearing at length her exasperation at the scare:

> Firstly, there was a critical mass of female parliamentarians eager to be seen to be doing something for women, and who used trafficking rhetoric and inflated trafficking figures which exploited migration fears ... Secondly, these were conveyed by a news media dependent on 'client journalism' and news agencies producing 'churnalism' from government press releases. Third, there were significant vested interests of politicized senior police officers who, using pseudo-scare tactics lobbied for more power and pressure groups influenced by USA prohibition research who supported the rise of 'spin' as an integral political tool. It was easy to spin material on sex work to a public who have little experience of or access to research material on sex work.

All in all, much of the news and comment about women and crime tends to smack of sexism and stereotyping, some of it promoted by radical campaigners perversely keen to portray the sisterhood as ready victims. Women are far less prone than men to suffer homicide or wounding; and females are quite as capable as males of making decisions on whether to work in an office, a factory or a knocking shop. In relationships with partners, most of them do not conform to the role of docile, submissive butt of violence; they often hit first or hit back. They do not need the courts to be prejudiced against men accused of rape and nor do they have to be sheltered from alcohol or drugs any more than the men they go out drinking with. The only question about women's emancipation is not whether they need ever more protection, but whether in time they may perpetrate more of the crimes that society needs protection from. That, self-evidently, is equality of a sort we could do without.

But what about that other fertile ground for prejudice: what about race?

13

BLACK AND BLUE: THE RACE ISSUE

Prejudice, which sees what it pleases, cannot see what is plain.
– Aubrey de Vere (1814–1902)

The British, or at any rate the English and Welsh, have achieved a spectacular feat of social integration. By the time of the 2011 census one in every seven citizens in England and Wales was from an 'ethnic minority'. Contrary to prophets of doom who had warned that rivers of blood would flow from racial differences, bigotry has palpably declined. After a decade of unprecedented immigration, opinion polls find widespread apprehension about 'too many' people coming into Britain but those concerns are partly about Eastern Europeans and the issue is no longer defined by colour. Detailed surveys show support for right-wing political parties is less about racism than real and imagined loss of 'Britishness', including traditions like nativity plays and the right to smack children. In any case the problem is largely conjectural – only 15 per cent think immigration causes problems in their own area – and racial attitudes are especially liberal where black people are most common, as in London. Most young people are embarrassed at the casual racism and xenophobia of past generations, which is now almost universally regarded as deplorable.

Yet in crime there remains a stubborn embarrassment to liberal bonhomie. People who describe themselves as black are far more likely to get into trouble than whites. Compared to whites there are one-and-a-half times as many mixed race and Asian people in prison in England and Wales, and four times more blacks. These are not trifling disparities. There is something very badly wrong.

But what? This has been one of the most bruisingly contentious questions since at least the 1980s: do immigrants cause crime or are ethnic minorities victims of discrimination?

Prejudice is not simply a legacy of colonialism. It is part of the human condition. It is latent deep within us and takes many forms: colour and religious intolerance, sectarianism, tribalism, caste systems, chauvinism, strident nationalism. We celebrate, even idealise, such partiality when people put their own families first. If there is a natural disaster, or if soldiers are killed in a conflict, it is perfectly acceptable to identify more closely with fellow countrymen than we do with foreigners. The more unfamiliar people seem, the less we empathise. There is a scale from love through affinity and indifference to antipathy which is essentially a measure of our sense of proximity.

But nowadays we deplore some versions of what are basically the same behaviours. We have made it a criminal offence to give preference to people 'like us' in most aspects of our daily lives. The word 'discrimination', which used to signify good taste, has become pejorative.

WHY WE'RE ALL PURE HYBRID STOCK

Migrants are only contentious for a while. Most countries, and Britain in particular, have seen waves of immigration through the centuries, transforming the very essence of the realm. The expression 'Anglo-Saxon' says much about the mongrel race that made up the English, with native Celts over-whelmed by Angles and Saxons long before the Picts, the Gauls, the Romans and the Normans came; before the Dutch and Flemish Huguenots, the Jews, the Irish, the Spanish and Portuguese; long before the post-war Commonwealth immi-grants, the exodus from former Soviet satellite states, the flow from European Union neighbours especially the French and Poles, the flamboyant trickle of Russian oligarchs and US bankers, and asylum seekers from around the world. Over the centuries some of these settlers brutalised the indigenous population when they arrived; others faced antagonism, even pogroms from the natives. Integration was occasion-ally protracted and difficult. But, on the whole and after a few generations, they all *became* the natives. Their differences were folded into the recipe that defined the nation. So it has been with the West Indians and East African Asians and will be with other Africans, Indians and Bangladeshis, Pakistanis and the rest. So it was in America with the Irish and Italians before blacks and Hispanics took on the role. Familiarity breeds respect. Prejudices tend to subside, and then move on…

While wariness of strangers may be universal, each community's prejudices are shaped by its history, and in post-war Britain, where the 1950s waves of immigration brought black faces to a land of mostly white ones, the issue was largely framed in terms of colour.

The first recruits from the West Indies received at best a mixed reception and were undoubtedly more sinned against than sinning. Many encountered open hostility, some were rebuffed or ripped off by inner-city landlords, and their very presence sparked the Notting Hill race riots of 1958, which (despite official attempts at the time to share blame equally) were mostly incited by whites. Up to the early 1970s it was generally held that blacks were more law-abiding than the natives. But, whether through alienation because of prejudice, maladaptive culture or just normal British adolescence, something started going wrong in the second generation. Black teenagers proved as difficult as white ones but with a distinctive twist. They reintroduced urban Britain to an affliction it had rarely encountered in a century: street robbery. Suddenly crime had racial overtones. The authorities responded with stops and searches under 'sus' laws dating back to the Napoleonic wars, and for years black youths complained they were being hounded by the police. Given that racism was tolerated and even widespread at the time, it would be surprising if prejudice was not a significant factor in policing. Formal monitoring was introduced in the early 1990s and grievances declined, but in 2010 black people were still seven times more likely, and Asians twice as likely, to be stopped and searched than their white counterparts. Blacks were three-and-a-half times more likely to be arrested than whites and then 25 per cent more likely to be sent to prison, on the face of it an accumulating chain of bias creating a blatantly lopsided prison population.

But was it bias? The question has dogged policing for decades and angrily divided public opinion; so let's try to drain the swamp of political inclination and look at some dry facts.

One event above all set the tone of the debate: the murder of a black teenager in south-east London in 1993. The stabbing of Stephen Lawrence by five self-proclaimed white racists was a watershed for race relations, not only because it exposed layers of ferocious prejudice in areas of London – and more discreetly among police – but because of the official inquiry that followed. A High Court judge, Sir William Macpherson, borrowed the black activist term 'institutional racism' to describe the Metropolitan

Police Service, and the phrase quickly become part of daily speech. It was now official doctrine that the police were racist. Yet that was not what Macpherson had intended to put across. While he was strongly critical of individual officers, and of a sometimes brusque and bigoted canteen culture, he emphatically rejected the idea that racism was officially sanctioned.

> It is vital to stress that neither academic debate nor the evidence presented to us leads us to say or to conclude that an accusation that institutional racism exists in the MPS implies that the policies of the MPS are racist. No such evidence is before us. *Indeed, the contrary is true.* [My emphasis.]

This 'vital' caveat got lost in the storm following publication. Macpherson's careless shorthand is held by some to have inflicted long-term damage to policing, race relations and, above all, crime control. It became an article of faith that there was systematic bias throughout the criminal justice system and that this bias helped explain why black people are so over-represented in criminal convictions and prisons.

Yet, at least in recent years, the facts don't fit the dogma. At no stage of the process, from people's encounters with police and through arrest rates to experience at court, is there a consistent pattern of unfairness that goes anywhere near explaining the huge preponderance of black people in British jails. There must be other, or at least additional, reasons young black people get into so much trouble.

Let's look first at street encounters with police. Complaints about harassment of black youths go back decades – in 1981 they sparked the Brixton riots, one of England's worst outbreaks of disorder in a century. The resulting Scarman Report led to a raft of reforms, and was well received both by the police and by local community leaders – but Lord Scarman specifically did *not* conclude that the police had been stopping young black men disproportionately. The police were often brusque (as one witness put it, 'We do not object to what they do so much as the way they do it') but white youths also complained to the inquiry, and reported levels of street crime were so high in Brixton that the police faced what Scarman called a genuine 'dilemma'.

So before we jump to conclusions about racist cops, we need to factor in that stop-and-search rates are bound to be a function of reported crime rates. There is another crucial qualifier too. Police can only stop people who are available to be stopped. If black youths tend to congregate on the street more than white youths then they are likely to be over-represented in these figures. This was checked after the Stephen Lawrence Inquiry and the research did indeed find that 'street populations' are very different from 'resident populations' – so much so that, in complete contrast to almost everyone's assumptions, in one location it was whites not blacks who were stopped most compared to the available population. Asians were generally under-represented, and black people had 'a more mixed experience, sometimes under-represented in stops and searches and sometimes over-represented'.

This was also the conclusion of a careful study of police stops in two Berkshire towns with high non-white populations, Slough and Reading. On raw figures it looked like stop-and-search was biased against blacks and Asians. But when the racial make-up of those towns' populations was compared with that of people on the streets, things looked very different, just as they had in London. In Reading, police stops were in proportion to racial groups available; while in Slough you were disproportionately more likely to be stopped if you were white.

In fact, fear of being seen as racist was corrupting police priorities. In an unpublished note the Thames Valley researchers concluded that in more than a third of cases officers had stopped white people just to try to get the racial proportions right. Since police generally only have powers to stop where they have 'reasonable suspicion', these actions were presumably unlawful. Similar concerns about unlawful stops on whites soon aroused formal complaints.

After bomb attacks on tube trains and a bus in 2005, the police, notably in London, began widespread street searches, almost doubling the number of white people stopped, but trebling searches of black and Asian people. Plainly there is a difference between targeting blacks and Asians out of prejudice and targeting them because these are the populations from which Islamic extremists are mostly drawn, and the official anti-terrorism watchdog accused the police of stopping white people unjustifiably to balance out the figures. Many of these searches, he said, were 'self-evidently unmerited' and 'almost certainly' illegal.

Getting the proportions right both in law and in perception may be an unwinnable issue for police. And there will always be loud complaints. As a quite different inquiry, the Philips Commission on criminal procedure concluded, young men easily feel alienated and, regardless of race, voice much the same complaints about what they see as oppressive behaviour.

In any case, street policing can't explain the vast preponderance of black people going through the courts and prisons. Fewer than 10 per cent of stop-and-searches result in an arrest. So how do all the others find their way into the criminal justice system? Is there racial prejudice higher up the process?

It certainly seems so given that startling fact that blacks are roughly three-and-a-half times more likely to be arrested in general than Caucasians. They are also a third less likely to be cautioned. Are they being singled out because of their skins or for their sins?

Let's dispense with the cautioning issue first. Cautions can only be issued for relatively minor offences, and the seriousness of their crimes may account for why black boys are less likely than whites to be let off with a warning. But also you can only get a caution if you admit the offence, and several studies have shown that black males are less likely to come clean than white people, either for cultural reasons or through mistrust of the system. This reluctance alone was long ago shown to be enough to explain the cautioning disparity.

There is also a compelling explanation for arrest rates. While black youths may be no more dishonest than their white counterparts, they seem prone to commit the sort of offence, the contact crimes, thefts and drug deals, most likely to lead to an arrest. This is partly because, like immigrants through history, they are more likely to live in rougher areas. In fact they are especially vulnerable to being victims of crime. But it is also because – and this is a potentially flammable assertion – there are cultural differences between different population groups. One obvious example is the migration of organised crimes from Italy. Sicilian, Calabrian and Neapolitan gangs first came to prominence in America in the 1860s, spreading from New Orleans to New York in the 1890s with their heyday in the 1920s and '30s. Even now, generations later, not many Cosa Nostra mobsters in America have non-Italian roots.

This does not mean there are inherent dispositions to act well or badly. But just as people take traditions like clothing, educational values, language and religion with them when they move abroad, often passing these impulses to subsequent generations, it would be surprising if they did not also carry bad habits or at least behaviours which do not sit comfortably with their changed circumstances. Some societies may be more familiar with extortion, some with corruption, and others with youth gang culture or with violent offending rather than pickpocketing, or with fraud rather than drugs. And some of these behaviours are more likely to result in police encounters than others. What's more, such issues may persist or even become amplified if, for whatever reason, second and third generations fail to thrive as well as their native peers.

The acid test is this: if racial prejudice were the driving factor in high arrest rates then all black people should suffer disadvantage because of their shared colour. After all, the essence of prejudice is that it lumps people together indiscriminately. But if we find big differences between how, say, Africans and West Indians fare, there may be other explanations. This seems to be the case. The first sign comes from school exclusions. When figures were disaggregated in 2004, it turned out that black Caribbeans were twice as likely to be banned as white kids. But black Africans were excluded at the same rate as white Britons. (Incidentally, whites of Irish traveller or Gypsy Roma extraction had most expulsions.)

More subtle ethnic differences emerged in evidence to a Home Affairs Select Committee which reported in 2007. Children from different backgrounds, even different Caribbean islands, had 'different issues' and accordingly hung out with different groups of friends and, if they got into trouble, were likely to participate in different types of crime. In Leeds the big concern was Caribbean groups supplying drugs, while in Manchester the problem seemed to be the growing involvement of Somalis in crime. In London, when the Trident task force was set up to tackle a spate of 'black-on-black' homicide, police found that most of the violence began with immigrants from Jamaica, as opposed to, say, Trinidad or Tobago. Partly as a result Jamaicans were hugely over-represented in prison.

These disparities should make us sharply aware of just how

racist the concept of race can be. By lumping together categories like black or Asian (or even white British) we often glossed over all the individuality of different civilisations, different traditions and different philosophies. Skin tone is usually our least important trait and even the continent we come from gives only a clue. Algerians are as different from Namibians as Icelanders are from Romanians.

At any rate, all the research and all the inquiries have reached a similar conclusion to that of the Select Committee: that 'it is difficult to quantify or pinpoint' bias by police. So the next question has to be, are certain ethnic groups being picked on by the courts?

Well, maybe, at least when it comes to remand – these are the suspects who are locked up before they come to trial, out of fear they might abscond or reoffend. Twice as many black as white youths are kept in pre-trial custody. It could be because of prejudice or perhaps because the cases are more serious with a skew towards robbery and drugs offences; the reasons aren't well researched. But what's really important is the disposals.

First let's look at the lower reaches of the law. So far as youth courts are concerned, black children are about twice as likely as whites to be given detention orders, but the numbers are small, there is huge variation between police force areas, and the differences may well be down to the offences and previous histories. In any case the real issue is with adults, and here the lower courts come out smelling of multicultural roses. Pilot studies of ethnic monitoring, and more recent statistics gathered from the courts by the Ministry of Justice, concur that proportionally more *white* defendants are convicted (60 per cent) than blacks (52 per cent) or Asians (44 per cent). Whites and blacks are just as likely to be given minor punishments or community sentences, and are equally liable to be sent to prison (10 per cent and 11 per cent respectively, and 8 per cent for Asians).

It does seem that the nature of the offence rather than the colour of the defendant is the decisive factor – and has been since at least the 1980s.

But magistrates can only deal with lesser offences. Less than a fifth of people found guilty by magistrates finish up inside – and in any case the maximum sentence is six months. So is there racial bias in the big courts, where two-thirds of those convicted go to jail, and the maximum sentence is life? It seems not, at least for verdicts. Court conviction data are deplorably incomplete and often fail to record ethnicity. But from what figures are available from Crown Courts, detailed analysis as far back as 1996 suggested that white defendants were again more likely to be convicted than suspects from ethnic minorities. On average 78 per cent of whites were convicted compared to 69 per cent of blacks and 68 per cent of Asians. This could be because black defendants were more likely to choose a high-risk strategy and plead not guilty, which self-evidently would result in more acquittals than a guilty plea. But a decade later an additional explanation emerged. A court case was simulated in front of racially mixed juries in London – in fact it was replicated twenty-seven times with high levels of authenticity. Black and ethnic minority jurors (and whites too, to some extent) were more lenient to black and Asian defendants than to white ones, apparently hoping to compensate for what they assumed was race bias in the system. Three years later a further large-scale simulation found even more emphatically that there was no evidence of unfair discrimination. If anything, all-white juries 'were least likely to convict the black defendant and most likely to convict the white defendant'.

Whatever the reasons, monitoring by the Ministry of Justice has found the results continue to be reflected in real-life trials: slightly more whites are convicted than blacks or Asians.

Of course that could mean one of two very different things: either that people from ethnic minorities are being let off more than they should be, or alternatively that they are more likely to be falsely accused in the first place. But either way it cannot explain why there are so many black faces in prison.

If juries are not unfair to black people, what about the judges who sentence them? The first review of this came in the early 1990s.

The study followed almost 3,000 male offenders through five Crown courts in the English West Midlands and found the proportion of blacks sentenced to prison (56 per cent) was higher than whites (48 per cent) and Asians (40 per cent). Of course a disparity is of itself hardly evidence of unfairness. There were big differences in the types of crimes, severity of offences, and previous convictions. But even when like was compared with like the race difference persisted, albeit less vividly. The chances of being sent down were 5 percentage points higher for whites than Asians and 5 percentage points higher for blacks than whites. Significantly, there was virtually no difference in the major crimes like robbery, rape or murder, nor for relatively minor ones – the problem was in the middling offences where the judges had most discretion. And there seemed to be one specific reason above all others. Black defendants were twice as likely to plead not guilty, and judges did not like it. Maybe black defendants were just less truthful, maybe they were more inclined to try to brag it out, maybe they were trying to play the race card, or perhaps they were simply less trusting of the courts. Whatever their motives, pleading not guilty was a gamble and if it failed the penalty for being caught lying was greater than the penalty for admitting the truth.

Remember, this was a survey conducted in the days when there was less formal emphasis on race equality, and when the race imbalance in prisons was even more striking than it is now; yet it concluded: 'The theory that this disparity is mostly caused by cumulative bias at the various stages of law enforcement and criminal process is implausible in the light of the fragmentary evidence available.'

Twenty years later, with ethnic monitoring now routine, the evidence is more emphatic. Black people convicted by a jury are still more likely to go to prison (around 70 per cent) than whites who have been in the same dock (60 per cent) but the proportions mostly 'reflect the seriousness of the offences committed'.

Finally there is another factor which is often overlooked – the effects of globalisation. At any one time, around a quarter of all blacks in British prisons are foreigners.

So, threading all of this together, it is hard to sustain the view that black people in Britain are hounded by police and persecuted by the courts. Unless all these studies are wrong or part of a giant conspiracy, blacks do more of the sorts of crime for which criminals get locked up. Maybe this reflects social factors like educational underachievement, but if so it seems likely that these themselves may flow from a culturally inherited disadvantage rather than straightforward prejudice.

There is a twist to this which it is worth recording. Such was the Establishment clamour in the 1990s to be seen to be institutionally colour-blind, that the view I have expressed here – that black people not white authorities are responsible for the penal imbalance – would have been regarded by many as racist. If it is acceptable today it is only because, after the turn of the millennium, opinion leaders like Trevor Phillips repudiated the chip-on-the-shoulder black mentality and helped break through the frigid white terror of saying the wrong thing. It is now OK to have dispassionate discussion – or even to cast a black man as a baddie in a movie, something that had been awkward for at least a decade. But at the time of the Macpherson report some things were unsayable.

Marian FitzGerald, the woman in charge of research into race relations at the Home Office, discovered this at the cost of her career. She had investigated the introduction of ethnic monitoring in detail but her draft report did not fit with the politics of the moment. Among other things she pointed out that police searches had *never* been indiscriminate – and nor could they be. (Imagine the outcry if old ladies were routinely stopped and frisked.) Accordingly, she warned, disproportionate stops of young black males could not simply be taken at face value to indicate bad policing. This was an important but inconvenient truth. Whitehall was in no mood to pick a fight with black activists. A powerful black lobby wanted a no-nonsense verdict of institutional racism, since that was the only finding that would uncompromisingly clear ethnic minorities of being more criminal than whites. At the time even the *Daily Mail* – the last national paper to have dropped racist crime reporting – was pressing the black agenda. Buckling under the pressure, the Macpherson report itself derided 'complex arguments' which could excuse the police and warned that anyone who considered 'other factors … simply exacerbates the climate of distrust'. Under intense pressure to support the pseudo-liberal agenda, Marian FitzGerald resigned in 1999.

With hindsight her caveats were plainly wise and she was sacrificed on the altar of white liberal guilt. Some of those who opposed her nuanced views went on to profit from a proliferation of training and other contracts to rid the police of their supposedly deep-seated bigotries. Yet, as prison figures show, it was largely a waste of money, with black people as badly over-represented now as ever. A further irony is that Marian FitzGerald is as unbigoted as they come. She continues to denounce simplistic interpretation of data on ethnicity and crime as 'statistical racism'.

But she has not yet won the argument for plain speaking on crime and race relations.

For several years, evidence emerged that networks of men, usually of south Asian origin, were grooming underage girls for sex, notably in South Yorkshire and the Midlands. *The Times* did much to reveal the scandal and showed that the police and social services had known about it for a decade though nothing had been done. This was a story in the dangerous no-man's land of race relations, and not just because the perpetrators were almost all from Pakistan, Bangladesh or Afghanistan; almost all the victims were white. Many praised *The Times* for its brave stand and some community leaders called for honest self-reflection. Mohammed Shafiq, of the Ramadhan Foundation, warned:

> Clearly, as members of the Pakistani community we've got to say to ourselves, yes, we've got a problem. We've got a problem because these people think white girls are worthless, they think they can use these girls. This is not sex, this is rape, these were children and I think we've got to speak out against this very openly.

Others were outraged at what they saw as the scapegoating of Pakistanis. One of hundreds of angry Muslim bloggers complained: 'The problem isn't Muslim men grooming girls; the problem is ... thousands of young English girls suffering from a breakdown of culture and society. The similarities between this sort of racial profiling and previous bigoted regimes is glaring; the Nazi regime regularly produced propaganda denouncing Jews as sexual perverts.'

But what was more interesting was how those in authority reacted. Officials from the children's watchdog were at pains to play down the Pakistani link. Sue Berelowitz, the Deputy

Children's Commissioner, said that it was 'irresponsible' to focus on Asian offenders. 'The only unifying factor is that, with rare exceptions, they're all male.'

Even on her own figures that was dubious if not wrong. After a two-year investigation into groups of men who were sexually exploiting children, the Office of the Children's Commissioner found that a quarter of offenders were Asian, some five times greater than the Asian share of population. The findings must be treated with great caution, partly because the data were incomplete (which meant they could be biased) and also because the victims were frequently uncertain or confused between ethnicity and nationality.

But that was not the only evidence. Official research compiled nationally by the policing agency CEOP also found Asians were massively over-represented as offenders. There appeared to be a distinctive racial pattern: that while white males predated on their own, Asian child abusers hunted in packs.

This is a very specific type of unusually nasty crime involving only a tiny proportion of British Asians. Overall Asians are little more likely than whites to commit the most serious offences. So it is hard not to feel sympathetic to the Sue Berelowitzes of this world. The target of prejudice has relocated from West Indians to south Asians, and specifically to Muslims. Many Bangladeshis and Pakistanis have yet to be absorbed by British culture and some make a point of disdaining it. Islamist terrorism hasn't helped. It is natural that people in authority are on edge when anything emerges which could inflame passions and deepen the divide.

But enlightenment is not about suppressing inconvenient truths. That tends to conceal awkward problems, not resolve them.

14

BROKEN WINDOWS

*Just as the constant increase of entropy is the basic law
of the universe, so it is the basic law of life.*
– Václav Havel

You are driving down an empty side street. Many of the buildings are derelict, some of them boarded up. There is broken glass and windblown litter, graffiti on the walls, and vandalised vehicles at the kerb. Would you want to park your car there? The idea behind the so-called 'broken windows' theory is that an unloved area becomes unfriendly and unnerving, and as things get worse, more people behave badly and fewer are prepared to linger – or be good samaritans.

In one form or another the 'broken windows' theory is probably as old as human habitation. Any cave, any house, any car that looks watched-over or well tended is likely to seem less vulnerable than places and possessions that appear to be neglected or abandoned. The concept was vividly demonstrated in 1969 by the psychologist Philip Zimbardo, whom we met in Chapter 7. He parked two ten-year-old Oldsmobiles, each without licence plates and with the bonnet propped open, one in a run-down area of the Bronx in New York State, where he himself had been brought up, and another in California on the far side of America in fashionable Palo Alto, across the road from Stanford University, where he was teaching. Within a few minutes the vehicle in the Bronx attracted passers-by who stole its battery and radiator, and soon it drew regular guests. After three days everything of value had been stripped and youngsters had moved in to rip up the upholstery and vandalise the remains. Meanwhile the car in Palo Alto stood untouched for over a week. Not an inquisitive visitor, not a scratch. The conventional assumption might be that the people were different: some rich, some poor. But Dr Zimbardo was not one to accept conventional thinking without putting it to the test. Intrigued, he and two students took a sledgehammer to the Palo Alto car and smashed a window to see if that would make a difference. It did, immediately. People came across to join the fun. Within a few hours that car too had been wrecked and finished up resting on its roof.

Zimbardo assumed that all of us are kept in line by what others do and think. If external controls are weakened – as when nobody else is around or no one else cares – we are more likely to lose our inhibitions. For a community to hold together we need to feel that other people care about the same things we do. If we let commonly agreed standards in our neighbourhood slide, we will edge towards nihilism. Accordingly, it is not just spectacular crime like homicide that matters, but the small things, like abandoned cars.

Some years later, his experiment caught the attention of two Harvard academics, James Q. Wilson and George Kelling, who wrote a popular article with, most importantly, a catchy title: 'Broken Windows'. In effect, they described a neighbourhood succumbing to entropy. Litter accumulates, people start drinking in public, teenagers gather, people use the street less often and move 'with averted eyes, silent lips, and hurried steps. "Don't get involved."'

Wilson and Kelling argued that the police and other agencies must take responsibility for restoring that sense of common ownership. Sort out the broken windows and the big stuff will take care of itself.

It was a bugle call for a return to neighbourhood policing. Get out of the patrol cars, they argued, and get back to the beat. The test should not be solving major crimes and making more arrests, but 'fostering health rather than simply treating illness'. The job of police was to liberate citizens so they need not cower; so they are free to look into each other's eyes, free to feel responsibility for their local streets, confident to chide naughty children and even to challenge suspicious intruders, and sufficiently at ease to intervene if someone is in trouble.

It was a compelling argument, especially at a time when no one else seemed to have anything new to say. The thesis won favour with think tanks and was put into effect with what seemed spectacular results. It has since been credited with transforming crime-fighting across America, and the prime example is New York.

In 1990 America's iconic city had been described on the cover of *Time* magazine as 'The Rotten Apple'. That year, New York State recorded 2,600 murders, almost a quarter of a million other violent crimes and nearly a million property crimes. As we saw in Chapter 3, the city had accumulated a massive budget deficit, had suffered riots and was haemorrhaging jobs. In 1993 in a closely fought election, a Democrat lawyer turned Republican, Rudy Giuliani, promised to control the city's budget and sort out crime. From the start he made it clear his main concern was quality of life. He deplored the trash storms, the drunks and homeless, the squeegee men shaking down the motorists, the graffiti on the subway trains and the daily sense of apprehension.

Giuliani took office at the start of 1994 and recruited Boston's police chief William J. Bratton as 38th commissioner of the NYPD. What followed became folklore. Crime in New York went into reverse. Within three years reported offences were down by a stunning 37 per cent and homicide was halved. It has been trumpeted as the greatest policing success in history and made Bratton the most celebrated copper in the world. But is the legend true?

The answer is yes, but only partly. Bratton, Giuliani and others at the helm in those few years deserve their halo of success but they are not quite the superheroes as generally portrayed. As so often we've been suckers for a splendid yarn and have skated over awkward truths that undermine it. History has conflated two quite different ideas: broken windows and zero tolerance. It has also neglected a fundamental feature first discovered by Sir Francis Galton: regression to the mean. What goes up most, usually comes down most. In fact New York's astonishing recovery from crime started before Giuliani and Bratton's arrival and persisted long after the entire cast in the story had moved on. Above all, the storytellers seem not to have noticed that what happened in New York also happened almost everywhere else in America and across much of the developed world.

Even so New York's salvation is an intriguing tale.

Bill Bratton is a smart operator with a flair for organisation and a no-nonsense approach which endears him to rank-and-file police. He recruited his deputy from Boston, Jack Maple, a flamboyant, podgy and irrepressible high-school drop-out who favoured two-tone shoes, bow ties and homburg hats and who had impressed Bratton years before when they worked together in New York's transit police. Maple was contemptuous of crimi-nologists and boasted if left to his own devices he could cut crime in half. Bratton made him deputy commissioner of crime control strategies. And he appointed John Timoney as his second in command, an athletic tough guy who had come up the hard way but who, like Bratton, is deceptively intellectual. Together they did a multitude of things, and did them fast – and therein lies the problem in deciding what caused what. Therein also lay the question of who should take the credit, for none of the four main characters, Giuliani, Bratton, Timoney and Maple lacked their share of ego or ideas, and all felt at times that others took more than their fair share of glory. Within three years the team had broken up.

There is no doubt a shared idea was: fix the broken windows. Bratton even described Kelling as his intellectual mentor. But what was done went way beyond anything Wilson and Kelling had proposed. Bratton needed to reclaim the streets and reassert police authority. 'Responding to 911 calls was random behaviour. We had lost all control over our police resources,' he recalls. Instead his cops were to be proactive. Following the broken windows model, police in large numbers were put back on the beat and took no nonsense. 'We had to take the beachhead. New York was an incredibly violent place so it took a very robust form of community policing at first. Later you can have a very different style of policing.' They intervened in even minor misdemeanours, and their high-visibility presence on the streets quickly restored a sense of authority and control, suppressing incivilities and driving out the petty criminals along with the culture of hopelessness and fear. This New York 'quality of life initiative' was sometimes dubbed the 'zero tolerance' approach, and was widely celebrated as the policy that turned the tide. It was applauded in the popular press and on TV shows as well as in political circles and academic journals. As crime rates fell spectacularly and with dramatic speed, Kelling and Wilson's original essay became one of the most influential writings on policing and crime control.

But while most people celebrated, and conservatives exulted, some on the left of politics were dismayed. At first there was disbelief and claims the police were cooking the books, though

incontrovertible falls in homicides put an end to that – especially when the trend persisted, down from 2,262 murders in
1990 to 629 in 1998. As Bill Bratton later wrote, 'It's hard to
hide that many bodies.' You could sense a new relaxed mood
in the subways and the canyons of Manhattan but also in the
streets in Queens or Brooklyn and the Bronx. Yet there was a
cost: police spending swelled while school budgets were being cut
(police numbers eventually increased by 50 per cent). More
disconcerting to liberals was what they saw as the price in civil
liberties. The NYPD was accused of being overbearing. Policing
in Gotham has always been muscular by European standards but
now there was a clampdown on the drunks, the panhandlers, the
squeegee men and young people congregating on the streets.

There was something else dismaying many on the left, including criminologists. They were wedded to the belief that crime
had 'root causes' in social injustice, and refused to believe that
policing could solve problems; it could merely suppress them.
They saw the city's deliverance from its crime pandemic not as
victory but as defeat. Bernard E. Harcourt, in *Illusion of Order:
The False Promise of Broken Windows Policing*, wrote:

> What we are left with today is a system of severe punishments
> for major offenders and severe treatments for minor offenders
> and ordinary citizens, especially minorities, a double-barrelled
> approach with significant effects on large numbers of our citi-
> zenry. The problem, in a nutshell, is that order-maintenance
> crackdowns permeate our streets and our police station houses
> while severe sentencing laws pack our prisons. We are left with
> the worst of both worlds.

It was an oddly mean-spirited assessment of a transformation
which had liberated the poor from crime at least as much as

the affluent. And it was plain wrong that severe sentencing was packing New York's prisons; despite all the talk of zero tolerance, incarceration rates remained pretty much the same. But was there something in the criticisms? *Had* the crackdown on misdemeanours made the difference, or had something else been going on?

In fact zero tolerance was a red herring. The phrase was never mentioned in 'Broken Windows' and if it conjures images of robocops swarming on the streets enforcing diktats from city hall it could scarcely be further from what Kelling and Wilson originally envisaged. Nor was the expression ever used by Bratton, except sometimes to disparage it. It belittles the complexity of policing, smacks of over-zealousness and is not a credible policy because it promises too much to law-abiding citizens and cries wolf to offenders. 'Consequently, zero tolerance is neither a phrase that I use nor one that captured the meaning of what happened in New York City.'

So what did happen? For one thing, New York was anyway emerging from its darkest hour. What had happened in the late 1980s had been an aberration. The city had been through an economic and employment crash, appalling fiscal and political mismanagement and staggering levels of police corruption. Things were getting back to normal long before the arrival of our heroes on the scene. Homicides and recorded robberies had dropped a third in the two years before Bratton's appointment, a rate of decline slightly faster than anything that followed.

What the new team did was to manage that decline. They had to reconnect with the mass of citizens and focus on the anxieties that ordinary people shared. There is no ringing slogan to encompass what they did and no fashionable academic theory, but they brought a quality that had hitherto been lacking: inspiring leadership.

GOOD COP, BAD COP

Before the police could win back New York, New York had to win back the police. Some time before Giuliani became mayor, I went out several times on patrol with New York's Finest. In fact over the years I tagged along with the NYPD, the housing police, the transit police and even the refuse police (yes, at one time they had a dedicated team to enforce recycling regulations). And I was shocked.

I am ambivalent about relating this because, just as they took me into their police houses and patrol cars, so they took me into their confidence. After all, I presented *Crimewatch*, the progenitor of *America's Most Wanted*, so in an honorary sense I was one of them. But they were not at one with the city they patrolled. We whisked from one location to another, hoping for action, often on sirens and flashing lights. We usually arrived at the same time as at least one other squad car, skidding in from another direction, and we disgorged like a small invading army. The officers were reasonably polite to people who were middle class and often disdainful of the rest.

Once, as we cruised down a less than salubrious street in Lower Manhattan, the officers spotted two men walking along the sidewalk minding their own business. We coasted to a halt beside them, and a cop peered through the window. 'You!' The men stopped.

'Yes, officer.'

'Don't give me that shit. What's in your pockets?'

'Nothing. Just going home from work.'

'Yeah, like fuck you are. What's your name?' And so it went on, until suddenly the officers lost interest and we pulled away.

'Did you know them?' I asked. 'No,' they said, 'but anyone round here is a piece of shit.'

Compared to life with New York's finest, even the sternest British bobbies I'd been out with seemed rather quaint.

An hour later on the roof of a block of flats I came face to face with someone nervously pointing a gun at me – the first time that had happened since I was a reporter in Northern Ireland in the 1970s. One pair of officers had gone up one flight of stairs, my lot had climbed another, and we had surprised each other. There were no crooks there; the biggest danger, at least on that occasion, was the cops themselves.

New York may have been healing itself but no one should underestimate the job that Bratton and his colleagues had to do in healing the police.

Having appointed his top team, Bratton applied two key doctrines of broken windows theory: he pulled lots of cops out of cars and out onto the streets, and he asserted a policy of ensuring a single standard of behaviour rather than ignoring beggars, gang members, prostitutes and drunks. But there was more to it than that, much more. For a start, led by Timoney, he amalgamated all the different New York police departments into one, and flattened the command structure, decentralising authority and pushing clear accountability onto his precinct commanders, in effect creating seventy-six business units each answerable for its own performance. He openly tackled corruption and set up twelve teams to review almost every aspect of police work, from training to technology. He set crime reduction targets and developed separate strategies to cut specific categories of crime like domestic violence, auto crime, drugs and guns. He gave his cops access to computers. He shifted responsibility to experienced leaders with clear goals and away from young recruits, many of whom were little more than kids who had never driven a car or were not old enough to drink, let alone solve complex problems of disorder. And he empowered his officers. Because of bribery scandals New York police had been prohibited from handing out citations, entering licensed premises, making drug arrests, or doing anything that might be open to corruption. Bratton scrapped all that. In addition, he, Timoney and Maple enthused their colleagues. They convinced them they could win back the city, and top cops frequently went out with fellow officers and made their own arrests.

They, or rather Maple, also found ways to target all this effort. Three or four years earlier, when trying to tackle New York subway crime, Jack Maple was frustrated that he was always one step behind the robbers and he started pinning big maps to the wall to try to get a broader sense of what was happening. If we could learn from the past, he reasoned, we could predict what will happen next, and he called the maps his 'charts of the future'. The idea was a great success and now, with overall responsibility for crime throughout New York, and with a boss impatient for results, he scribbled out a bolder plan on a napkin in an Upper East Side restaurant.

His charts would be computerised.

CompStat brought the cops from a primitive age of mostly seeing crimes as isolated incidents to seeing them as patterns. Many police forces have since adopted hotspot mapping but Maple wanted more: he demanded that his commanders should take ownership of everything that was going on. Jack Maple 'drove everybody nuts', especially in a double act with his chief of police patrol, Louis Anemone. Each precinct commander could expect a grilling roughly once a month and woe betide anyone who was ill prepared. One advantage of a CompStat meeting was that commanders came to Maple, not the other way around. Until then he was out morning, noon and night, piling pressure on his cops out on the streets, but the city was too big and there weren't enough hours in the day. CompStat gave cops time to think.

INSIDE A COMPSTAT MEETING

CompStat can be a rough business. I never experienced one led by Jack Maple but I have seen others including the nearest thing: one under John Timoney when he moved to be chief of police in Philadelphia. Imagine a darkened hall, dominated by a projection screen, with tables lined up in a square and with precinct commanders on three sides, surrounded by their experts and lieutenants. On the fourth side are the top brass, with all the status that comes not just from knowledge and experience but from paramilitary rank. The purpose, as everyone knows, is to keep every commander's feet to the fire, and each side is armed to the teeth with paperwork.

This exchange gives an idea of how tough these dialogues could be.

'What about sexual assaults in that area?'

'They're down about 2 per cent, sir. That's not statistically significant but it's going the right way.'

'That's not what I hear.'

'Pardon me, sir?'

(Without looking up) 'That's not what I hear.'

Shuffling of papers, urgent consultation with two colleagues. A projected graph is changed.

'There are the figures, sir.'

(Still without looking up.) 'Did you talk to the ER? Have you been to the rape crisis centre?'

Silence.

'I said, did you talk to the rape crisis centre?'

'No, sir.'

'Then how do you know assaults are down?'

I cite that because it exemplifies how area commanders were placed under intense pressure to come up with results, but also how their bosses often needed to see quality of life improvements too, and not just measure performance against lists of legally defined offences. For the first time, cops were required to manage their crime portfolio like business executives might be expected to manage production or sales.

I was so impressed with CompStat that I arranged for British officers (from Thames Valley Police) to go and see it for themselves and they in turn were so impressed that they set up their own version. But CompStat itself alters little. Turning out the lights and projecting maps and blobs on a screen changes nothing on the streets. I have watched the process in another American city where they were just going through the motions. But back in New York when CompStat started, there was no play-acting. It was urgent, it was real, and if anyone didn't perform, then he or she would soon be looking for a new job.

A crisis can bring out the best in leaders and Bratton's team excelled. But a crisis also allows leaders to be bolder than in normal times. So they had unusual latitude: it is rarely possible for management to force through so many rapid changes. And it is rare that police chiefs inherit such a massive increase in resources. Above all, with the benefit of hindsight we can see just how lucky they were in the most important respect of all. The drop in New

York's crime rate, already precipitous when Giuliani came to office, actually went down less steeply from then on. Maybe these radical surgeons would have encountered more resistance had it been clearer that the patient was already so rapidly on the mend.

And maybe New York's story would not have become so legendary had people noticed what was going on elsewhere in America. In fact for years something fundamental had been changing. The public, the politicians and the media had become so used to rising rates of murder, rape and robbery that no one could believe it when lines on the charts began to turn. Falling crime was not part of the script. But bit by bit crime was running out of steam and New York was not the first city to experience the change. Pittsburgh went through a renaissance and had already experienced an unprecedented drop in homicide a decade earlier (down by 61 per cent between 1984 and 1989). During the 1990s while Bill Bratton worked wonders in the Big Apple, the city he'd left, Boston, did just as well without him, matching almost precisely New York's fall in homicides. Way across the continent Dallas and Houston were only a short way behind, as were St Louis in the south and San Diego, Los Angeles and San Francisco over in the west. As one thorough study concluded, 'New York's homicide trend during the 1990s did not differ significantly from those of other large cities.' It wasn't uniform, it wasn't predictable. Some places did better with murder, some with robbery, some with drug offences, some with burglary. Yet it happened across the board.

This is not to belittle what was achieved in the Big Apple. Forget the much-trumpeted fact that its burglary rate is lower than London's – that is because far more New Yorkers live in apartments than in houses, and flats are less vulnerable to burglary. New York still has five times the homicide rate of London. But taking the long view, it has seen a reduction twice as fast and twice as long as the average for major cities in America. Whether broken windows theory was in part responsible we shall never know; it is impossible to disentangle so many things that happened simultaneously and interacted unpredictably. But James Wilson and George Kelling got what they wanted: policing that cared about the hassles in daily life.

There is an important postscript to all of this. University researchers have tested the broken windows theory in controlled experiments and proved it works. There are examples of how we follow social cues, going back at least to pioneering work by the psychologist Solomon Asch in the 1950s, who used stooges to induce students to give wrong answers to simple questions. Another psychologist, Robert Cialdini, once got several people to look up at the sky and, as more and more passers-by joined in, the crowd began to spill into the street and stop the traffic. But more significantly, forty years after Zimbardo's pioneering work, Dutch behavioural scientists conducted several field experiments which showed spectacularly how significant these effects can be for crime.

First they chose a wide and tidy alleyway which was used as a cycle park for a nearby shopping centre. It had a prominent 'No Graffiti' sign, but no refuse bins. The researchers provoked littering by using elastic bands to fix advertising hand-outs to every bike. Cyclists would either have to dump the fliers in the street, or take them with them. Almost a third of riders dropped the hand-outs, but the rest folded them up and took them away. Soon afterwards, the trio plastered the place with graffiti and repeated the experiment. This time more than two-thirds of the cyclists dropped the handbills on the ground.

Later the scientists got a similar effect with fliers on car windscreens in a supermarket car park. About 30 per cent of the drivers scooped the paper straight onto the floor even when the place was spotless; but when the researchers left shopping trolleys strewn around haphazardly the proportion of litter louts more than doubled.

People also broke rules on trespassing once they saw rule-breaking was the norm. The scientists put up a temporary fence blocking access to a car park, requiring drivers to make a detour when they went to get their vehicles. Most motorists took the longer route, but about a quarter ignored a sign that said 'No Throughway' and squeezed through a small gap in the fence. Then, in an ingenious and subtle indication of disorder, the researchers left four bicycles leaning on the fence in defiance of a 'No Cycles' sign. After that, the proportion of people squeezing through the fence more than trebled to 82 per cent.

Perhaps littering and taking a short cut are such minor misde-meanours that they can't be considered as crime. So next the Dutch team checked if they could provoke more serious misconduct, like theft. A stamped addressed envelope clearly containing cash was left hanging from a post box. Most passers-by ignored it, and others pushed it through into the mail, but 13 per cent took it out and pocketed it. After the letter box was sprayed with graffiti or surrounded with discarded rubbish, twice as many people stole the money. Disorder begets disorder.

Broken windows should be fixed.

Next stop, broken theories. For while Wilson and Kelling felt vindicated, most conventional ideas about crime had been confounded. The grand assumption, that crime is caused by criminals, had been shown wanting. There had been no short-age of supply: the population of young men had grown during the great decline. There had been no big increase in incarceration rates. And there had been no sweeping interventions to reform those who got into trouble.

Whatever happened in New York it wrong-footed mainstream criminology.

15

CRIMINOLOGY

An ology! He gets an ology…
– BT commercial, 1987

Afamous British TV commercial in the 1980s had a Jewish student talking to his grandmother on the phone, telling her he had passed an exam, but confessing it was only 'sociology'. His grandma would have none of it: 'Anthony,' she trilled, 'you get an ology, you're a scientist!' The joke struck a chord because everybody grasps that some -ologies are soft options. Sadly, criminology tends to be one of them.

Given the political importance of reducing crime, one might have expected universities would have flocked to the task. Academics are by nature inquisitive, and criminology is more popular than philosophy, zoology, geology or dentistry and almost as fashionable as journalism. But very little of this endeavour has been directed at cutting crime. And few of its approaches would pass muster in the natural or life sciences. In reality, criminology is grounded in the arts. Sometimes it is combined with psychology or law but almost all the 7,500 students who apply for courses each year will mix it with sociology or subjects like film studies, counselling and creative digital music. Most will learn little about real scientific methodology.

There are some fine exceptions. This book draws heavily on

their work and I hope they will not bridle at my generalisations for they know they are in a small minority. There have always been half a dozen British university departments, mostly led by psychologists rather than sociologists, and there is the Institute of Criminology at Cambridge, which was set up by the Home Office in 1960 in the hope of guiding it on penal policy. But as a general rule when police and public-policy-makers need practical, evidence-based advice on what works and what does not, their local criminologists are more likely to be political polemicists than crime reduction experts.

Criminology is a branch of sociology and is thoroughly steeped in politics; most of it is highly partisan. Tactful critics say it has a 'sentimental attachment to any breed of "underdog"' – by which they really mean it is grounded in left-wing ideology. Its teachings almost invariably assert that crime is caused by disaffection and usually assume that this is caused by inequality. Accordingly it is more concerned with social factors rather than immediate precursors to any crime. That in turn leads to a fascination with criminals, their backgrounds and how they are treated. Except for its feminist wing it has discovered victims only recently; and while all preventable crime has yet to take place, most criminology has little stated interest in the future. When it does engage in practical research it is often poorly done if not downright pseudoscientific.

Take the partisanship first, which is mostly far to the left of political consensus. Ever since the 1960s much of the teaching has been little short of indoctrination, as lots of graduates will attest. Even now, with students keener on clubbing than collectivism and in finding a job rather than rising up against the system, the centre of gravity remains somewhere between communist and old Labour. The dominant theory is known as critical criminology, where the world 'critical' is code for Marxist.

This is a typical syllabus: 'Key issues include surveillance and police powers, the politics of imprisonment, the criminalisation of children and young people and international frameworks for rights and justice.'

Many of today's criminology teachers were brought up on a textbook called *The New Criminology*, which saw society as a prison, police as the instruments of oppression and the mugger as a crypto-Robin Hood. Believe it or not, the Soviet dissident Alexander Solzhenitsyn was used as the authors' model for a convict. And here is the crux: 'It should be clear that a criminology which is not normatively committed to the abolition of inequalities of wealth and power, and in particular of inequalities in property and life chances, is inevitably bound to fall into correctionalism.'

In other words, the biggest problem of crime is capitalism, with its unequal distribution of wealth and power. Crime is a reaction, capitalism responds with imprisonment, and the only answer is the abolition of capitalism.

Any challenge to this assertion is seen by many criminologists as right-wing stupidity or denial. But that's untrue and unfair. On the contrary, it is astonishing that under the guise of academic freedom such one-sided views have for so long gone uncontested by the Universities Funding Council. It is hard to imagine learned authorities allowing equivalent theories from the far right (propounding the view that the largest problem in crime is immigrants, for example). And it is inconceivable that the National Union of Students would have tolerated such flagrant bias had the boot been on the right foot rather than the left.

Nor was this revolutionary zeal confined to Britain. It was rampant in Australia and much of Europe and to a surprising extent in North America. The Critical Criminology Division is now the largest section in the American Society of Criminology, home for what its members call 'progressive scholars' but which most people might well regard as old-fashioned left-wing ideologies peppered with strident feminism and politics of resistance. Crime as they see it is a 'moral panic' whipped up by the Establishment in collusion with the media, and the real problems of offending are 'crimes of domination' by the government, police and business.

The inconsequentiality of the discipline was at its starkest in the 1980s and 1990s as crime approached its peak and often dominated the news. Here was a field of study at the heart of one of society's most pressing problems, but with few significant exceptions, criminologists either dismissed the headlines as middle-class hysteria or regarded it as payback for the iniquities of free enterprise.

There has been a slow climb back to relevance since then. The consensus has migrated from 'Left Idealism' to 'Left Realism' and more recently been camouflaged as 'cultural criminology'. There are now more decent textbooks, though most dwell on theory, are silent on statistics or even go out of their way to distance themselves from science. The politics, while still intrinsic, has become more discreet in reputable universities like York or LSE.

Not surprisingly this hardly makes criminologists attractive to employers, even – perhaps especially – employers who have to deal with crime. One don complained bitterly he had heard from the Home Office that 'it's very rare that we employ people who have got degrees in criminology, because they don't have any skills'. He was so outraged that he called for a boycott. But in setting out his 'criminology of resistance' he expressed lucidly why his students might find themselves redundant. He railed against research that focused on 'state-defined notions of criminality' which were 'regulating the poor and the powerless' through 'an intolerant, punitive and [im]moral authoritarian state'. He dismissed 'evidence-based research' wholesale – 'the mainstream is nothing more than knowledge corruption' – and complained of the Home Office research department: 'If it were concerned with understanding and explaining the most violent aspect of contemporary British society (notably the modern corporation) it would fund projects that analyse corporate negligence, commercial disasters and workplace injuries – but it doesn't.'

As it happens, other government departments, not the Home Office, are responsible for corporate negligence, commercial disasters and workplace injuries; and these, especially workplace injuries, are reasonably well managed – in fact some would say the health and safety culture has been taken to excess. But in any case what he regards as 'the most violent aspect of contemporary British society' is far removed from the anxieties of the very people, the 'poor and powerless', whom he claims to represent and who are most often victims of crime and most likely to be arrested for it.

Nor, if crime is a reaction to oppression, is it clear why so much of it, as he complains, is caused by pampered and well-heeled capitalists.

In quoting this extensively I am not being unfair to criminology. This was a routine article in what passes in criminology for a mainstream 'scientific' journal; and few in the field have had the courage to denounce the bias and lack of intellectual rigour. There is nothing wrong with theory, only with bad theory, irrelevant theory and untested theory. Universities should be expected to challenge the status quo – and most great insights and discoveries arise through observation, description and reflection. But too many assumptions in criminology are tethered to this sort of dogma.

Sadly, even when criminology does try to do research it tends to do it in ways that many scientists would not regard as decent science. This has always been a problem. In 1932 a devastating critique concluded that while an empirical science of criminology is possible, 'it does not now exist'. This so-called Michael-Adler

Report had been commissioned in New York to evaluate the desirability of establishing a national institute to train criminological researchers. It warned that researchers were so incompetent that scientists should be imported from other fields.

Professor David Kennedy is one of the few criminologists to make a big and measurable cut in crime rates, having tackled gun crime in several US cities. But he acknowledges there are not many who do research as he does with such practical and palpable outcomes. 'The literature on the theoretical and descriptive side is rich on this subject; on the action side it is almost silent.'

Many criminologists do no research at all. This is particularly serious in the UK, where several professors of criminology are ex-probation officers or prison staff who are relatively unfamiliar with research or scientific methodology. In fact some of them have never done or commissioned any research at all – they were awarded PhDs 'by publication', which means by writing articles or books. (Sadly I shan't expect a science PhD for writing this one.)

Since few criminologists are good at maths the emphasis is on what they call 'qualitative research', a term that covers just about everything – especially interviews – as opposed to quantitative research, which involves measurement and statistics. There is nothing wrong with anecdotes which can enrich our understanding, or better still act as a precursor to testing a hypothesis; but as the saying goes, the plural of anecdote is not data. Perhaps unsurprisingly, criminology's reliance on general observations rather than detailed statistics is a touchy issue. When once I addressed the British Criminology Society, comparing qualitative research to journalism and urging the adoption of more scientific methodology, I was dismissed in the BCS's journal as empty-headed: 'Someone who thinks we should understand a little less and control a little more … In future, perhaps an opening speaker "fit for purpose" would be better suited.'

Tellingly, though, the newsletter editor added a rider in my support:

> The fact remains that [Nick Ross's] view is widely shared and accepted by all the key constituencies in which criminology operates. The basis for this shared view is the almost total absence of any UK criminal justice evaluation research in the past thirty years which comes close to meeting the scientific standards which should be seen as part of the human rights entitlement of both offenders and victims of crime.

Support like that was extremely welcome – but extremely unusual. And it was certainly not official, as I discovered when, exasperated by criminology, I helped set up the Institute of Crime Science at University College London (see below). The social science research council almost rejected UCL's application for a grant because there was neither enough sociological explanation for criminality nor qualitative research.

CRIME SCIENCE

I had always assumed criminology had the answers to the challenges of crime – or at least was asking the right questions. In the early days of *Crimewatch* I so often drew a blank from my inquiries that I stopped ringing criminologists for help. When I asked the social science research council for examples of work they had funded which had helped to tackle crime, the answer was that they could think of nothing. Yet I knew there was talent out there, some of it where I had not expected it in the Home Office research department, and I had met several brilliant criminologists through government committees set up to tackle crime. I proposed the creation of a new discipline distilling the best of criminology and enriching it with researchers from other fields. Above all it would be preoccupied with the task of measurably cutting victimisation. Since criminology was so patchy, and since the new approach was multidisciplinary, I called it Crime Science.

When my *Crimewatch* co-presenter, Jill Dando, was murdered in April 1999, I approached her fiancé with the idea of creating a lasting memorial to her and proposed we should found a Jill Dando Institute at a leading university. Together with her friends and colleagues, and Lord Stevens (then head of the Met), we launched an appeal which raised enough cash to whet the appetites of several top-rank institutions, all of which had disdained criminology. We settled on UCL, one of the world's top universities with a long history of ground-breaking and interdisciplinary innovation, and the Jill Dando Institute of Crime Science is the only institution of its sort to be based in a science and engineering faculty. It has spawned a substantial department called security and crime science, and has attracted funding not just through the social sciences but also from the research councils that finance engineering, the hard sciences and the arts.

Around the same time as the JDI was founded, social science researchers set out to put their own house in order. The Campbell Collaboration is an international network of investigators based on an influential development in medicine called the Cochrane Collaboration, which weeds out the best research from the bad and mediocre. Campbell's systematic reviews of evidence are setting criminology on the road to being a real science.

A start has been made.

Science is humankind's most powerful invention. It is sometimes so badly taught at school that many people think of it as people in white coats or as a set of academic subjects such as physics or biology rather than as a methodology or tool kit for testing our beliefs. But science provides the most rigorous way to explore things, to provoke ideas, to test theories and to defend ourselves against being misled by chance or bias. It has proved spectacularly successful across most of the vast terrain of human endeavour. Science has been responsible for such colossal leaps in imagination as that the earth moves round the sun, that living things evolved, and that solid matter is really just a force field. It underpins most practical activities from accountancy to zookeeping and detective work to plumbing; and in the last few generations has propelled us with breathtaking speed and rising cadence from a horse-drawn lifestyle which had lasted millennia to a microprocessed space age.

Whereas ideology places cherished beliefs on a pedestal and protects them from sacrilege and dissent, science puts them on a plinth and throws bricks at them to see if they fall over.

We all demand such testing when our lives depend upon it: the crashworthiness of a car, the purity of tap water, the integrity of a high-rise building, the safety of a medicine. We ought to demand it for public policy. Yet science has rarely been applied systematically to crime prevention.

In fact, some criminologists assert there is no such thing as objectivity, or tangible evidence of natural laws, merely competing evidence, each bit of which is as valid as any other. Science is a tyranny devised to impose one world view upon all others. This load of piffle has been dignified with terms like 'constructivism' or 'postmodernism', and has the singular advantage that you can ignore facts that don't fit with your beliefs. In fact its advocates claim the rest of us are just deluding ourselves about reality.

For others the plodding and methodical process of science – its reliance on measurement, experimentation and mathematical proof – restricts us to reductionism and to extrapolating from what we already know: 'scientists have to look under the street-light' whereas faith can light up the darkness. On the contrary, of course, it is science that literally lit up the darkness and has done most to challenge accepted wisdoms.

Yet this is dismissed as 'scientific positivism'. One textbook, *Criminology*, says the discipline should instead be judged by 'complexity, erudition, elegance, profundity, reflexivity, originality and ethical stance'.

As I say, things are improving, and in some respects substantially. Recognising its weaknesses, the Economics and Social Research Council appointed a statistician as chief executive, who, at least in private, echoed my despair at what had been going on and began to put things right. He was succeeded by a geographer who was the President of Science Europe and the council began to support centres of excellence where people understand numbers and know how to do proper experiments. Some critical criminology courses are being withdrawn and elsewhere the politics are less overt. Meanwhile the funding body for science and engineering has moved in, supporting a wide variety of projects such as tackling gun crime, and the Arts and Humanities Research Council has applied itself, for example with a project to cut bike theft.

At last the mainstream British Society of Criminology became embarrassed by its threadbare reputation. In 2006 the editor of its journal (the one who had supported me) went off to start a scientific research group, and soon afterwards the president himself conceded that criminology was in 'a pretty parlous state of affairs', with its researchers 'more or less irrelevant to policymakers'. More recently the American Society of Criminology was told much the same thing: 'The time has come for crimi-nologists to choose a different future.'

As I say, some have. There are breakaway groups including experimental criminologists who conduct hard-nosed research, and I am proud to be one of their honorary fellows. There are environmental criminologists who seek ways to design out unnecessary provocations and opportunities for crime and who, in the past ten or twenty years, have contributed more to fresh thinking about crime than all the classic criminologists together. There is a growing cadre of crime analysts and there is good work going on in many places, including Cambridge, Huddersfield, Loughborough and UCL. These are people who will come up with solutions. Perhaps one day the discipline will demonstrate its coming of age by the appointment of some of its number as Fellows of the Royal Society.

Just don't hold your breath.

Meanwhile watch out for something odd. While the dominant influence remains sociological and the instinctive leaning of many criminologists is still a tad rebellious, there is often something incongruously traditionalist in criminology – a conservative faith in the old-fashioned virtues of courtroom justice.

That too ought to be challenged.

16

THE CRIMINAL JUSTICE SYSTEM

Make crime pay. Become a lawyer.
– Will Rogers

Almost everyone seems to believe in British justice.
People argue about specific laws. Not everyone has confidence in the police. Some may think the judiciary is fuddy-duddy, or campaign for procedural reform. But hardly anyone appears to doubt that the natural consequence of crime should be to go before a court, and that in general the process is a good one. It is as though we imbibe confidence in British justice with our mothers' milk. Yet in many respects we should be literally in contempt of court. It is neither as open nor just as it pretends, it is unnecessarily expensive and it is not very good at assessing evidence. These are in-house failings more interesting for the fact they are so readily overlooked than for the effect they have outside the system. More importantly from a crime prevention point of view, the criminal justice process is little more than a breakwater against the tidal rise and fall of crime. Most crime just swirls on by.

These flaws are all the more remarkable because this and similar criminal justice systems command huge prestige throughout the democratic world and employ some of the sharpest minds on the planet.

In what follows, the model is the British, and specifically the

English and Welsh, legal approach, but where its defects are not shared by other jurisdictions they have other failings of their own.

There are huge and unseen obstacles in bringing prosecutions in the first place. Even if a suspect is identified, officers frequently have to decide on their own whether the evidence is strong enough to warrant an arrest. There can be great temptation for police to gild the lily but there is also a resigned acceptance that the defendant may say they are lying anyway or at least invent a story of his own. Then there is a problem of physical capacity. I have witnessed a handbag thief who fled with his booty from a pub, was chased across the street and subdued by the bar manager, was brought back to the bar and arrested by police, and was later that evening released without charge because the police station was busy. It is rarely understood how much discretion custody sergeants have as gatekeepers to the system, and how bottlenecks, like having enough cells, can be a decisive factor in whether or not a case ever gets to court.

After the sergeant comes the next stumbling block: the prosecuting lawyers. In England and Wales, decisions on whether or not to charge a suspect are taken by the Crown Prosecution Service, which cherry-picks cases it thinks are 'more likely than not' to succeed. In other words, long before a public trial there is a private one and its outcome is highly subjective. This is a big task employing 6,000 people at a cost of over half a billion pounds a year. As one of their most senior lawyers told me, 'We're almost a judicial function at an earlier stage.' And as a local CPS solicitor put it, 'Prosecuting is quite a lonely job.'

Theirs is a steeply uphill task. This is an adversarial system and for the most part the suspect need not help the process in any way. Despite the famous caution that saying nothing might count against defendants, it rarely does. On the contrary, silence can be golden. It makes things much harder for the prosecution without incurring any jeopardy, especially if things ever get as far as trial and the defendant eventually speaks up in court. Since the prosecution has to make all the running, police officers wait fretfully to make their case to the prosecuting lawyers, sometimes surprised to get the go-ahead, and sometimes crestfallen when very serious crimes, including many rapes and other violent offences, are ejected from the system.

So the purportedly rigorous and open judicial system has a decidedly private, opinionated and one-sided start. The principle of open justice falls heavily, albeit unseen, at the first hurdles.

The next problem is what happens if a case makes it through the labyrinth and proceeds towards a trial. Despite big improvements by the CPS *more than half of all cases* fail to make the grade. They are what the Ministry of Justice calls 'cracked' or 'ineffective' trials, usually because of lack of courtrooms or judges, the unpreparedness of lawyers, or because witnesses don't turn up or defendants fail to appear.

Set aside the attrition and look at the quality of getting at the truth even if a case secures a proper hearing. Everyone seems to insist that the British courtroom process is as good as it gets, and it is certainly a beacon to legal systems all around the world. We all know that debate is a good way of challenging opinions. But how reliable is it at the task of assessing facts?

The question goes to the heart of the adversarial approach, so let's examine it with what is commonly held to be the gold standard: trial by jury. Suppose a verdict conspicuously mattered in terms of public safety: say, after a series of crashes whether to certify an airliner as fit to fly. Would we really leave it to a focus group of twelve people selected for their naivety – literally their ignorance? Indeed in English law they would be deselected if they knew anything about aviation or aeronautical engineering. Once appointed they would be subjected to arguments from barristers hired as spin doctors. They might be excluded from large parts of the hearing while lawyers debated how much evidence should be withheld from them. They would be forbidden to question witnesses or make their own inquiries but be expected to listen mutely to what others chose to set before them. They would not even be permitted to read scientific evidence from source materials – jurors have been imprisoned themselves for looking things up online. It is as though the information age has passed the system by. After that they would go into a room on their own in secret, and after a while would come out and be permitted a one-word answer: 'no' or 'yes'. Once again there is a conspicuous lack of openness at the crucial decision-making moment. There is no peer review. There is no replication to check for factual accuracy or logical consistency. In fact any second opinion would be illegal unless entirely novel facts emerged or unless some bureaucratic flaw could be found in the way the inquiry was conducted.

To continue with our aircraft analogy, suppose the plane was cleared to fly. Would you be happy to travel in it? Probably not. Nor if they had any sense would any of the judges, barristers, solicitors and legislators who champion our criminal justice system. They might disagree with the aircraft safety comparison, perhaps on the grounds that aeronautics are matters of simple engineering fact, quite unlike the complex and hazy issue of innocence or guilt. If so they would be wrong. Science and engineering are often intensely complicated and almost always embody uncertainty; but in any case juries are indeed required to assess deeply technical issues in criminal trials.

When Australian researchers were given unprecedented access to jurors immediately after trials had concluded, they found three-quarters of juries were not even agreed on whether the defendant had been acquitted or found guilty. When asked the simplest question, 'What was the verdict in this case?', in nineteen cases out of twenty-five, at least one juror was wrong or unsure. In one trial four jurors thought they had convicted a man when court records showed they had acquitted him. Jurors believed they had acted properly and took their responsibilities seriously but in reality confusion and bewilderment were routine. Judges' directions were widely misunderstood, and in a high proportion of acquittals jury members had misinterpreted warnings about fairness as warnings against conviction; in 40 per cent of cases at least one juror believed the judge had ordered an acquittal when no such direction had been made.

In Britain, juries are 'remarkably effective decision-makers' even if the decision-making process is less than perfect. The former editor of *The Times*, Simon Jenkins, describes how a jury he served on 'let a killer loose' largely because 'a couple of taxi drivers wanted to get back to work'. A large-scale simulation of trials in Britain found a majority of jurors failed to understand the judge's directions and many of them defied instructions, including trawling the internet for evidence that had not been presented in the courtroom. Jury members often wrestle with the idea that they cannot consider evidence unless it has been raised in court. And many, maybe most, are baffled by what is meant by 'beyond reasonable doubt'. The words may be plain English but the concept is anything but clear. Occasionally the mutual incomprehension between jurors and lawyers becomes too hard to ignore, but the legal establishment convinces itself that such things are exceptional and blames the jury for 'fundamental deficits', not their precious system.

In America, the largest study ever undertaken on juries found that judges hearing the same evidence considered many of the verdicts perverse, including a majority of acquittals.

Much is made of the fact that juries go way back in history, far pre-dating Magna Carta, but less often is it conceded that we have neutered and infantilised them. The original point of jurors was that they should be well acquainted with the people and the facts and had a duty to find out everything they could. Somehow we have migrated to the antithesis of this. Now they must be ignorant of everything at issue and unqualified to make judgements on any interpretations of the facts that are not spoon-fed to them in court.

Many people who have served on juries will swear that they were scrupulously fair, while others complain that their experiences appalled them. You might imagine that liberty and public safety are too important to rely on personal impressions and tittle-tattle and that the authorities would be keen to demonstrate that the system really gets things right, as we mostly suppose. This they refuse to do. On the contrary it is official policy to maintain the secrecy of what goes on and jurors can be sent to prison if they speak about their experiences – even if they feared for the 'propriety of the verdict' and acted in good faith. The 1981 Contempt of Court Act went further and banned formal research on juries.

It is extraordinary that British citizens believe their freedom is so well protected by such clandestine procedures. One might expect vigilant libertarians to see through these weaknesses, but they do not. Lawyers and most journalists instinctively recoil each time governments try to restrict the proportion of trials that take place before a jury. There is a widely held view that juries are democracy in action and a bulwark of freedom against abuse and tyranny. In fact there is a case for juries at the highest court of appeal (the very last place they are permitted now) so that ordinary people can take a stand against laws, procedures or outcomes which seem patently unjust. Yet as things stand, there is arguably no more guarantee of liberty or justice in jury trials than there is of secrecy and impenetrability.

Contrast jury trials with the Diplock courts in Northern Ireland – judge-only trials introduced at the height of the Troubles in 1973. They were in response to jury intimidation, which is a problem not just with terrorism but with serious organised crime and inner-city gangs. Inevitably they were anathema to a legal profession suckled on the milk of tradition. Yet when Lord Carlile QC, a Liberal Democrat politician and human rights lawyer, was appointed by the British government to review terrorist legislation he reported, 'There is general and justified agreement that the quality of judgment in the Diplock courts is very high.' The process was open and judges gave reasons for their decisions, which meant they could be challenged on appeal about the facts, not just on legal issues. In the mystery of the jury room, bigotry or mistaken reasoning is suppressed for ever. For all the huffing, puffing and inherent disdain for Diplock procedures, the courts worked so well that, according to Lord Carlile, they created wide public acceptance and consensus: 'I have yet to discover any high level of interest in the Diplock courts issue outside the community of politicians, lawyers, academics, interest groups and lobbyists.' As a result Crown Court trial without jury was permitted in England and Wales, though so far only in exceptional cases.

As a means of tackling crime, courts are also long-winded. The government has acknowledged that 'unforgiveable delays' are endemic, and the wheels of justice grind especially slowly in the upper courts. Jury trials can be laborious affairs even when they get under way, but there are immense delays before they start. Defendants held on remand can expect to kick their heels for four months on average; those on bail a good deal more; meanwhile witnesses and victims are in the doldrums too.

Nor do trials come cheap. It is said that a Crown Court trial costs £10,000 a day, but the real bill will be far higher. As well as the overheads of buildings, staff and logistics, not to mention lawyers' fees, there is the almost incalculable cost of lost time for all the jurors, police officers, witnesses and suspects, mostly spent waiting around. Big trials are notoriously profligate, often costing millions, and few people working in the system have much incentive to save money. To make matters worse, complex cases are also prone to failure because of juror incomprehension or frustration. A corruption trial into backhanders over London's Jubilee Line Underground lasted two years, cost £60 million, heard evidence for only 17 per cent of its existence and finally collapsed when three of the jurors rebelled against their enforced stay in the court.

In any case, for the most part juries are an irrelevance. Some 97 per cent of criminal cases that come before the British courts are heard by magistrates. If lawyers, politicians or the media believe that magistrates' courts do not dispense decent justice then they have been strangely quiet about it.

BAD MEMORIES

Does any of this matter? Maybe not in terms of crime prevention. But perhaps what should concern us is the way that criminal law assesses evidence. Unless we learn from its mistakes we are likely to make similar errors of logic ourselves.

It has long been known that witnesses are intrinsically unreliable. Jeremy Bentham was vexed about courtroom evidence back in the 1820s, and in 1901 a celebrated experiment proved the point. Professor Franz von Liszt, a lawyer and relative of the famous composer who shared his name, had his lecture at Berlin University disrupted by a violent argument between two undergraduates, one of whom discharged a pistol.

Understandably everyone was shocked. But the whole thing had been staged and when the students were asked to recall what happened they got almost all the details wrong.

'Words were put into the mouths of men who had been silent spectators during the whole short episode; actions were attributed to the chief participants of which not the slightest trace existed; and essential parts of the tragi-comedy were completely eliminated from the memory of a number of witnesses.'

We don't see and record things like a camera. Our brains are guessing and inventing all the time, struggling to make sense of impulses from our eyes and ears that represent the world around us. Nor do we file away those images in a folder. Memory is dynamic. It tidies up each dust storm of experience into orderly piles. And, like a good housekeeper, it never stops spring cleaning. Even the process of retrieving the memory will alter the way it is stockpiled and later recalled.

Liszt's demonstration has been repeated in dozens of forms ever since and in the 1970s an American psychologist, Elizabeth Loftus, became a celebrity for demonstrating how fickle we are. In one of her presentations she showed film of a road accident and then asked people how fast the cars had been travelling at the point of the collision. But half the group was asked how fast the cars had been going when they 'hit each other'; while the others were asked about when they 'smashed into each other'. You guessed it: the second lot thought the crash was more violent. They were even more likely to recollect broken glass, though none had been shown in the film. Professor Loftus later conducted the biggest false memory test ever and showed that half of us can easily be convinced we saw things that never happened. She became so successful in picking holes in eyewitness testimony that she became sought-after by attorneys across America. She summed up three decades of research thus: 'People's memories are not only the sum of all that they have done, but ... also the sum of what they have thought, what they have been told, what they believe. We seem to reinvent our memories, and in doing so we become the person of our own imagination.'

You might suppose that at least dramatic experiences – so-called 'flashbulb events' – would burn themselves into our memories. After all, these are things we think we will remember for the rest of our lives. But as Liszt had shown, the opposite may be true. Six Dutch psychologists explored people's recall of the most explosive moment in contemporary Dutch history, the assassination of the flamboyant politician Pim Fortuyn in 2002. Almost two-thirds of the people questioned recalled the actual footage of the murder, and almost a quarter were able to remember details from the video. The only problem was: the assassination was not caught on camera. All these 'memories' were false.

Little wonder that it's hard to tell whether people are lying or just wrong.

London's former police chief Sir Ian Blair showed how memory can be fallible even for a copper who is experienced with evidence and is on the record. 'It was a very defining moment,' he said, describing how as a young constable he came face to face with IRA men in London in 1976 who opened fire on him. 'It was just a sudden astonishing moment when you actually hear the bullets going over your head.' The drama had happened three decades earlier in the prelude to what became known as the Balcombe Street Siege, but Sir Ian was mistaken. No one shot anywhere near him. But I can sympathise; I was there, reporting for the BBC. Yet had he said these things on oath, his honest mistake would almost certainly have got him into trouble. I call this the 'delusion of deceit': when witnesses are caught out we are too quick to assume they are mendacious.

Not that we are any better at judging when people tell the truth. Psychologists have been testing this for years and, as one of them puts it, 'The results have been remarkably consistent – when it comes to lie detection, the public might as well simply toss a coin.' Yet at the heart of the courtroom ideal is the belief that ordinary men and women are able to judge whether someone can be believed.

No one is immune to errors of perception. Fingerprints, for example, have to be examined by specialists to see if they come from the same person. In 2005 psychologists took old fingerprints that had already been matched and gave them back to the same experts. But this time they implied the prints were simply for elimination. Given that context, four of the five experts changed their opinion – reporting that the prints did not match even though five years previously they had said that they did. The experiment was subsequently repeated on a much larger scale with similar results.

Lawyers are vaguely aware of all this, of course. They certainly know about leading questions and adopt rules of evidence that supposedly avoid contamination. But judges and magistrates do not read the scientific literature and juries have no training at all. All around the world, courts place huge emphasis on what witnesses have 'seen with their own eyes', and the assumed reliability of this so-called *direct* evidence is often contrasted with the limitations of *circumstantial* evidence. In fact this presumption may be diametrically wrong.

And what of the lawyers who mediate the process? Apart from the recent history of investment banks, there is no other professional group whose pay and costs are so unrelated to their performance. There was a time when arrest, charge, trial and even hanging followed in quick succession. The most spectacular murder hearings took only a few days, while juries often retired for just a few minutes before delivering their verdicts. In 1910 the trial of Hawley Harvey Crippen gripped the nation and, as was typical of the time, the trial took four days, the verdict twenty-seven minutes and, even allowing time for an appeal, his execution followed four weeks later. That was the pattern right up to the 1950s. In a gruesome and complex case, Britain's most notorious post-war killer, John Christie, was arrested at the end of March 1953, was in the dock of the Old Bailey ten weeks later and, after a four-day trial and eighty-two minutes of jury deliberation, he was hanged within a month. Nowadays important cases face so much delay that many trials have to be abandoned, and if they get before a jury, a lesser charge will run into at least two days while major trials drag on for weeks or even months. It is not clear this inflation is in the interests of victims or accused, let alone that it has been responsible for helping to curb crime.

While virtually every other field of endeavour – research, design, manufacturing, processing, mining, engineering, supply chain management, communications, transport – has transformed its procedures and its cost base, the criminal legal process has become bloated while lawyers become incensed at every cost-saving endeavour.

It is not even clear that lawyers are always necessary. The only randomised trial ever conducted into their efficiency was in civil not criminal hearings, and in tribunals rather than courts, but returned the 'unexpected' result that their involvement caused expensive delays and that their clients would have been better off without them.

There is another, and more worrying, way that the system puts

its own needs ahead of the public good. Concerns for legal nice-
ties are more important than concerns for truth – or even for
public safety. Thus a serial rapist could be freed because of a technical error, or a police officer twice accused of rape (and who had
lost the confidence of his chief constable and colleagues) could
remain in uniform because of a procedural error in disclosing a
witness statement. This is not in the public interest. Of course
there must be a process for disciplining the criminal justice
system, but it is reckless to do so by throwing out cases where
the rules have not been followed. If police or lawyers need to be
chastised because they cheat or make mistakes, it should be at
risk to them and not to public safety.

In time some of these weaknesses will be resolved. It is a slow
process, since the system is more comfortable with precedent
than change. And the legal profession is famously conservative
– indeed, lawyers who consider themselves radicals are often
the most reactionary. But bit by bit, archaic rules are jettisoned,
including some totemic ones. In 2003, for example, the double
jeopardy rule was finally abolished; for 800 years it had suppressed
any new evidence from being heard once a case had been
through court. After a while the waters close over the old rites as
though they had never existed, and maybe in time many of the
weaknesses with evidence and problems of secrecy, costs, delays
and inefficiency can be overcome.

Yet the fundamentals will remain the same: the courtroom is
wholly focused on apportioning blame. The only crime prevention benefit is very much secondary to the needs of justice and
is assumed to flow from punishing the suspect in the event of
a guilty verdict. If the way courts dispose of cases has an effect
on crime rates, they would never know. It is not their job. And
if a pattern of crime emerges (for example, a rash of burglaries
because of a technique known as lock-snapping, as happened

around 2010) the courts would not be conscious of it. They have eyes only for the suspect.

This is vividly expressed in verdicts. Unlike an inquest, which seeks the truth, a criminal justice system only pursues a crude conclusion: guilt or innocence. But risk does not come in binary packages and if you calibrate justice to defend the suspect, you jeopardise the victim. It is a splendid principle that rather ten guilty persons should escape than that one innocent should suffer. But it is smugly detached from reality outside the bubble of the courtroom, because in truth, innocent people, including victims or future victims of crime, are likely to suffer either way. And while a guilty verdict is extremely hard to overturn, a not guilty verdict means that many offenders have their past eradicated as though their crime had never happened. It is hard to think of any other aspect of human affairs, where public safety is at stake, which remains trapped in such an austere dichotomy.

And with the suspect as the centre of attention, there is little interest in the victim. Private prosecutions were the norm in most parts of the country until at least the 1860s and only fell into disuse in the early twentieth century. Taking the law into one's own hands was difficult and burdensome and so it was a huge advance when the state became a proxy for the victim. But the reform had an unintended consequence. The intensely personal process of prosecution became the property of a distant bureaucracy, and from being at the centre of the process, victims suddenly became irrelevant. Unless they were needed as witnesses, victims had no role in the proceedings.

On the other hand, if they will not appear as witnesses the case may well collapse. This is a frequent problem with sex assaults and domestic violence but also with vulnerable witnesses like children or the very old – even when there is a wealth of other evidence available.

UNRELIABLE WITNESS

When my father-in-law woke one night to find an intruder in the house, the police, at first, were all one could have asked of them. When controllers heard he was ninety years of age they dispatched officers to the scene on blues and twos – something they would usually do only if a burglar was still on the scene. His front room was strewn with glass, drawers and cupboards had been rifled and a random selection of trinkets had been stolen. My father-in-law had come down the staircase brandishing his walking stick ('Well,' he told us, 'I had been in the army'), had shouted at the intruder to get out, and got a vague impression of someone climbing back out through the broken window. The police made sure he had a cup of tea while they checked that no one was hiding in the garden, and they stayed a reassuring half an hour. Next day a forensic officer arrived and found a bloody fingerprint – the burglar had cut himself as he fled through the broken shards. So far, so good.

And that was the last we heard. Or at least, it was until we called them and were told they had identified the villain – a rather hopeless and prolific burglar – but would not press charges because, at ninety, my father-in-law would not make a good witness. The description he had given did not match the offender. The matter had been dropped.

It was a classic illustration of how the legal process has hijacked decency and common sense: he was no good as a witness, as a victim he didn't count, so the machine had no further use for him. It should not have mattered that my father-in-law, nonagenarian, living alone, frightened and in semi-darkness, got the description wrong. The fingerprint and blood left by the burglar were proof enough. The offender went on offending and the victim was abandoned. What police will not have known (and since nobody kept in touch how could they?) was how that small nocturnal trauma ruined the rest of my father-in-law's life. Thereafter he couldn't sleep. He began hallucinating, seeing a strange man in his room and wandering round his house, a man who used his toothpaste and toyed with his possessions. His confusion and anxiety were not caused by the burglar – it was diagnosed as a form of dementia – but the form it took undoubtedly was. At his insistence, after a life-time of domestic tranquillity, his house was thereafter encased with burglar-proof steel mesh.

Nor are witnesses always treated with the value they deserve. There is no general duty in English law to give evidence against another citizen in a criminal trial, so in general the system relies on people's sense of goodwill and civic duty. Yet the criminal justice system has traditionally treated witnesses with such high-handed indifference that many are deterred from coming forward. It is a wonder that so many citizens are still prepared to go through with it at all. They are often made to hang around for hours, or even days, sometimes alongside those they are about to give evidence against. Unsurprisingly, around a quarter say they feel intimidated. If they ever take the stand they may be challenged as though they are fools or inveterate liars; but, insultingly, almost half of all witnesses who wait at court are told they are not needed and are never called to speak.

Some things have improved over the years. The charity Victim Support had a huge impact and procedures were overhauled in 2003 after the Law Commission acknowledged that the rules of evidence were defective (often exposing witnesses to 'gratuitous and humiliating exposure of long-forgotten misconduct'). Major surveys suggest that after a decade of reform some of this is bearing fruit – but while more than three-quarters of witnesses were satisfied with their experience overall, a third said they would not be happy to be a witness again.

It is hard to exaggerate the extent to which the criminal justice process is dissociated from the business of protecting victims and cutting crime. It measures its impact on the world by measuring itself, and even then, as one official report noted, 'each part of the system has little regard for the consequences of its actions on the other parts'. There is little realistic prospect of radical change to the process, grounded as it is in much-admired tradition, and defining as it does so much about our nation and the way we think about ourselves. What we *can* do is recognise its failings, and adjust our course accordingly.

And what that means is that we cannot rely on it as the main tool in our toolbox. Indeed, nor do we. As we shall see in the next chapter, only a small proportion of crimes gets into the system, and only a tiny proportion results in any meaningful disposal. What's more, when it comes to sentencing, the system is full of untested assumptions, and is based on lies.

17

PUNISHMENT

All punishment in itself is evil. Upon the principle of utility,
if it ought at all to be admitted, it ought only to be admitted
in as far as it promises to exclude some greater evil.
– Jeremy Bentham

Punishment has always been the natural response when someone has broken the rules. The assumption is that as penalties get bigger, crime declines. But like so many 'obvious' truths, once you start to dig into the facts you find grand castles are built on shifting sands.

And in our hearts we know it. There are no league tables of any court's community safety outcomes and nobody bothers to check. Punishments are not based on actuarial evaluation so much as administrative convenience, cultural norms and political whim. This is why neither magistrates nor judges are trained in crime prevention or held responsible for cutting crime. As Mick Cavadino, one of Britain's best-known penologists, observes, 'It remains the case that the main method of "perfecting the art" of sentencing is by practising on actual offenders.'

For a process vested with such political, social and academic importance, it is a remarkably haphazard business.

Since most crimes are not reported, and the majority of those which are reported remain undetected or unproven, legal sanctions reach only a fraction of the problem. Just how small a fraction we shall see. But even if an offence gets past all those hurdles there is a substantial chance in England and Wales that it will never go before a magistrate or judge. The courts are unable to cope. Instead what happens is officially described as 'a series of pragmatic responses to particular operational challenges'. That means hundreds of thousands of offences are processed through 'out-of-court disposal' and that in turn means they will not result in any formal punishment beyond a ticking-off or, at most, a small fixed penalty. Police cautions and out-of-court disposals have declined sharply but are not restricted to minor misdemeanours. According to the Magistrates' Association, almost half of them involve repeat offenders, many of them violent.

There is a similar outcome for some of those that do go before a court and result in a conviction. Around 50,000 cases a year lead to an absolute discharge or to a conditional sentence, which in practice is largely a promise of good behaviour. That means perhaps over half a million hours are spent by police each year in detecting and convicting crimes after which nothing happens.

Actually, more than half of all punishments amount to nothing at all in practice. The main reason is that fines make up two-thirds of all disposals – and they routinely go unpaid.

Fines are by no means always trivial. They are the law's response to a huge range of offences including stealing cars, hit-and-run, fishing in protected waters, trading in stolen body parts and assaulting a police officer. About the only things financial penalties can't be used for are homicide and treason.

But they are often imposed on people who are saddled with other debts or are simply disinclined to pay. Many courts have no way of checking a defendant's proper address let alone his financial means or if there is a history of fine defaulting. Record-keeping is so poor that in 2011 the National Audit Office refused to sign off the HM

Court Service's accounts. Almost £2 billion worth of penalties were then unpaid, with less than half a million likely to be collected. Over £100 million of fines were being written off each year.

This was actually an improvement. Ten years previously the NAO had found that fewer than a third of the financial penalties imposed by magistrates in England and Wales were paid without enforcement and even after enormous costs in bailiffs' fees a fifth of offenders could not even be traced.

Complaining of the farce, Lord Justice Leveson, the top presiding judge in England and Wales, cited cases where an offender gave his name and address as a local war memorial and another who had collected eight fines for drunkenness, shoplifting and theft but which were 'all unpaid with no real prospect of [the offender] ever being able to pay a single one of them'.

If penalties are watered down because a lot of people can't afford to pay them, and are then further diluted because a lot of people don't, fines become the judicial equivalent of homeopathy. Certainly no one has ever demonstrated what effect, if any, they have on crime rates. In any case research would be difficult because information kept by courts is so 'unreliable'. What we do know, from Scottish figures, is that 40 per cent of people who are fined are convicted of further offences within two years.

Community sentences

By volume our second biggest response (at 13 per cent and rising) is community sentencing, which covers a multitude of sins in a multitude of ways: unpaid work, probation, drug testing, curfews, tagging, or being made to write a letter of apology. It has the great virtue of being cheap – about £2,500 a year, whereas prison can cost fifteen times that. Ministers worry that voters think it's simply a soft option and like to rebrand it as 'Community

Payback' or pledge to make it more punitive. Hence the Justice Secretary pledged in 2012: 'We're today putting punishment back into community sentencing. This is about sending a clear message.' But essentially the successive governments insist it is effective and anti-prison campaigners heartily agree.

The truth is, we just can't tell.

What we do know is that a third of offenders given supervision orders commit a 'proven offence' within twelve months. Heaven knows how many crimes they commit without being caught. And many of these people continue in their old ways when the sentence is completed. In Scotland, 42 per cent given community service and 58 per cent on probation are reconvicted within two years. In England and Wales, 75 per cent of offenders given tagging and curfews reoffend within a year of completing the scheme, compared to 69 per cent of all young offenders who serve custodial sentences.

But there has never been a head-to-head evaluation of community sentencing and prison. As Mark Henderson of *The Times* has pointed out, when it comes to sentencing, the legal system is 'an evidence-free zone'. We should really set up *real* trials, with selected courts randomly assigning offenders, some to prison, some to community punishments and some simply getting a telling-off. Since courts and magistrates are inconsistent anyway, there is nothing to be lost in testing this systematically – and the public deserves to know what works and what does not. But ministers are rarely noted for their scientific literacy or political courage.

Instead we usually get palmed off with simplistic results using reconviction rates. Invariably these seem to show that people who are not locked up reoffend less than those who are. But this is a built-in bias. People sent home are likely to have offended less seriously – and less often – than those who get sent to jail. Like so many studies in crime and justice, these are not comparing like with like.

Worse still, these reviews then go on to apply different yard-sticks. Plainly both types of punishment should be assessed from the same starting point. But while community penalties are measured from the moment the sentence is imposed, those sent to jail tend to be measured from the day of their release. Why the difference? Apologists for community sentences say this comparison is fair because prisoners *can't* reoffend while they're incarcerated. But that's the point! As far as you or I are concerned as citizens, we want to know which method makes us safer. In other words, we need to work out which approach results in less offending. For a fair comparison we need the clocks to start ticking at the same time.

Around a quarter of those given community sentences get reconvicted while the average prisoner is still inside. That amounts to 20,000 extra crimes each year *for which the offender is caught and reconvicted*. Since we know that convictions account for only a small fraction of the crimes actually committed, it is quite possible that hundreds of thousands of crimes are commit-ted each year by offenders who have been left in the community rather than put away in prison. The crime scientist Ken Pease spotted this research bias back in the 1990s and complained about it to the House of Commons Select Committee on Home Affairs. But almost all the most influential reconviction studies continue to give the false impression that community sentencing is at least as effective as prison or better.

PROBATION

Around 15,000 front-line probation staff supervise over 225,000 offenders, including 13,000 officially regarded as at 'high or very high risk of committing serious offences'. In effect prisoners serve much, and sometimes most, of their sentence *not* in prison (a piece of mendacity we shall come to shortly). Those on release are supposed to be under supervision, but this rarely amounts to more than a half-hour meeting once a week – if that. Even when offenders are obliged to live in bail hostels, the staff, however well intentioned, have no resources to tail people in their charge, no powers to search them for drugs or paedophile pornography, and often become cynical at the blatant mismatch between political rhetoric and the practical realities. Every year spectacular crimes are committed by people on probation or parole, including some seventy-five murders, attempted murders or manslaughters. There is just not the time to keep everyone under surveillance.

Because of paperwork, travel, training and court appearances, probation officers can spend only a quarter of their time dealing directly with offenders, yet their caseload has risen by more than a third since the turn of the millennium. In fact, several probation officers have told me that with fifty (and in one case eighty) clients to look after they have less than an hour a day to meet the people they are supposed to be in charge of. Keeping tabs on people who move requires enormous coordination between probation, police, social services, court officials and sometimes other agencies as well.

I have a soft spot for the probation service – it employs many good and decent people who at very least strike up relationships with troubled people. Indeed many regard that as their main role. But once again we need real scientific trials to see if, that apart, they do any good. Until then so far as crime reduction is concerned there is little evidence that probation works better than doing nothing at all.

Proponents of community sentences might argue that non-custodial schemes *could* work if only they were properly resourced. That may well be true, but if parole and probation really did mean 24/7 surveillance and support it would cost at least as much as prison. In any case, exhaustive – and expensive – supervision has been tried before, and failed.

For example, from 2001 a concerted effort was made to redeem persistent offenders. On top of routine probation costs it had dedicated staff and an annual budget rising to over £30 million. They tried carrot as well as stick, with a programme of interpersonal skills and family support along with community punishments, police surveillance and electronic tagging. Over a four-year period about 18,000 teenagers were recruited, all of whom had committed a major crime or been caught four times for lesser crimes in the past year.

There is a time-honoured fashion whereby advocates of new ways of treating offenders are convinced they have found the Holy Grail, and, in the words of David Green of the think tank Civitas, the first report on the experiment reads 'like a press release, instead of an independent appraisal'. But by 2005 it became clear that offenders who had been on the scheme were reoffending at a prodigious rate. Over 90 per cent of them were reconvicted, each for an average of seven further crimes over the next two years.

All we can say with certainty is that non-custodial reoffending rates are disappointing to say the least, and the only way magistrates can ever learn whether their sentencing was beneficial is if they recognise an offender when he is back before the court.

Prison

What then of prison, the one sentence almost everybody associates with crime? The slogan 'prison works' is often quoted as an article of faith. And in one sense it is manifestly true. Prison satisfies a sense of justice and a desire for retribution. It is payback time without the lynchings.

But does it help cut crime? If so the evidence needs to be persuasive. After all, locking people up is a dangerous incursion into civil liberties. It is extremely expensive. (It costs twice as much to send a teenager to a young offender institution as to Eton; or as they say in America, it costs more to send someone to jail than to Yale.) And it is often corrupting, as we shall see. Except in the abstract, it is also unpopular: who do you know who wants a prison built nearby? So if prison really does work we should see vivid evidence that it cuts crime in at least one of three ways, by:

- incapacitation: preventing reoffending through physical restraint;
- rehabilitation: persuading the individual not to reoffend;
- deterring others.

As with non-custodial sentences this all cries out for randomised control trials so we can make honest comparisons, but (with one noble exception – experiments with something called restorative justice) the judicial system has yet to see the light. In the absence of fair tests, the prison thesis seems far less credible than its proponents swear it is. In fact it looks positively ragged. Little wonder that Prison Service targets do not include preventing reoffending.

Let's start with the good news. If enough crime results in the clang of a cell door then many of the people most inclined to behave badly will be taken off the streets. At very least it will postpone a future offence so our communities are safer for as long as they remain behind bars. But how many citizens do you need to lock away to have a meaningful effect?

As it happens the United States has been conducting a huge experiment on captivity. In thirty years from 1973 the US prison population rose more than ten-fold to over 2.3 million before the numbers began to stabilise. That meant more than one in every fifty males of working age was in the slammer, easily catapulting the US into global incarceration leadership. Americans are five times more likely to be locked up than Britons.

Here was a golden opportunity to test the effects of custody on a vast research canvass.

There was enough variation in different years and different states for conservatives and liberals to cherry-pick outcomes that suited their point of view. But the consensus from independent research is that mass imprisonment *did* cause a drop in crime, even if the effect was far too small to explain the radical turnaround in crime rates at the time. Some think incarceration might have accounted for as much as a quarter of the cut in violence and a third of the drop in theft. British researchers on the whole concurred. One Home Office model suggested that a single 15 per cent rise in the prison population might achieve a 1 per cent drop in crime. At any rate this was quoted in a big government inquiry into prisons, but the report was so tentative and its conclusions so wallpapered over with caveats that they amount to little more than hopeful guesswork.

What about targeting high-risk offenders? America's new punitive mood led to a policy of 'three strikes and you're out', which volleyed thousands of offenders to extremely long terms in jail for a third offence. This could mean twenty-five years or life for shoplifting or, in one case, for stealing a slice of pizza. Even when the criteria were tightened there was still a lot of arbitrariness, and states which embraced the approach failed to achieve better crime rates than those which shunned such a rigid rule. Eventually, because of its evident unfairness and financial burden 'three strikes' lost much of its voter appeal.

On the other hand the Dutch have tried a much more carefully focused approach. In effect they introduced a '*ten* strikes' rule, jailing prolific offenders who proved resistant to everything else. It was shown to be highly cost-effective. But the initiative had to be extremely selective or its effects quickly faded away. From a strictly crime reduction point of view this is plainly a very promising approach – if only for a tiny cohort of highly recidivist offenders.

So prison *can* help lower crime rates simply by keeping known offenders out of circulation – albeit the effect is limited and seems to be subject to the law of diminishing returns.

Even then for the most part we are only postponing trouble. In a masterly survey, Jeremy Travis, one of America's leading lights on penal policy, set out the predicament starkly: you can put more people into prison but they almost all come back. Well over half a million prisoners are released every year in the United States, most with no honest job to go to, many with fractured family ties, quite a few with mental illness, and 'it is hard to imagine another identifiable group of people who exhibit such a high rate of criminal behaviour'.

In Britain too, the revolving door goes round rapidly and relentlessly. In England and Wales over 40 per cent of adults are caught and sentenced for further crimes within a year of getting out of jail, sometimes for multiple offences. For young offenders the record is even worse: over half reoffended within a month of discharge and over three-quarters are reconvicted within a year. *Actual* reoffending is vastly higher. In confidential self-report questionnaires, prisoners confess to huge rates of reoffending without being caught – in one survey inmates admitted to an average of 140 offences in the year before they were convicted. In other words many of those who are thought to have gone straight will really just have been evading detection. As for the rest, the assumed successes for rehabilitation, the figures will be flattered by crimes that are one-offs (including most murders) and by last-throw offenders who have in any case reached the end of their criminal careers.

Maybe more prisoners would see the error of their ways if we made prison life much harsher. Four out of five Britons tell pollsters they think sentencing for convicted offenders is too lenient; and common sense tells us that the nastier the punishment the more likely it is that people will learn to behave. But just as the earth ought to be flat, common sense turns out to be wrong. The US has tried all sorts of 'boot camps' and 'scared straight' regimes, and from the 1980s to the mid-1990s Britain added 'short, sharp shock' and military drill to incarceration. All decent evaluations – including a highly reputable compilation of many studies – showed they simply didn't work.

In short, if being behind bars helps some people find the path of righteousness, for others it might makes things worse.

OUT OF SIGHT, OUT OF MIND

We may prefer to think that people can't offend while they are locked away but prison walls do not a sanctuary make. Bullying is rampant and roughly four out of every ten inmates report feeling unsafe – a figure that climbs to two-thirds in high-security prisons like Long Lartin. One report catalogued twenty-five violent offences for each 100 inmates and in another survey one in five prisoners said they had been assaulted in the previous month. Even the murder rate tends to be higher in prisons. Bribery, smuggling and drug deals are commonplace. According to official government reports, mandatory blood tests are often dodged and a quarter of prisoners say they can easily get heroin, cannabis, buprenorphine or addictive prescription medicines like Tramadol. Some offenders have operated major criminal operations from the inside of a prison.

But in any case prisons often encourage cultures which are substantially at odds with those we might be hoping to advance. Time and again prison inspectors have denounced the conditions they report on. There is little training or formal work, a lot of enforced laziness and many prison governors submit 'seriously misleading' reports that 'greatly inflate' the amount of time prisoners spend out of their cells or in training or any other purposeful activity.

Compliance, security and economy tend to trump most other considerations, and behind high walls, beyond the eyes or concerns of the general public, the quality of humanitarianism or concern for fairness, safety, rehabilitation, and even of staff honesty is extremely variable. Depression is a major theme and about sixty prisoners kill themselves each year, mostly by hanging.

A lot of prisons are well run despite the odds, according to the prisons inspectorate, and some prison officers are exceptionally capable and dedicated. If conditions were improved, if more emphasis was on rehabilitation, perhaps it might be different. We will check the evidence for that in Chapter 18. But money is tight and British prisons are one of the last bastions of old-style trade unionism.

Maybe we should not be surprised that a lot of people come out of the system unreformed.

Deterrence

Prison may not be conducive to redemption but at least it acts as a deterrent. That is the theory, anyway, and you would think it self-evidently true. Suppose you could do whatever you wanted without unpleasant repercussions – eat without getting fat, drive as fast as you can, have sex with whoever takes your fancy, put your hand in the fire without getting burned ... it would be strange if deterrence didn't work.

Yet life *is* strange. Or rather, deterrence works in strange ways. We have less fear of cars, which are dangerous, than flying, which is not. In fact the study of risk perception is becoming a science in its own right. Jeopardy can be thrilling as well as frightening; immediate rewards can easily outweigh distant danger; punishments which are not consistent can do more harm than good.

CARROT AND STICK

Back in the 1950s Fred Skinner, one of the fathers of behavioural psychology, gave rats and pigeons either food pellets or mild electric shocks and discovered what is known as operant conditioning: reward will encourage actions but punishment will not extinguish an undesirable behaviour, it merely suppresses it. Worse still, it has long been shown in humans, not just rodents, that punishment can cause aggression. So reinforcing good behaviour is more effective than penalising bad. (Perhaps that is why we praise children while potty-training rather than slapping them when they soil their nappies.)

Brain scans help explain why deterrents don't work as effectively as we think they should. It turns out that we are hardwired for instant gratification. The limbic system helps govern emotions and often overrides the more calculating prefrontal cortex. Hence it is so easy to promise to be good but so difficult to avoid temptation and why the threat of punishment tomorrow may not translate into compliant behaviour today.

Cognitive neuroscience also explains why this is especially true of the people who commit by far the most crime: juveniles. Experiments have shown adolescents find thrills even more rewarding when they know they have cheated danger – and their tolerance for novelty and risk is magnified because of inexperience in understanding consequences. A Home Office study in England found offenders hugely overestimate their chances of being caught but even so nearly three-quarters were 'not worried' about the penalties. In other words, the generation principally targeted by deterrence is the cohort most immune to it.

Nor will a deterrent work the same for those who prosper and those who are less fortunate. There is an evolutionary logic for people to be short-sighted and self-indulgent if their long-term prospects are poor: it makes sense to eat, drink and be merry for tomorrow they may be dead. Academics call it 'discounting the future'.

So while rational choice theory might help explain *which* temptations people are most likely to give in to, the *risks* offenders will tolerate may not seem rational at all. In other words, what frightens you may for someone else be water off a duck's back. In fact, each year in England and Wales around 5,000 prisoners turn down the chance of early release. They would rather stay in jail.

Public health physicians have wrestled with these issues for years. We know as an uncontested fact that the penalty for smoking is death and that half of those who smoke will die of it, often in horrible ways and losing on average fourteen years of life. Tobacco use kills more people than illegal drugs, alcohol, road accidents, AIDS/HIV, suicides and murders combined. But there is a fatal delay between pleasure and pain. Even the threat of a horrible and premature death does not stop millions smoking. Let those who believe in punishment put that in their pipe and consider it.

Much the same is true of obesity. Around half of British adults are overweight and about a fifth are clinically obese, risking heart disease and stroke, diabetes, loss of mobility and an early grave.

Health risks are strongly analogous with the threat of prison (which is perhaps why the average prisoner is four times more likely than normal to be a smoker). The reward is now but the chance of being caught is hazy, and if there is any pain to come it is remote in time. In fact penal risks are very much more obscure than you might expect. Even if you are convicted and expect to go to prison you will almost certainly need a lawyer to give you an idea of what's in store. I remember asking an inmate at HM Prison Pentonville what he was inside for; all he knew was he was 'done for stealing'. Very few prisoners are clear about which statutes they infringed, let alone what the tariff is for their offences, what the fashion is for sentencing or what the predilections are of local courts. Did you know life sentences more than doubled between 1994 and 2004? Or that you are three times more likely to get a life sentence in one crown court than in another? Do villains in Cambridgeshire know that they are two-and-a-half times more likely to be sent to prison than if they carried out the same offence in neighbouring Lincolnshire? Does a crook in Bedfordshire feel any more vulnerable than his counterpart in Warwickshire, where his risk of prison is almost three times lower? What are the chances his sentence will be suspended or served concurrently? To understand the tariff in different places for different types of crime you would have to carry round a whole folder full of tables. Like getting cancer or late-onset diabetes, it must feel like a lottery.

In any case all this assumes that people make any calcula-tions at all before committing crimes. Frequently they don't. A great deal of theft is impulsive, most violence is spontaneous and almost half of all murders in England and Wales result from angry quarrels that get out of hand. How can the threat of prison deter them?

HANGING ON THE EVIDENCE

Is capital punishment the ultimate deterrent or is it just a touchstone for political attitudes?

Ultra-conservative Saudi Arabia is often cited as a country where it has proved effective, but many countries have propor-tionally no more homicides than Saudi. Iceland had its last peacetime hanging in 1830 and Norway in 1860.

On the other hand, Jamaica, which *does* still hang people, has a murder rate some fifty times higher.

Given that international comparisons may be equating oranges with lemons, there has been a lot of interest in the United States, whose fifty different states share a common culture but are split about the issue of judicial killing. Maine abolished the death penalty in 1846, since when about a third of other US states have followed suit, including Illinois in 2011 and Connecticut in 2012. In the 1950s there was a classic study by Thorsten Sellin of the University of Pennsylvania, who meticulously crunched the numbers and famously deduced, 'Executions have no discernible effect on homicide rates.' Since then every similar review has come to the same conclusion.

But that may be because there have been too *few* executions. Capital punishment was stopped altogether by the Supreme Court between 1972 and 1976 and after that, even in its peak year of 1999, fewer than 100 people were put to death. That's about one execution for every 1,500 homicides, always after lengthy and costly appeals. On that basis even the most calculating killer is unlikely to be deterred. He would be five times more likely to die from cardiovascular disease.

At any rate, if there is a deterrent effect it is very hard to see. An analysis of FBI Uniform Crime Reports in 2004 showed the murder rate in states with the death penalty was 5.1 per 100,000 population; among those without the death penalty it averaged 2.9. The ten states with most murders all had capital punishment; only half the safest states did. So, whatever other factors are at work, judicial killing in America may actually be a *reaction* to high homicide rates, not the *cause* of low ones.

And there may be positive effects from abolition: it has long been known that the death penalty makes prosecutions harder. (Of course it also risks grievous miscarriages of justice.)

In the United Kingdom, hanging was effectively abolished in 1965, at a time when homicide was rising. The upward trend continued to the turn of the millennium, then peaked and fell back to the level of the 1970s.

You may think hanging is justifiable as a matter of retribution and just deserts, or alternatively that it is intrinsically immoral. But it is very hard to argue from the data that bringing back the gallows would have an appreciable effect on crime.

For those who do think through the consequences – who premeditate their crimes – surveys consistently show they are far less concerned with penalties than with getting caught. Even people who use spreadsheets for a living are unlikely to calculate the odds of punishment if they do wrong. David Myers, the former Comptroller of WorldCom who was convicted of an

$11 billion accounting fraud, told me he and his colleagues had no idea what the penalties were when they under-reported costs and inflated revenues. And as a bank robber once told me, 'I wouldn't have done it if I thought I'd be found out.'

Deceit

Whatever the dearth of evidence about the effectiveness of deterrence, whenever there is heightened concern or outrage about crime there are calls to make sentencing harsher. Sometimes politicians actually do so – pledging mandatory jail for knife crime, for example – though any changes they make are forgotten by everyone as soon as they cease to make headlines.

But there is a worse consequence that flows from the clamour to be tougher. It has a profoundly corrupting influence on British justice. As a result, prison sentencing is based on lies.

Maybe that word is excessively derogatory and even undignified; but see if you can find a better way of expressing what really happens. Criminal courts routinely say what they do not mean. They do so despite the fact that the media appear to take them at face value. And it's possible, even intentional, that the public is deceived.

At very least the system is obscure. You have to read the small print to understand what is going on and the calculations are seriously complicated. In essence a prisoner sent down for under twelve months is entitled to be released after serving half of that; and in practice the same applies to any term up to four years. So when a judge says, 'I sentence you to three years,' the culprit will *automatically* be out in eighteen months.

For convictions after 2005, even long-term prisoners can expect to be released after half their time is done. So in most cases ten years means five. And naturally life does not mean life.

Even more bafflingly, sentences can be served concurrently. In the bizarre mathematics of the English justice system, a ten-year sentence for aggravated rape and a further ten years for GBH does not mean twenty; it means free in five. Then there is a discount for time spent on remand. While defendants acquitted of a crime get no compensation, those found guilty do. In one case a fraudster who was jailed for nineteen years was out in eighteen months.

This parallel world used to be even more baffling. Take one *Crimewatch* case, where a minicab driver raped his passengers, was convicted of two of the attacks and got two terms of twelve years. I asked the lawyers, police officers and fellow journalists when he was likely to be released. No one knew. Eventually I was advised that one of his twelve-year terms should be ignored, the other should be divided by three and multiplied by two, and time on remand should be deducted.

Policy-makers have often told me they are afraid that if the sentencing is unambiguously transparent the public will mutiny. But maybe voters can be trusted more than those in authority think. In 2002, along with Fiona Bruce I presented a live experiment for the BBC, perhaps the biggest of its sort ever conducted anywhere in the world. We showed reconstructions of actual crimes, explained briefly what happened in court, and invited viewers to vote by phone for the most appropriate sentence. In three out of four cases the judges were in line with the majority of viewers.

This accords with a great deal of research and measurement, including a Royal Commission in Britain and a sweeping international comparative evaluation. It does seem most people are only vindictive when they feel disempowered: 'The less information people have about any specific case the more likely they are to advocate a punitive response to it.'

Perhaps it is not the public that cannot be trusted so much as the politicians. The debate over penal policy is not merely lacking in scientific data; where there is evidence it tends to be systematically abused. While the right claim Britain is a soft touch, the liberal left claim it is one of the most punitive cultures in Europe. In reality UK incarceration rates have been middling by international comparisons, higher than Spain, Hungary or Poland; lower than Germany, France or Norway. In any case such figures are misleading. They relate to population not to recorded crime. An official inquiry found England and Wales sent only twelve people to prison for every 1,000 recorded crimes compared to forty-eight in Spain – but we are prison-mad compared to Sweden, which jailed fewer than five.

However, set aside corrupting politics, the costs, the mendacity, the lack of evidence for deterrence or reform; from a strictly crime reduction perspective, prison is peripheral. It is right at the bottom of what is known as the criminal justice funnel: however much you put in at the top, not a lot comes out at the other end.

Put simply, of all the crimes we know about, slightly more than half are reported to the police, slightly fewer than half are officially recorded for investigation and about a quarter of those are regarded as detected. But only half of those result in a charge, of which a third are dropped or discontinued, leaving four of the original 100 cases left to go to trial. Of these, just one in sixteen results in a custodial sentence.

To describe that graphically, let's take a hundred personal crimes of the sort that are revealed by crime surveys. They include everything from bike thefts to rape and from minor assaults to GBH (but excluding commercial fraud and other dark crime we rarely get to hear about which entirely evades the criminal justice system).

- Fifty-five are reported to the police;
- Fifty-one are officially recorded;
- Twelve are regarded as 'detected' (about 25 per cent of recorded crime);
- Six have charges dropped or 'taken into consideration' (i.e. *not* taken into consideration);
- Six are charged or summonsed;
- Four are sent for trial (the other two are dropped or discontinued);
- Three are convicted (55 per cent conviction rate in magistrates' courts, 74 per cent in Crown courts);
- and 0.25 result in a custodial sentence.

The gap between actual crime and punishment has been growing rapidly. In 1950, half of all recorded crimes were detected and half of those resulted in a caution or conviction. By 2000, recorded crimes had rocketed ten-fold, but cautions and convictions had only doubled. In other words villains were five times more likely to get away with it. The old criminal justice model is simply floundering in modern times.

All in all:

- 97.7 per cent of crime does not result in formal punishment of any form.
- 99.75 per cent of crime does not result in a custodial sentence.

Naturally, since many crimes are committed by repeat offenders, very many more than 0.25 per cent of criminals will see the inside of a prison. But the message is clear. Punishment is a bit of a distraction. We must mostly look for other means to conquer crime.

18

REHAB

What most persons consider as virtue, after
the age of forty is simply a loss of energy.
– Voltaire

One of the most endearing views about humanity is that it can be purged of badness. Americans actually call their prisons 'correctional' institutions. Perhaps the idea had its origins in religion, in notions of a struggle between good and evil with the prospect of redemption in the eyes of God. In these more secular times we talk less of spiritual salvation than of treatment or rehabilitation, as though there was a medicine or therapeutic cure, but it is routinely taken as a fact that if only we dealt with offenders properly we would have less crime. Every now and then striking examples are cited where young tearaways or old lags have reformed, and indeed there are countless examples of deliverance.

But so what? Most offenders see the light. Very few go on committing crimes all through their lives. Some take to antisocial behaviour in childhood and give it up soon afterwards. Most people who go off the rails do so in adolescence and return to the straight and narrow in their late teens or early twenties. A few behave badly until their thirties or their forties. But hardly any keep up vandalising, mugging, burgling, hijacking or beating people up much beyond middle age. I recently did some research with the help of one of Britain's most notorious armed robbers, who simply grew out of being wayward – and he is as trustworthy now as anyone I know. We should be wholly unconvinced by examples of 'successful treatment' that are probably just illustrating the natural course of criminal careers. On the contrary, if there really are some therapies or other interventions which truly shorten criminal behaviour, we should be able to see consistent and widespread effects involving thousands of offenders.

We can't.

And that's not through lack of trying. In the United States faith in rehabilitation was once so strong that almost all prison sentences were indeterminate – in other words the courts set maximum terms and parole boards would then decide when the offender was sufficiently reformed to justify his release. The whole process was torpedoed in the 1970s by a devastating study which looked back over 231 evaluations that had taken place between 1945 and 1967. In a robust summary for a political journal, one of the authors, sociologist Robert Martinson, concluded that with 'few and isolated exceptions the rehabilitative efforts that have been reported so far have had no appreciable effect on recidivism'.

He pursued his case with evangelical fervour, appearing on chat shows and in debates across the country and was hugely influential, perhaps more so than he could ever have dared imagine – and certainly not in the way he had intended. Martinson was a penal reformer who two years previously had written for a liberal magazine claiming nothing made much difference and therefore people languished too long in jail because the authorities played safe before releasing them. It was just the sort of thing a leftish periodical would say and it was barely noticed. Only when he published the same thesis in a right-wing journal did the storm break, and he played straight to a conservative agenda. The previous decade had seen a surge in US crime, provoking a punitive mood across the nation. His 'What Works' article was seized on by the national press as the 'nothing works' report, and in the following years across the country maximum sentences became de facto tariffs as rehabilitation was phased out. There was talk of the 'death of liberal criminology'. In 1979 Martinson tried retracting some of his more forthright comments but it was too late; and the following year he leapt to his death from a ninth-floor window of his apartment in New York. Finally rehabilitation was officially killed off by the US Supreme Court.

In fact Martinson's flamboyant writing had been less guarded and more compelling than the facts that underpinned it. He had come late to the research, though his pithy articles pre-empted its academic publication and were written without consulting his co-authors.

In the ensuing hullabaloo the US National Academy of Science appointed a panel to try to sort out what the evidence really was. They were appalled. A few things seemed worth further evaluation but, on the evidence they had, nothing much seemed to reduce reoffending – whether tagging, boot camps and the short, sharp, shock beloved of authoritarians, or supportive interventions like counselling favoured by more charitable souls. But it was the slapdash, amateur approach to rehabilitation that bugged them most. It wasn't that nothing worked so much as that almost nothing had been properly tried out or given a fair test. Most rehabilitation programmes had been weak, piecemeal and poorly managed, and the research programmes used to appraise them had been unimaginative, unsystematic and lacking rigour.

But bad science has its uses. Helping ex-offenders is big business, with large numbers of voluntary organisations (many backed with taxpayers' money) promoting dozens of different flavours of deliverance: psychotherapy, counselling, holidays, education, family therapy, art lessons, skills training, housing, healthcare, drug treatment, reparation, prayer, family support and so on. Then there are official groups like the probation services where social workers, traditionally from the liberal left, feared 'a real danger that probation is slipping away from us'. And since everyone needs grants and donations there is a veritable cottage industry of studies claiming to prove that each pet theory works.

When there was a big controlled trial in Britain in the 1970s, it reinforced the increasingly gloomy consensus emerging in America. Home Office researchers randomly divided 1,000 offenders so that half were left to their own devices while the other 500 had intensive help with family dynamics, housing practicalities, leisure pursuits and finding work. It made no difference (or rather, while there were slight differences for some offenders they were not statistically significant, which amounts to the same thing). A flurry of other reports around this time reached similar conclusions and an official review for British ministers, hoping to find some crumbs of comfort, finished up 'confirming the pessimism of previous reviewers'.

Liberals were appalled – 'harshness has replaced hope, retribution has replaced rehabilitation, and prevention has eroded proportionality'. It is hard not to be sympathetic: we all feel a moral imperative that we must try to help people in trouble. Apart from that, so much hope and effort had been invested in social interventions that supporters of the sociological tradition were bound to fight on, convinced their babies had been thrown out with the bathwater. They pointed out that no one could be sure that nothing works; the case was simply unproven. They argued that rehabilitation had not had a fair trial: many of the tested interventions had been ill defined and poorly funded, counsellors had often had little formal training, prisoners had sometimes been seen only intermittently (in one case five times in a year), and crude reconviction rates could fail to spot that an offender was scaling back to less serious transgressions.

Accordingly, in 1998 the US Justice Department stepped in to try to sort criminology's empirical wheat from its pseudo-scientific chaff. A team led by Larry Sherman at the University of Maryland was asked to assemble as many academic studies as it could and subject them to a 'scientific methods' test. A score of 1 meant the research was well designed with proper random assignment to rule out bias and sufficient statistical power to minimise the play of chance. A score of 5 meant, in effect, the claims were junk. Based on these ratings the Maryland survey set out to show what works, what doesn't and what looks promising.

Doris MacKenzie, an expert on experimental design, was put in charge of the penal rehabilitation section and her team came up with 184 studies which at least tried to make some comparisons between offenders who had been treated and those who had not. Of an astonishingly diverse field – from physical exercise through restitution and apology to group counselling – most could not be shown to work. Boot camps, 'scared straight' programmes and 'tough love' therapeutic camps came out badly – they are always found to make things worse. But, significantly, some interventions did seem to work to some extent. These included some of the vocational training and post-release employment programmes, and a few sex offender treatments.

What's more, the Maryland findings were soon supported by a Canadian review and the good news was greeted with glee by rehabilitationists.

But these big evaluations, though a huge advance, were only as good as the research they were revisiting. Almost none of the tens of thousands of well-meant interventions across the whole of North America had reported any outcomes at all, and only two of all the schemes the Americans and Canadians had looked at had been properly tested by randomised trials. Accordingly, Professors Sherman and MacKenzie could only aggregate research that was second-rate to start with – using a process called meta-analysis, which can magnify underlying errors as well as hidden truths.

Some statisticians thought we were trying to make a silk purse out of a sow's ear.

Weak evaluation remains the hallmark of the rehabilitation field, and indeed of criminology in general. In 2003, in a hugely ambitious piece of work, two investigators from Missouri went through all the hundreds of published and unpublished pieces of academic literature on rehabilitation over the quarter-century between 1975 and 2001 and, excluding drug treatment programmes, found only nine credible academic papers. Three years later another highly rigorous review looked back even further, over half a century, and found only fourteen studies which they regarded as top-quality and well-controlled trials. They were all from North America.

In Britain too, the science has been poor, and where there has been high-quality research, the results have been disappointing.

For a time community courts were the great hope of penal reformers. Based on a Community Justice Center in New York, they embody every reasonable liberal view of how to stop offending. Criminals are seen as problematic individuals who need help, and are embraced by as many agencies as possible to deal with what are thought to be their underlying problems. They go before dedicated courts and their drug use, housing, education or employment and their relationships are addressed, in the expectation that once they get their lives straight they will go straight. It didn't work. The North Liverpool Community Justice Centre opened in 2005 and swallowed £13 million before a decent evaluation showed that reoffending rates were just the same as at conventional courts. A smaller trial in Salford turned out equally disappointing results.

There are always ready objections to research that fails to turn up clinching evidence. Defenders claimed that 'bald' reconviction rates don't tell the whole story. 'We should look at other benefits,' said the judge who presided over the experiment. Which is true; but it ducks the point that these were heralded as important crime reduction measures.

Some of the more impassioned supporters of rehab programmes are so resigned to negative results that they reject all sceptical evaluations. In Britain, some criminologists have denounced them as a capitalist excuse to impose more 'social control and exclusion of those citizens deemed "intransigent" or "irresponsible"'. Others say it is wholly unreasonable that treatment should be challenged by 'methodological idealists' using 'unimaginative evaluation [which] divert[s] resources from delivery', and one or two researchers promptly disavowed randomised trials which had not come up with the results they expected.

This is a classic resort of quackery, which claims support from science when it can, and reviles the methodology when the answers don't suit. Another school of thought says quantitative assessments can never come up with 'clinching evidence' because of 'a failure to recognise that work with offenders is a highly reflexive process [so] the effectiveness of interventions will be highly context-specific. What works in one culture at one time may be ineffective in other settings and at other times.' But this really will not do. If a given treatment might or might not work, depending on 'context-specific' factors we can't identify, then what use is it in the real world? We are playing here not just with vast amounts of public money, but with public safety too. We deserve better than evidence which flickers green from time to time but amber and red at others.

Real science is based on starting with a null hypothesis – a presumption that there is no effect – and the onus is on researchers to prove, consistently, the opposite. In social science, on the other hand, the burden of proof has tended to be reversed, with a keenness to believe that something works unless you can demonstrate decisively that it does not. These large-scale rethinks of the evidence underscored how little really rigorous research there is, how tentative our conclusions need to be, how modest the effects are, and how difficult it is to transplant an effective scheme from one setting to another.

A good example is something that *can* work, at least in theory: CBT.

STRAIGHT THINKING

In the late 1950s an American psychiatrist, Aaron T. Beck, came up with a remarkable new approach. He was working on psychoanalytic theories of depression at the University of Pennsylvania, but was disillusioned. The prevailing dogmas had no scientific basis and, frankly, many were not far removed from the notion that depressive patients were possessed by demons (though this was given a suitably fancy pseudoscientific term: 'introjected hostility'). It occurred to Dr Beck that maybe these people's sense of despair was because they had learned to feel that way – in other words they had acquired a *bias against themselves*. If this were so, it should be possible to help them adjust to a more rational appraisal. He demonstrated in laboratory experiments that this is indeed sometimes the case: if such people were shown concrete evidence that their gloomy views were wrong, they brightened up. Dr Beck refined his approach and called it cognitive behaviour therapy.

CBT is not a magic wand – some severe depressions, and disorders like bipolar disease and schizophrenia, are clearly associated with brain damage or biochemical imbalances – but CBT was the one form of psychotherapy that could be shown experimentally to work, and it has since been adapted to treat a whole range of other psychiatric conditions including bulimia, phobia, obsessive-compulsive disorder and addiction.

It was not long before the cognitive approach began to be applied to criminals – and once again it was the failure of Freudian psychoanalysis that was the spur. In the 1970s a charismatic psychiatrist, Samuel Yochelson, and a brilliant young clinical psychologist, Stanton Samenow, were investigating criminal behaviour with offenders in St Elizabeth's psychiatric hospital in Washington DC. Being Freudians, and following psychoanalytic protocol, they talked through childhood dreams and traumas, family conflicts, Oedipal complexes, and every other subconscious experience and dynamic that could have caused the criminal behaviour. This being the 1970s, they also looked for social causes. Then they talked through their findings with the patients – and it seemed to work. Offenders began to report changed attitudes and in gratitude some even threw parties in the hospital for the researchers. But, much to his consternation, Yochelson discovered the patients were continuing to commit crimes. In fact, the thank-you parties had been stocked with supplies stolen from the hospital.

Either the offenders were trying to please the researchers or they were hoping for early release. Worse still, psychoanalytic raking through of early memories, and especially childhood traumas, seemed to entrench their view that they were a product of their past and not responsible for their own actions. Yochelson and Samenow abandoned the search for deterministic 'causes' of crime, and started looking for solutions.

It occurred to them that as we grow up some of us experience bad luck, or bad treatment at the hands of others, which gives us distorted views about ourselves. This often results in offenders regarding themselves as victims ('the world is against me') and blaming everyone other than themselves – even those they victimise (as in 'he deserved it').

That required getting offenders to reason differently, which led them to CBT. Incidentally, Stanton Samenow insisted on calling his work 'habilitation', as opposed to rehabilitation, on the grounds that with CBT offenders were not being turned back onto the path of righteousness, but were learning skills and behaviours – a new and rational mindset – for the first time in their lives. It is a far remove from other psycho-therapies, and far more mechanistic, but in 1979 two Canadian psychologists, Paul Gendreau and Robert Ross, reviewed the evidence and confirmed it seemed to work.

Cognitive behaviour therapy was not much loved by psycho-analysts and is unsatisfying to those who think society, not the individual, is responsible for crime. But over the years a persuasive body of evidence was built up and by 2005 the case seemed irrefutable. When results were pooled from fifty-eight broadly comparable studies across the US and Canada, CBT showed a drop in rates of re-arrest or conviction, or revocation of probation or parole of 25 per cent. What is more, and rather surprising, is that the results were consistently better with serious offenders than with minor ones. A similar if smaller effect was found in Europe.

So far so exciting. But, and there is a big but, another American report warned that the reality of CBT fell a long way short of the academic promise. Perhaps practitioners were poorly trained, or maybe they reverted to old-fashioned psychotherapy rather than sticking closely to the protocols. Whatever the reason, the assessors warned it was not clear that 'the impressive effects on recidivism can be routinely attained under everyday circumstances'.

Nor did US successes travel well. The holy grail of crime reduction is to find what works in different places and different contexts so that we can pick it off the shelf and apply it anywhere. But when CBT for recidivism was tried in Britain, a review conducted for the Home Office found its effect was 'inconclusive … mixed and limited'. There were some positive outcomes but researchers warned that even those gains might not have been caused by the therapy and, in any case, 'can be quickly lost'. Actually, while the authors went out of their way to sound encouraging, they were hard-pressed to prove that *anything* had much effect on reducing reoffending.

And so it goes on. Even when results seem encouraging they tend to dissipate over time. Another wide-ranging official report, this time for the government in Northern Ireland, described the outcomes of all the British evaluations as 'uniformly disappointing'.

These dismal conclusions even apply to tangible help for offenders, like finding them accommodation and a job on their release. Many studies have shown that homelessness and unemployment are strongly correlated with recidivism – and prisoners' welfare charities take such truths to be self-evident – but it is far from clear which causes what. Most likely the people least likely to reoffend are those who can find somewhere to live and hold down a job, while more dysfunctional people have a syndrome of problem behaviour. The news on jobs is rather better than for housing – ex-cons in employment tend to reoffend less. That is to say their rate of getting caught is somewhat lower than those who hang around on welfare, and when they do offend it is rarely against their bosses. But though the big Northern Ireland survey of British and American research concludes that the best schemes 'can be at least modestly effective in reducing re-offending among ex-offenders', as always when it comes to rehabilitation, not much research has 'met the highest standards for programme evaluations'. In other words schemes often cherry-pick offenders who cherry-pick themselves for help.

It's all just enough to keep up the spirits of those who believe in reforming people but not enough to make much difference to the crime rates.

Nonetheless hope often triumphs over demoralising facts, and in 2004 the British government dived headlong into the rehab movement, launching NOMS, its National Offender Management Service. The idea was to bring together the prison and probation services so as to build a bridge between life behind bars and life outside the wall. Intrinsically this is worthwhile stuff, inasmuch as many ex-offenders need jobs or housing and many have health or drug problems, sometimes with little family support. Whatever your anger at crime in general, you usually feel sorry for individual offenders when you meet them in their prison garb, and it's plain that most of them could do with help. I have seen an audience melt with fellow-feeling and warmly applaud an orchestra made up of young offenders, some of whom were serving time for savage violence. Who would deny it is sensible to find them accommodation and a job before they are released; who would refuse them medical access if they are physically unwell or have trouble with mental health; who would turn them down for help with family problems or addiction; and who would argue that it is wrong to offer them reading and writing classes or employment skills? These things are all signs of generosity and graciousness that some of the offenders have experienced too rarely. But that does not guarantee substantial and measurable cuts in crime.

Nonetheless, for reasons best known to itself, NOMS continues to imply that it does. It acknowledges that treatments can '*increase* reoffending rates' and must be 'evidence-based', but then is selective in the evidence. It gives prominence to a US study that suggested reoffending rates can be cut 'by an average of 17 per cent if delivered in custody and 35 per cent if delivered in the community'. But it chooses not to cite a study of its own which concluded that 'there is a paucity of robust evaluations' and that 'the overall evidence remains tentative'.

A British psychologist, Iain Crow, summed up the state of affairs, and this from a man who has himself worked for years on community-based projects for offenders: 'We are still a long way from being able to say what, if anything, does work. Indeed, it seems more likely that nothing works in a universal sense, but that some things can be effective in reducing the likelihood of reconviction for certain people in certain circumstances.'

It is hardly a call to arms.

But maybe something much more radical could help. In 1994, under a scheme called *Moving To Opportunity*, the US government undertook about the most comprehensive sort of social engineering that a democratic society could engage in. Almost 5,000 lucky families were plucked at random from crime-ridden public housing estates in Baltimore, Boston, Chicago, LA and New York, and given housing vouchers that let them pick properties in much more affluent areas. Researchers then tracked how they fared in health, drug use, education and offending. Curiously, the results were good for girls and deeply disappointing for their brothers. Girls tended to stay longer in school, with fewer mental health problems, and were a third less likely to have been arrested for a violent or property crime. On the other hand, males were far more likely to take alcohol and drugs than youths on their old estates, they engaged in more risky behaviours and were 13 per cent more likely to have been arrested, notably for theft. It seems the upwardly mobile boys experienced more *opportunity* for bad behaviour; sadly, if predictably, their predispositions did not seem to change.

There is, though, one more social intervention that *does* look promising – trying to stop people from being predisposed to bad behaviour in the first place. Suppose we get in very early indeed, at home when children are developing their personalities?

GET THEM WHEN THEY'RE YOUNG

We need to be cautious here because nowadays geneticists and neuroscientists play down the role of parenthood in moulding temperament. In particular Judith Rich Harris has shaken many of our cherished views about child development. As a mother as well as a psychologist she herself once shared the popular assumption that providing a good upbringing is what mums and dads are all about, but found that, frustratingly, the theory just wouldn't fit the facts. She described her struggle with the evidence as trying to get a double sheet to fit a queen-size bed: 'The corners kept popping out.' When you track what happens to twins or to adopted babies, you find inheritance moulds their personalities far more than had generally been supposed. Genetics accounts for the general tendency of antisocial parents to have antisocial children whether or not the children live with them. It also explains how apparently uniform upbringing styles can produce very different children – the 'black sheep of the family' phenomenon. In fact what happens outside the home is often far more influential than what happens in it, which is why children of immigrant parents do not have immigrant accents. This still leaves a lot to play for. Even Judith Rich Harris concedes that a child with an innate ability to be a swimming champion might never learn to swim at all if he never has the opportunity to try. Conversely, presumably, bad parenting can limit children's horizons and make them more vulnerable to peer pressure. Yet as Steven Pinker puts it succinctly, 'The greatest contribution parents make is in their genes and where they choose to set up home.'

So bad behaviour does not always mean bad parenting. The cause might be innate or what happened in the playground. But at very least parents can make things worse. As you might expect, risk factors include harsh discipline, poor supervision and lack of the mother or father's involvement with their children, parental conflict, family breakdown, parental criminality or drug use, physical violence, sexual abuse and maternal deprivation. In particular mothers who were themselves brought up badly are likely to lack child-rearing skills with their own offspring.

Accordingly, pioneers in the 1970s tried teaching mums-to-be to be better at their task. In part of New York State, nurses visited pregnant girls who were regarded as high-risk first-time parents and gave advice on child-rearing, behaviour management, nutrition and development. They kept up regular house calls for two years, and a fifteen-year follow-up found the women who experienced these visits were less likely to finish up on welfare, be arrested or come to attention for neglect or child abuse than equivalent mothers who had not been part of the parent-education scheme. What's more, their children were less likely to get into trouble with the law. Similar studies started in the 1990s in Tennessee and Colorado hint at similar improvements.

But the best support for early intervention comes from pooling fifty-five studies from across the world covering almost 10,000 under-fives who were exhibiting aggressive and troublesome behaviour. All of the trials were proper randomised controlled experiments – in each case arbitrarily assigning families to be left alone or to take part in a parent-training programme. The results were emphatic. About half the toddlers in the control arm of the experiment just grew out of their behaviour problems, leaving five out of every ten growing up with worrying antisocial tendencies. But in families who *did* take part in the programme only three in ten continued to have problems. The investigators concluded: 'Family/parent training programs help reduce the number of little trouble-makers and in doing so, in the long term, the number of big trouble-makers.'

So get in early. As the Jesuits put it: give me a child until he is seven and I will give you the man. The existence of so many rehab schemes is more a proof of hope than of effectiveness. You could try CBT and maybe helping with employment – and by all means do more research. Or we could follow the advice of Shadd Maruna, a professor at my alma mater, the Queen's University of Belfast: offer recidivists a wheelchair to renovate…

> Many prisoners struggle to find a sense of meaning in their lives. They seek to fill empty lives with cocaine binges, joy rides and violence. Some find they can fill this void equally well with creative writing, raising children or even volunteering. This is how rehabilitation works. Or maybe not. If volunteer work fails as a panacea – as has every other magic bullet in offender rehabilitation – at least the world will have more respite care and more repaired wheelchairs.

If there was a clear-cut way of cutting crime by changing people, it would surely have shone out by now. In fact, the more research there is, the more disheartening the results become. Doris

MacKenzie, who led the US Justice Department 'What Works' inquiry on offenders in the 1990s, is even more gloomy, having spent a further fifteen years trawling through studies and statistics. She acknowledges that CBT might help, but for the rest she is now emphatic: 'Deterrence, incapacitation and increased control do not reduce the future criminal activity of offenders and delinquents. Nor have programs targeting social opportunities such as employment.'

On the contrary some well-meaning projects turned out to do quite a lot of harm, including hug-a-hoodie ones. A group of delinquents was given 'friendly understanding implying a degree of love', but when the boys were followed up for thirty years the results were not just counterintuitive, they were 'shocking'. Those who had been given therapy grew up with more problems and committed more serious crime than those who had been left to their own devices.

Large-scale British and other European evaluations have proved as dispiriting as those in North America.

Changing people is difficult stuff, a far remove from simplistic slogans like 'reforming' or 'correcting' criminals. As with Humpty Dumpty, once people's personalities have been damaged, all the king's courses and all the king's men find it hard to put them together again. Or as Andrew Bridges, England's chief inspector of probation, put it, whatever we do we can only make a 10 per cent difference to reoffending rates, 'at best, at very best'.

Thank heavens there are other things we can do to bring down crime.

19

DRUGS

All sins tend to be addictive.
– W. H. Auden

Back in the 1980s I was overruled by colleagues at the BBC about what drugs we should take into the studio. I was presenting a one-hour special on BBC One, along with Esther Rantzen and the Princess of Wales, and an opening sequence had me describing a huge array of street drugs available in Britain. They were heaped like sparkling confectionery on a long table in the studio: heroin and cocaine, barbiturates and amphetamines, marijuana and ketamine, solvents and benzodiazepines, and a blizzard of acronyms like GHB, MDMA and LSD.

But where were by far the most common and the most danger-ous psychotropic substances: booze and baccy? Mention of these had been excised from my script the day before the show. 'You're being naive,' said our exasperated producer. 'People don't think of those as drugs. It'll just cause a distraction.'

Well, let me cause that distraction now. In crime, as with health, sweeping alcohol and tobacco off the table would amount to censorship and delusion. They are The Big Ones. Alcohol is implicated in a large proportion of violent crime. It is hard to be specific because police statistics are hopelessly inadequate. Cops count offences, not causes, and in any case, as we saw in Chapter 9, most assaults including serious ones pass them by in the night. But almost half of all victims of violence say their assailant was 'under the influence of alcohol' and surveys of wounded patients in A&E come up with similar responses. As for tobacco, it has become what one reporter called the 'new cash cow' for criminal gangs from the Mafia to the Triads. Intercepts and intelligence show it is big business for counterfeiters as well as for smugglers big and small. The Revenue estimates cigarette frauds swindle taxpayers out of £2 billion a year.

Government ministers know this but have often had an uneasy relationship with scientists over what is really a political issue dressed up as a scientific one, and culminating in the sacking of their top adviser in 2009.

So let's stick with what most people think of as the 'drugs problem', the stuff my producer let us pile up on the table. Despite the fact that drug use has declined substantially in the new millennium, our studio exhibits would have been consumed in seconds. Around a third of British adults admit to taking illegal substances at some stage in their lives and only half of this is cannabis. Self-report questionnaires suggest about 5 million people have tried class A drugs and half a million are current class A users. This is law-breaking on a grand scale. But set aside illegality as such; what harm does it do to others?

According to the government, a lot.

In 2004 a ministerial strategy paper made the sensational claim that '280,000 problem drug users cause around half of all crime'.

I know it is becoming a tiresome refrain to say that the politics of crime lack scientific credibility, but the most striking characteristic of the whole subject is that grand claims and assumptions are routinely woven out of airy nothings and in this case no evidence was offered at all. Perhaps a ministerial adviser noted that 280,000 addicts were known to health authorities at the time and simply painted in their culpability for about 5 million crimes.

So how much crime really is caused because people are on drugs?

For the police it is axiomatic that crime and addiction are closely conjoined. Go out with a police response unit and, at least in larger towns and cities, a lot of shoplifting and perhaps the majority of burglaries are caused by addicts. Most is amateurish but on a few occasions it gets nasty. I once filmed a habitual user almost dying in hospital from an overdose but who, a few hours later, staggered out of bed to a nearby house and terrorised an elderly couple until they gave him money. Soon afterwards we came across a whole family in the throes of moving home because their student son had been threatened by a dealer with a hammer. So the supply chain is not always benign and nor are all those who get caught up in it. According to victim surveys, a sixth of all violence is caused by people high on drugs. Drugtakers are also vastly over-represented in our prisons.

But the picture is not as straightforward as it seems.

First, let's remember that arrests and convictions account for only a tiny proportion of crime that is committed. Could it be that these offenders are so conspicuous on our radar simply because they are more likely to be caught? They are certainly not very professional – bunglers and muddlers as well as burglars and muggers. Offenders who use drugs are twice as likely to be arrested as offenders who do not, which automatically doubles the perceived scale of the problem.

In any case, maybe habitual drug users are just the sort of people for whom bad behaviour and getting high were both part of the same culture or personality malaise. Almost all confess to having had one or more of three teenage behaviours which bridge drug dependency and crime: low self-esteem, being easily led, or being out of control. Addicts often compare the rush they get from drugs with the buzz they get from committing an offence, and some users actually talk of being *addicted to crime*. Maybe the poet W. H. Auden was right that *all* sins tend to be addictive.

Which raises the third question: did the drugs cause the crime, or were offenders drawn to crime long before they got involved with serious drug-taking? Police and policy-makers reflexively see drugs as a motive rather than a symptom. (Revealingly, confidential crime documents compiled by the Prime Minister's Strategy Unit in 2003 spoke of 'crime *linked* to alcohol', but of 'drug-*motivated* crime'). But it has been known for a long time that spending on drugs often follows success at crime rather than crime just being a consequence of the need for drugs. As one investigator put it, 'day to day, crime was a better explanation of drug use than drug use was of crime'.

We also know that even occasional recreational drug use is linked to a general pattern of disdain for the law. A systematic review found the odds of offending were one-and-a-half times higher than normal for cannabis users, with the odds of offending rising in line with what one might call the delinquency of the favoured drug rather than its addictiveness or price. If one thinks of a hierarchy of social acceptance of street drugs, with marijuana at the bottom and crack cocaine at the top, offending rates climbed with each rung up the ladder.

In any case, the acid test (no pun intended) is this: according to simplistic theory, junkies should stop thieving when they have enough money for their fix – but generally they don't. Even those seeking official help and given free drugs frequently don't stop offending. I have been on police searches where a prolific burglar was found to have bags full of stolen property on one side of his bed and two large prescribed bottles of methadone on the other.

The messy truth is that different drug users have different

routes to crime and that, for the great majority of those arrested and found to be on drugs, getting high and getting caught are parallel careers. As one group of researchers put it: 'Stated simply, acquisitive crime provides people with enough surplus cash to develop a drug habit, and the drug habit locks them into acquisitive crime.'

This leads us in turn to two big drug-related misconceptions.

The first is the *need-for-money myth*. We picture an addict desperate for a fix – an image which some of them like to propagate. The reality, long known but rarely publicised for fear of giving the 'wrong message', is that only a tiny proportion of regular drug users lose all control. The overwhelming majority have relatively stable lives. Even those who are on opiates often have legitimate jobs and when they don't they wheedle money out of family and friends, live off their partners, use up welfare benefits, plunder savings, or at worst indulge in non-theft crimes like small drug deals or prostitution. In one particularly intriguing study, psychologists from Glasgow tracked down over a hundred people who had regularly injected heroin – on average they each had one fix every four days for seven years – but none had had addiction treatment or been in custody. Almost all binge-drank at times and took other drugs as well and a third acknowledged their habit had caused problems with education or at work. Yet in only once case did heroin use cause the break-up of a relationship and only 15 per cent were unemployed.

So beware stereotypes derived from addicts who get noticed only when in prison or receiving treatment. And beware the presumption that narcotics invariably set people on the path to perdition, or to crime.

The second canard is what I call the *desperation fallacy* – the assumption that users need a fix so badly they will do anything to get it. The notion is swallowed whole by many lawyers, drugs workers and doctors – and, of course, is promoted by delinquent addicts who can blame bad behaviour not on themselves but on their drugs. This is to misunderstand addiction.

DEPENDING ON ADDICTION

Addictive drugs alter our mood by mimicking naturally occurring chemicals like dopamines or endorphins and if taken for long enough the body eventually reduces its own production or cuts the number of chemical receptors. Sudden withdrawal can upset the balance and in rare cases can cause seizures, notably in chronic alcoholics or heavy users of barbiturates. Contrary to folklore, heroin and cocaine are more forgiving: going cold turkey from opiates can pass unnoticed or at worst feels like a nasty tummy bug. But hard-core addiction is much more than a chemical dependency. It is a learned sequence of behaviours.

This is why patients don't have pathological yearnings for a fix when they come off morphine after surgery or withdraw from pills prescribed to keep them calm or help them sleep. They may be uncomfortable or restless for a while – insomnia or depression can be torture – but they rarely get red-mist cravings. It is different when drug-taking is part of a recreational ritual. As Alcoholics Anonymous knows, once an alcoholic always an alcoholic. Here the compulsion is much more than slavery to a chemical compound. It is a swooning promise of reward triggered by circumstance or memory. Pathways in the brain, like tracks through the forest, become wider and deeper the longer they are used. After prolonged and heavy traffic, nature takes time to reclaim them. This is why simple 'detox' programmes rarely have long-term benefits. It is why smokers discover they can kick the habit many times before they really stop and even after years of abstinence something can trigger a massive relapse. And it is why some people can become dependent on any sort of fix, substituting one drug for another or getting hooked on gambling, sex, eating or even shopping – in fact anything that holds the promise of euphoria, including, it seems, risk-taking like violence, burglary or robbery.

It is not the drug that addicts become dependent on so much as addiction itself.

This is not to retreat to the old view that addiction is no more than moral imbecility. It is plainly influenced by genetics and mediated by complex physiological cascades. But so is impulsiveness, aggression and risk-taking. So is all behaviour. Drug users do not represent a novel, discrete class of offenders who should be regarded with more – or less – sympathy than any other miscreant.

So how effective is drug rehabilitation? It is a big and hungry industry. Each year in England and Wales, getting on for half a billion pounds is invested by the state to wean people off street drugs, and an unquantifiable fortune more is spent by charities and through private clinics. Some of this is science-based to some degree or other, most is good intention and a lot is pop psychology and pre-Enlightenment quackery. Addiction is a godsend for charlatans, including doctors who never did quite grasp scientific methodology and who bamboozle well-meaning politicians and philanthropists. It is also deeply rooted in ideology, so that followers of different flavours of rehabilitation often regard their approach as the only true path to redemption. Naturally almost everyone's appraisals 'prove' that their approach to treatment works.

Some of the private clinics allege they can 'consistently' solve almost any substance dependency, including alcohol, heroin, methadone, benzodiazepines or cocaine. At least one is a front for scientology. There are promises of quick treatments ('our programme for most addictive substances is just ten days long'), 'non-judgemental' processes and 'complementary treatments' including 'auricular acupuncture', hypnosis and herbal teas, and some resort to scaremongering. They invariably charge thousands, sometimes tens of thousands, for a course, none of which is refundable if things don't turn out quite as intended.

Successive governments have long been in thrall to the medical model of addiction, have poured billions into treatment centres, and have always trumpeted success. According to press handouts, Britain's National Treatment Agency achieved a 'watershed' in drug treatment in 2007/8, supervising 200,000 people, half of whom 'completed treatment successfully'. But at the most generous interpretation only 11,000 of the patients were judged as drug-free by the end of the process, and they may be the ones who would have given up drugs anyway. That cost £400 million.

Since everyone *wants* rehab to work no one has much incentive to be a party pooper. Yet what is so extraordinary is that even with involvement of the NHS there has been such little decent science. When a team of researchers trawled through 8,000 published research reports on drug-user interventions they found only twenty-four which made the grade for what medical scientists would regard as decent evidence. Accordingly, 'very limited conclusions' could be drawn. Disappointing studies get drowned out while optimistic ones are trumpeted. In 2012 the government's annual drugs strategy review claimed: 'For every £1 spent on young people's treatment services, there is a return of up to almost £2 over a two-year period and up to £8 over the long term.'

Which sounds impressive until you read the original source of that arithmetic and note the 'important caveats', including 'lack of robust evidence', a 'limited sample', a 'partial picture', the fact that 'long-term benefits are very difficult to assess' and the hugely significant warning that researchers had been 'unable to distinguish from the data the impact that treatment has on outcomes compared to the impact of other factors'.

There are similar caveats galore from US studies, along with warnings about 'publication bias', meaning negative findings tend to get buried while positive outcomes are hyped. Even so the consensus seems to be that some rehab does produce 'modest' improvements, at least for addicts who are already about to turn their lives around. And being drug-free, or even crime-free, is not the only thing that matters. Intervening can be the decent thing to do and at least gives hope to family and friends. But we should all be sceptical about an industry which is buoyed up more by politics and self-belief than by science.

There is a simple answer to all this. Every treatment programme which attracts government money should be recruited into a massive and definitive therapeutic trial. Every drug user seeking help or referred by courts should be randomly assigned to either treatment or non-treatment options and then followed up to see what happened over many years. It is the only way to make a fair comparison. Given the huge amounts of public money involved it would be irresponsible not to do it; and given the fashion for paying local treatment centres by results it would be reckless not to insist on it. Oversight should be handed over to the National Institute for Health Research, which knows how to do these things properly. Otherwise I fear we will be no wiser in fifty years than we are now, half a century since the first research on this got under way.

It is understandable that mandarins from the ministries of justice and education might find this a moral challenge, or that economists who advise the civil servants are ignorant of bioethics norms and think fair comparisons would fail 'obvious' ethical objections: 'Having established a treatment need, treatment providers have an obligation to treat these individuals, rather than monitor them as part of a control group.'

But on the contrary, to submit people to unproven treatments is wrong, unless it is part of a formal experiment with the informed consent of all of those involved. This should be second nature to the NHS. As should be the ethical imperative to put things right. Decades ago doctors bridled at the thought of 'arbitrary' trials – denying some patients while treating others – but disasters like thalidomide convinced the professional leadership of the need to check for safety and efficacy. Nowadays medical research is unique in giving oversight and veto to independent ethics boards – and no new medicine or treatment is likely to gain traction without randomised controls. If rehab really does work then users and their families deserve proper information, practitioners deserve feedback so interventions are best targeted, and those who balance budgets deserve to know how best to spend them. Those concerned with crime would also find it useful to have a better understanding of what their options are.

WHERE TO DRAW THE LINE?

What else could we do to cut links between drugs and crime? One obvious answer is to change the law so that drugs simply cease to be illegal – and more and more commentators have been toying with the idea of such a radical reform.

At present drugs are given grades rather like school marks in reverse. Scoring a C can put you on the naughty step while class A drugs are wicked and could get you a detention. The categories are allocated with agonising care, but the criteria are so subjective that one year cannabis might rise from C to B and next year Ecstasy tumbles from A to B. Users have scant idea where a drug comes on the classification alphabet, the police often ignore the grades and use discretion, and the courts try cases on their intrinsic merits. The whole process is a political distraction. In any case, the final judgement has to be political – and should be seen as such.

Which leads back to the idea of a wholesale political solution. It is said that the war on drugs has failed and that ending prohibition is the answer. At a stroke it would decriminalise users and cut out the criminal supply chain.

Well, the war on drugs analogy was always just a slogan. And no one bothered to define success so anyone can tell you what they like about whether it worked or failed. We can say for sure that, despite extensive intelligence operations and global cooperation to disrupt drug trafficking, quite a bit of stuff gets through. We can be reasonably sure that education programmes can do harm as well as good – controlled experiments showed students came out better informed but no less likely to take drugs. We can be confident that haphazardly arresting drug-takers who come into our view will make no difference – as the cop who ran Chicago's narcotic division put it, 'There is as much cocaine in the Stock Exchange as there is in the black community. But those guys are harder to catch.'

Yet we can also reasonably assume that interdiction cuts supplies, raises prices, displaces casual users from the market and obliges heavy-duty users to cut down, to seek help or to downgrade to less satisfying products. A drought of heroin in Melbourne in 2001 shifted users to replacement drugs but, even so, cut overdose admissions to hospital by 75 per cent.

And we can say with reasonable certainty that things have not been getting noticeably worse. Self-report questionnaires suggest that the number of drug users has been falling steadily and 2012 recorded the lowest level since measurement began in 1996. The floodgates are leaky but there are a lot of important questions still to be addressed by those who insist it would be wise to open them.

For example, how far do abolitionists want to go? Just marijuana? Would we have it on open sale? Would PR and advertising be permitted? If so, what would the consequences be? The idea that hash is a gateway drug has been derided but the arrow of evolution only points one way: while few cannabis users progress to crack cocaine almost all class-A users report that they started on cannabis. It is also toxic and, worse, it is smoked with tobacco, which is the most carcinogenic substance citizens ordinarily ingest. At a time when we are progressively banning the use of cigarettes is it wise to remove controls on an equally pernicious and symbiotic habit, and one that is as provocative of accidents as alcohol?

Should we remove drug controls altogether? If so could anyone buy any medicine or poison they liked without prescription? Or should we only liberalise drugs thought to be addictive and leave others as they are? Given how dangerous drug interactions can be, physicians and pharmacologists go through seven or eight years of intensive study. Is theirs just a patronising cartel or are there dangers in having an unregulated market?

Would newly legitimised drugs, whether cannabis or crack cocaine, be taxed? For governments that would surely be irresistible, not just for commercial consistency and treaty obligations but to raise revenue and to curb demand. Yet if prices remain high so will the temptation to go on smuggling and dealing on the side – especially now that the supply chain is so heavily colonised by organised crime.

How elastic is the market? Does anybody know? High prices can check demand. We know this from cigarettes but also from cocaine. (Economists Ilyana Kuziemko from Oxford and Steven Levitt from Chicago calculated that when cocaine prices rose by 10–15 per cent, consumption dropped by 20 per cent.) But what happens with low prices? Is there a natural floor to demand or might we create an epidemic? And given Britain's bingeing culture is this the smartest place to try such a fundamental experiment? Who can even quantify the risks?

How would we stop a laissez-faire Britain from being a haven for drug tourism? When Zurich tolerated open drug dealing in the late 1980s about 2,000 users flocked each day to what became called Needle Park, followed by a rash of robberies, car break-ins and violence. The experiment was abandoned in 1992. There were similar experiences in Basle, Berne, Frankfurt and Rotterdam, in each case reining back from open markets.

More generally, what would be the implications for health? Every year in Britain some 2,000 recreational users die from overdose or directly attributable side effects like infectious disease or hepatitis. More common consequences include injury through accident or crime.

What will be the effect on children? It is said that drugs attract the young because they are illicit, but the evidence points overwhelmingly the other way. There is unimpeach-able experimental evidence that unambiguous rules help keep people young and old on the straight and narrow.

Then there are ethical and philosophical enigmas. Since psychoactive drugs are habit forming and interfere with normal intellectual function, how can someone who takes them be assumed to be making decisions out of sentient free will? And if individual liberty is a motive for liberalising drugs how does that square with the consistent finding that 80 per cent of heroin users say they would like to stop but can't?

And finally there are the practical – and possibly insurmountable – political objections. Over the past thirty years there has been growing public tolerance of cannabis. But rightly or wrongly most people still want it banned and a huge majority of the electorate is content to keep the status quo on other drugs, even relatively harmless ones like Ecstasy.

Thus the easiest course, and the one most countries adopt, is to continue to muddle through.

Ultimately there are only two coherent positions: prohibition or legitimisation. Logical consistency is not always congenial with cultural norms so we can mix and match the two. But that is not to say we should do neither efficiently or effectively. There is an argument that we make things worse by giving out mixed messages. If you have a car crash, being drunk is an aggravating factor. Yet if you rob someone the fact that you were high on drugs is likely to be cited in mitigation. It is surely worth piloting consistency. And if we set aside the moral or health issues about drugs and simply concentrate on crime, the problem that affects most people is relatively small. It is not the global trafficking or the clubbing kids who smoke dope or swallow pills, the media executives with their lines of coke or even the heroin injectors who keep up jobs and family commitments. It is the revolving door through which a tiny group of highly chaotic and prolific offenders repeatedly goes into the criminal justice system and back out to steal from shops and houses and sometimes passersby. It may be time to try the Dutch approach we touched on in Chapter 17, removing from circulation offenders who have proved resistant to everything else.

Instead of giving them support to live in the community where they repeatedly cause mayhem, and instead of requiring them to go through rehab or sending them to prison on a judicial tariff calibrated for each offence, perhaps we should try non-punitive detention. Quite how one would square this with human rights I cannot say, but there is nothing novel in principle. We have long reserved powers to detain people under mental health legislation for their own good and for that of the community. It might be more tranquil (and cheaper) for society, and better for the health and well-being of repeat-offender junkies, if we experimented with long-term secure but benevolent residential care. At very least this is something that deserves more thought and experimentation.

And experimentation is not a soft idea, a cop-out. In the end the only reliable solution is the appliance of science right across the field. Crime research is not always amenable to large-scale randomised experiments, as with redesigning a town centre. And you can't test the crime-proofing of a new car by selling an unmodified version to half the unsuspecting customers. But no challenge could be better suited to controlled trials than drugs. So whatever we do we should test it first. Most strong opinions about drug policy are based on slender and partisan facts. When discussing drug problems, as with almost every other political conundrum, too many people are addicted to an ideology.

20

PREVENTION IS BETTER THAN CURE

The wise man avoids evil by anticipating it.
– Publilius Syrus

There is nothing new in the idea of thwarting crime by making it harder. That is why people dwelt in caves, branded livestock and, as technology advanced, invented keys and installed burglar alarms. It is why we lock our cars, keep money in the bank, guard our handbags and tap in PIN codes. It is why we have tickets and turnstiles, gas meters and passports, registration plates and parking barriers. Many solutions are invisible, like chassis numbers; or matters of policy, such as requesting receipts. The best improve the quality of life, like litter bins. Sometimes the security intentions are so obscure that we are mystified at first, as with bar seats at bus stops which you can lean on but not lie on, or see-through bin bags in places that are vulnerable to terrorist bombs. Individually and collectively, piecemeal and coherently, we habitually take precautions, often scarcely thinking of it as crime prevention. And that can be a problem. This stuff is so ubiquitous that we don't see it for what it is: the biggest and most important crime prevention strategy we have.

What is so remarkable is that it still occupies a backwater in political and criminological thinking.

And this is not a zero-sum game. We are not deflecting crime – that would just be dumping problems on our neighbours. What we are engaged in is making honesty easier.

MINTING IT

Has it ever occurred to you why coins like the US quarter or the Euro have milled edges, or like the British 50p, unusual shapes? The answer is that when money was hammered by hand out of precious metal it was easy to scrape gold or silver off the edges, a process known as clipping. Things got so bad in Tudor England that Good Queen Bess had to be warned how severely it was robbing her Treasury: 'Thus all your ffine goold was convayd ought of this your realm.' Happily, around this time the first machines had been invented for minting coins, and soon new techniques emerged that left striations on the edge of them. These tell-tale crenulations disappeared if someone tried to shave away the metal, and by the end of the seventeenth century accepting a coin without examining the edge was like accepting a €500 note without checking for a watermark. Handmade currency ceased to be legal tender in 1696 and so the great debasement was brought to an end.

Banknotes developed at around the same time out of private IOUs, some of which were made out to 'the bearer' so that the client could pass them on. When the Bank of England was established in 1694 to raise funds for the war with France, it borrowed the idea and issued handwritten notes signed by its cashiers. These were for vast amounts, the equivalent of merchant banking, and were rare enough for forgery to be conspicuous; but with the advent of £5 and £1 notes a century later, counterfeiting became a more serious problem. It wasn't until 1855 that fully printed notes were issued. But the lessons from clipping had been learned, and banknotes now have distinctive paper, unique inks, raised lettering, ultrafine print, metallic threads, watermarks, holograms, fluorescent features and foil patches. Central banks understand that design against crime is easily their best defence.

The challenge is to arrange the world so that honesty is the default position. And intriguingly this idea was first developed not by criminologists but by a journalist-cum-activist sometimes dismissed as an interfering housewife.

In the 1950s Jane Jacobs was in her thirties, was married to an architect, had settled in Greenwich Village in New York and had got a job on an architectural magazine. She was soon dispatched to report on a splendid new slum clearance in Philadelphia. But instead of writing a favourable endorsement of post-war urban regeneration, she hated what she saw and railed against it. It was impersonal, it broke up communities, and with great prescience she realised by removing 'eyes on the streets' it would lead to indifference and crime. She became even more impassioned when she discovered developers planned to bulldoze much of her own neighbourhood for a new expressway lined with tower blocks. She had chosen to live in Greenwich Village precisely because it was one of those 'strips of chaos that have a weird wisdom of their own', rather than part of Manhattan's regimented grid. Jane Jacobs became an energetic activist but she made by far her biggest impact with a book which became an instant classic.

The Death and Life of Great American Cities is as furiously artic-ulate, as satirical and as relevant now as it was when it emerged in 1961. 'This is not the rebuilding of cities,' she fulminated. 'This is the sacking of cities.' And in her opening chapter she went straight to the heart of it: 'The bedrock attribute of a successful city is that a person must feel personally safe and secure on the street among all those strangers.' Without what she called the 'ballet of the sidewalk', there would be no sharing or caring and no 'natural policing mechanisms' so that the regimented order imposed by design would lead to disorder and decline. 'An all-important question about any street is, "How much easy opportunity does it offer to crime?"'

Sadly the combined momentum of property development and of brutalist urban planning was unstoppable and, as Jane Jacobs had warned, many inner cities did indeed become concrete jungles full of barbarism and fear, 'centres of delinquency, vandalism and general social hopelessness sealed against any buoyancy or vitality of city life'. But a decade later powerful reinforcements rode to her aid from within the architectural profession. In 1972 Oscar Newman's book, *Defensible Space: Crime Prevention through Urban Design*, called for a complete rethink of town planning. Like Jane Jacobs he realised that ordinary people create the best form of communal safety and that sending in police is a substitute for natural surveillance, almost an admission of failure. Each resident should be able to look out at what is going on. And each passer-by should feel there is friendly supervision at hand while any potential predator should fear the sense of natural surveillance.

But while Jacobs had focused on the streets, Newman's approach went into the detail of building design. And while Jacobs saw strangers as a source of safety, Newman saw them as a source of danger. Each home should have a sense of territoriality which family members naturally feel responsible for and able to protect. Hence *defensible space*.

Over the years these apparent differences led to some arcane and ridiculously damaging squabbles. Should estates be open, where people would mingle and visibility was all? Or should they be fenced off, where strangers would be conspicuous and be challenged as intruders? Actually there is no real contradiction. One works for public spaces; one for private ones. But where should the boundary be between the two? A private house is one thing; but what about a private estate?

The question gained a politically raw edge with the advent of gated communities, which were often seen as a way to deny access to a particular class of people – those who lived in social housing round the corner. There was even a row when pedestrians were barred from Downing Street in 1982. But strip out the associations with political vanity or financial exclusiveness and the idea makes perfect sense. In part of Liverpool where burglary was rampant, a maze of alleyways running at the back of terraced housing was blocked with lockable gates so that only residents had access. The scheme (inevitably called 'alley-gating') immediately proved popular and sustainably cut break-ins by more than a third with a drop in crime radiating to surrounding areas.

The point is, design can make a huge difference. When it is done well people are authors of their own destiny rather than feeling awed by security precautions. We choose not to go up a dead end because we have the impression we might be invading privacy, not because we are banned from it; we feel protected because spaces are sociable and overlooked not because they are shielded by forbidding walls. We enjoy a sense of ownership where we live and work and play, not an awareness of powerlessness and alienation.

The principle has even been extended to school lavatories. Some have an obscured glass wall so, on the Jacobs principle, teachers can see enough to prevent bullying, but on the Newman principle, even the most fastidious pupils have a sense of privacy.

The Pepys Estate in Deptford, south-east London is one of

many places where, albeit half a century late, these principles finally delivered whole populations from despair. The area had been redeveloped in the 1960s with just the sort of Utopian designs that Jacobs and Newman had raged against. There was a labyrinthine network of high-rise stairwells, walkways and subterranean car parks, all with dark, dank nooks and crannies. Residents ran a gauntlet of crime and antisocial behaviour, and the car parks became unusable except for dealing drugs. Finally, at the turn of the millennium, work began on demolition and architects were hired to rebuild the estate as a natural crime-free environment. Large glass areas from floor to ceiling gave views directly to the streetscape where cars could be left and children could play safely in full view of everyone above. When the residents moved back they loved it. 'This is better,' they told me. 'No need for CCTV now, they've taken all that down. It's open. Trees. No drug-taking. No houses getting broken into. No rubbish dumped. No crime.'

And so far it has stayed that way.

Given the huge importance of design against crime it is extraordinary how little it figures in conversation or political priorities.

Commendably, in 1989 police chiefs took the initiative and adopted a set of standards for house-builders called *Secured by Design*. A researcher, Rachel Armitage, soon demonstrated that SBD homes were almost a third less likely to suffer burglaries than otherwise comparable homes and that the effects persisted. The Association of British Insurers endorsed the idea but even so it was so hard to get traction that the initiative had to be relaunched. No one seriously doubts that it works but there are competing interests between developers, landlords and local authorities as well as conflicting guidelines and hazy definitions of 'sustainability'.

Perhaps above all, in their hearts most of those involved think crime is caused by criminals, not bad design.

ARTIFICIAL EYES

Bad things are more likely to happen unseen. You can light up the darkness, which helps to some extent, but as Jane Jacobs put it: 'Horrifying crimes can, and do, occur in well-lighted subway stations when no eyewitnesses are present. They virtually never happen in a darkened theatre when many people and eyes are present.'

To get more eyes on the street, Britain has seen the world's biggest boom in CCTV. By 2011 there were perhaps 2 million cameras – though almost all are private and most are indoors not facing the street. I must confess I find it hard to share anxieties over CCTV provided there is proper accountability. Being noticed when in public was always part of the human condition until urban life became so crowded that people could melt into a crowd. And it seems to reduce harm more than it threatens it. One systematic review of well-run experiments shows British CCTV has had 'a modest but significant desirable effect on crime'; another that it cuts crime by about a fifth. Other studies suggest it improves reporting rates, gives people a feeling of security, is an effective tool in prosecutions and, by directing resources to where violence is taking place, it significantly improves police responsiveness.

This research is mostly based on car park or city centre schemes. It is less clear that DIY installations have much effect. But the fact that so many of us install cameras for our own protection shows it is mostly fellow citizens who we think pose a threat to us rather than Big Brother.

In any case, artificial eyes are everywhere. Paradoxically, as cameras become omnipresent in phones and who knows what to come, we are returning to a simpler age where no one could take anonymity for granted.

The techniques used to make us honest in the built environment work in another form of architecture too: cyberspace. Not since the development of language has there been a greater advance in the cause of democratising access to information. But we have allowed the web to become unsafe. We call it virtual, but the effects of spam, spyware, malware, hacking, trolling, incitements, insults and obscenities cause very real distress; and the internet's material wounds run into billions every year, defrauding uncounted millions of individuals, facilitating grooming, paedophilia, rioting and terrorism, damaging corporations and posing a risk to infrastructure and to safety. Malware has already been discovered that can turn on microphones and cameras and so spy on homes and offices and it is only a matter of time before technology helps proliferate very physical crimes too. Just as robotics are enabling warfare to be conducted remotely, so-called haptic devices will give sensory feedback, closing the gap between avatars and the real world and maybe even delivering physical sex and violence.

In the beginning, safeguards existed naturally. The first computer networks simply linked adjacent workstations. In the 1950s a few researchers began to lease bundles of phone lines so they could collaborate with colleagues on other campuses, and by the 1960s people began to see the advantages of interlinking different private networks. Along came ARPANET, funded by the US military to create resilient communications, followed by a separate British academic network, a technical protocol so they could interact and finally, in 1991, Tim Berners-Lee connected everything together by creating the world wide web and inventing the browser.

What runs through this history is that users were all very much part of the same community of interests. But that began to change. Companies soon offered private access to the web, the 1990s saw the dotcom revolution, and before long the world wide web was a sprawling city with few rules, no police and almost no thought given to control. By 2007 Vint Cerf, one of the founders of the net, claimed that a quarter of all the world's PCs had been infiltrated and recruited into 'botnets' – slave robots used to launch coordinated spam and denial-of-service attacks. Soon afterwards Spamhaus, a voluntary security consortium, reckoned there were 70 billion spam messages sent every day.

Nowadays we can all be hoodies. We can have aliases as usernames, disguise our addresses (even our countries) through virtual private networks and use Bitcoins to dive into the dark economy. If we choose we can make illegal downloads, hack other people's secrets, send anonymous hate mail, surf violent pornography, steal identities or con people around the world from the comfort of our homes. Phishing, smishing and then vishing. The internet has proved how easy it is to recruit a whole new army of lawbreakers, most of whom (as the Motion Picture Association's antipiracy campaign points out) would never have burgled a home or stolen a car.

Yet many pioneers revel in the anarchy. The internet so impudently challenged the might and secrecy of the old establishments that proposals to curb it are denounced as attacks on liberty itself. After all, web censorship is imposed by totalitarian regimes so any curbs must be anti-democratic.

It is nonsense, of course, for the same logic would require us to scrap policing in real life, repeal most laws and remove every constraint except personal responsibility. It is also odd to the point of being hypocritical that those who believe in openness defend so much faceless secrecy. Cyberspace is not populated by a different form of humanity; it is merely powered by a different form of technology. In fact distance lends detachment, and the Disneyesque remoteness of any consequences makes the internet an especially fertile breeding ground for irresponsibility.

We must build on what we know from building. We need natural surveillance, defensible space and built-in resilience. And if we do not act decisively there is a risk that the openness of the web will disaggregate of its own accord. Companies and governments have already turned their systems into gated communities, and as cybercrime gets worse private users too will club together to create walled gardens or build chicanes that disrupt the superhighway.

Corporate giants who depend on the web understand this. One of the most significant advances in situational crime prevention was the Trustworthy Computing memo sent round Microsoft by Bill Gates in 2002 in which he said for the sake of the whole industry the operating system must be made secure, even if there was no immediate money to be made out of the improvements. It put security at the heart of the Vista/Longhorn project and every Windows upgrade ever since.

Even so, there will always be an arms race between those who build and those who seek to take advantage. Just as Moore's Law predicts that computer power will continue to double every two years, so the opportunities for cybercrime will grow in direct proportion.

And people whose machines have been spammed or corrupted can't go to superhighway patrolmen to report it. Policing is hopelessly behind the curve. The Americans led the way with IC3, linked to the FBI, but it was always absurdly underfunded: half a dozen federal agents and fifty or so analysts attempting to police the world. Microsoft itself has often had to shoulder the role of law enforcement but it takes court orders and months of persuasion to have criminal sites taken down. Botnets with names like Rustock, Kelihos, Waledac, Bredolab, Zeus and Nitol act like locust swarms of pickpockets, spies and swindlers. When one, called McColo, was shut down there was a two-thirds drop in the amount of spam circulating on the web, yet it had taken civil action to get anything done. And the crooks invariably get away with it. Microsoft and other companies have won millions in damages from individual spammers but have rarely been able to collect a cent.

Like it or not we have to remove the absurd and dangerous privilege of internet anonymity. And whatever libertarians protest, privacy and anonymity are not the same thing. Privacy is what protects you; anonymity is what threatens others. We should seek out the choke point, the place where we as a democratic society can most easily impose constraints, and in web terms that is the ISP.

Internet service providers are the people you contract to provide your broadband, the equivalent of mail sorting rooms or telephone exchanges, and they protest that phone companies don't tap calls and mail companies don't censor letters. As it happens, phone companies will cut off abusive, threatening or obscene calls and postal companies ban many things including dangerous or illegal goods. In any case the internet represents a much higher risk, which is why most ISPs now offer filters anyway, scanning for viruses and spam and blocking paedophilia or websites deemed unsuitable for children. They need to adapt their business models, as Microsoft has done, to take responsibility for web security; because if they don't deliver us from cyberspace evil, nothing can.

The internet is where some of the worst crime of the future

will be carried out. In fact if trends continue, cybercrime is likely to become the greatest threat short of plague or nuclear war. We have solutions. The question is, will we design potential gremlins out or respond belatedly only when beset by bigger demons?

DEATH IN A BOTTLE

Packaging is a form of crime prevention and none more so than with food and medicines.

In September 1982 an apparently healthy twelve-year-old girl in Chicago collapsed and died and within three days city authorities learned of six other fatalities, three from the same family and all with the same symptoms. Their skin went cherry-red, they developed rapid breathing, became confused and weak and fell into a coma. It quickly emerged that they had all swallowed Tylenol, America's leading brand of paracetamol. When the bottles of Tylenol were taken from the victims' homes, tests showed the remaining pills were laced with cyanide.

Immediately Tylenol was stripped from pharmacies and supermarket shelves and police with loudspeakers toured the Windy City to warn people not to take the stuff. The story became a media sensation and the whole of the US appeared to be at risk. But the toxic bottles came from different factories, so whoever tampered with them did so in Chicago. Either there was a saboteur in the warehouse or someone must have bought the bottles, switched the contents and then replaced them on the shelves. In a masterpiece of brilliant if hugely expensive crisis management the makers, Johnson & Johnson, recalled over 30 million jars and quickly redesigned the packaging with triple seals. Within a year their market share of analgesics had rebounded, and the FDA, which regulates the US drugs market, required all pharmaceutical companies to follow Johnson & Johnson's tamper-proof approach.

The Chicago poisonings were never solved (though an extortionist was caught masquerading as the killer; a suspect who was cleared later shot someone whom he thought, mistakenly, had informed on him to the police; and there were some copycat attacks soon afterwards). But the Tylenol murders led to a fundamental rethink of packaging which has helped prevent adulteration ever since.

As a by-product, secure packaging has also helped thwart counterfeiting, product switching and several other crimes. Next time you open any food or medicine packaging, bear in mind the seven deaths which caused manufacturers to think about your security.

In all these examples, and there are countless more, the police have not been our front-line defence; nor should they be. They are the long-stop. In a free economy it is largely up to private enterprise to make sure its services and products lead us not into temptation and deliver us from the evil aims of others. But why should companies bother? Sometimes there is a common interest between supplier and consumer. In the case of Microsoft, Bill Gates could see its whole business model failing if customers thought its products were too vulnerable or that rival systems like Apple were much safer. But sometimes there is no shared purpose between supplier and consumer. Take mobile phones.

When cell phones were introduced in the early 1980s they were the size of bricks and far from a mass-market product. No thought was given to security. But after a decade or so the technology became ubiquitous and cell phone crime became pandemic. In America it was the phone companies that suffered. People gave false names to take out a subscription and so never paid their bills. Stolen mobiles could be used for weeks before the service was cut off. Handsets could be 'tumbled' or reprogrammed with different phone numbers to impersonate other subscribers. Handheld scanners could be used to pick up serial numbers transmitted by the phones themselves so individual handsets could be 'cloned'. Fraud became widespread so quickly that it was easy to find people selling cut-rate long-distance and global calls. By 1995 the US cellular industry was writing off $800 million a year in unpaid or disputed bills.

At last it dawned on them: either they react or go under. So they fought back. They introduced computer profiling to detect unusual or impossible call patterns (such as a phone being in two places at once), had operators intercept suspicious calls to verify the owner, and, as digital networks replaced the old analogue ones, they built in electronic validation to check that phone numbers matched their allocated handsets. By the end of 1999 major airtime frauds had all but been eliminated. The crime-proofing had cost maybe a quarter of a billion dollars but repaid itself ten times over in a year. As a bonus it solved a lot of other problems too. Since stolen cell phones were hard to clone, thefts of handsets plunged, as did their use in drug deals and other crime.

Things were different in Britain, though. Instead of the carriers being targeted by crime, it was users. In the UK market, mobile phones were sold as fashion items and quickly became trophies for the young. And, unlike in America, where each phone had a signature, British ones were practically unidentifiable. What's more, while different US carriers used incompatible technologies, European handsets could be used around the world, especially after the GSM standard was introduced in 1991. So here were prized items, pocketable, concealable, untraceable and international currency. You did not need to be a genius to work out what would happen next.

In 1993 I was appointed to a British government crime prevention board where at the inaugural meeting the minister asked us what the next crime wave would consist of. I found a kindred spirit in the then Manchester academic, Ken Pease, and we both predicted the target would be mobile phones. By the time of the next meeting the minister had been reshuffled.

Seven years later, when nothing had been done, I returned to the theme in a joint lecture with the Metropolitan Police Commissioner in 2000:

> The shareholders of Nokia or Orange are 'decent' law-abiding people, as are their managers and employees. Yet, it is hard to resist the conclusion that the results of legitimate well-intentioned actions are that their industry is pimping for crime. They lead to misery, injury and death, unintentionally but as inevitably as drug peddlers or the Mafia.

Again the industry would not be distracted. And the police had no mechanism for dealing with hypothetical crimes that might take place in the future. Around this time I sat on a plane with an executive from Nokia and asked him why he was not doing more. His answer was disarmingly honest: 'What do you think people do when their phone is stolen?'

Of course. They go out and buy another.

An entirely predictable crime contagion was allowed to develop into a crisis. By 2001 around 700,000 mobiles were reported stolen in London alone, mostly when unattended but accounting for more than half of all street attacks. Mugging had become the most pressing crime issue in Britain, so much so that the government was obliged to call an emergency summit to which all the mobile phone industry was summoned, and from whom ministers demanded urgent action. Only then did business leaders work together and start to install security procedures that should have been built in from the start.

Reliable figures of phone thefts are hard to come by because people report what is insured rather than what is stolen, but when the industry finally did get its act together crime surveys showed theft levelled out at 2 per cent around 2006 and was almost wholly a crime by and against the young. In 2012 Sussex police launched Operation Mobli and planted handsets in pubs and bars to catch out thieves. Each device was protectively marked and fitted with a tracker. None was stolen. In fact every single phone was handed in.

The pity is that the plague was allowed to become established in the first place. And the lesson is that government must create a level playing field so that every firm has a duty to protect its customers. That has long been the case with health and safety. It should be so with crime.

Displacement

So, to cut crime we should look first at what tempts, and then at what prevents.

But if I stop someone from stealing from me how do we know that the thief won't go round and steal from you instead? And if he can't get your phone might he not steal cars or resort to violence? It would be frustrating if every time we thought we'd solved a problem it simply reappeared in another place or in another form. Thankfully we know that happens much less than one might expect.

The reason comes back to the central thesis of this book. Crime rates do not dance to an imperceptible tune of evil but to the strings pulled by all-too-corporeal temptation. In fact if only we could remove temptation altogether we would be left with just a residue of pathological offending.

Of course we can't go quite that far. And even if we could it would be a Taliban world devoid of attractions.

Accordingly there are lots of examples where determined offenders move on to secondary targets, usually less attractive or more risky ones, and in rare cases a small proportion of criminals do become more violent when passive crimes are blocked. Car stealing is a good example. As vehicles became much more secure, car theft plunged 75 per cent but it did not become extinct. Some of it managed to evolve. An analysis of West Midlands Police data between 1998 and 2004 found a big increase in burglaries in which the main purpose was to steal car keys. Elsewhere, as noted in Chapter 2, thieves tried poking fishing rods through letterboxes, hoping to hook car keys off hall tables. A more disturbing response in the US was a growth of carjacking. Throughout the 1990s there were almost 50,000 cases every year, after which the crime subsided.

But there is now overwhelming evidence that you gain far more on the roundabouts than you lose on the swings. Overall crime rates make the point, of course, showing massive net gains, with Britain experiencing the biggest crime falls in all of the EU. Several detailed studies have proved the point by drilling down into what happens locally. It turns out that sometimes there is no substitution at all – even quite the opposite.

KEEPING MOTORCYCLISTS SAFE

In the 1970s West Germany began to bring in laws requiring bikers to wear helmets, and in 1980 introduced on-the-spot fines. One unexpected consequence was that recorded theft of motorbikes quickly dropped to a third of its former level (from 150,000 in 1980 to 50,000 in 1986). This was in sharp contrast to other types of theft which in those days were continuing to climb. The same pattern emerged when helmets were required in other countries as disparate as the Netherlands, the UK, India and Taiwan.

Motorbikes had always been easier to steal than cars. They were fun for joyriders and easy to dispose of, so opportunism was a major factor in their theft. But if you didn't have a helmet the opportunity was severely compromised: any thief was suddenly conspicuous.

Thus, a law designed to save lives also saved on crime. Incidentally, there was very little displacement to stealing cars or bicycles.

In the mid-1980s a comprehensive anti-burglary approach was put in place in Kirkholt in Rochdale, Lancashire, including better home security. At a time when crime was rising in the UK, recorded burglaries in Kirkholt fell by almost half within a year and by three-quarters over three years. More significantly there was no sign of the intruders moving elsewhere or escalating to more serious offences. A decade later the same thing was tried in the Royds area of Bradford, which went from being the most prolifically burgled housing estate in Britain to one which was essentially burglary-free. Here too burglary also fell in surrounding areas. Similar analysis of bank and post office robberies shows that good security has good outcomes overall, and several studies have shown the reverse of displacement, with what has become known as 'diffusion of benefits' or what others describe as 'free riding', a 'windfall' or the 'bonus'. I call it the 'halo effect'.

Almost certainly this was why vandalism fell as dramatically as it did. In response to the spiralling costs of criminal damage, more and more vandal-proofing was introduced in the 1990s. Hooligans didn't just move and wreck something else instead. The protective effect seemed to promote better behaviour. At any rate, crime surveys showed a fall of almost 50 per cent from the peak in the mid-1990s and recorded offences plunged 3.5 million to below 2 million in 2012.

Criminologists are an argumentative lot but when it comes to crime displacement the accumulating evidence is strong and the consensus is compelling.

BLESSING IN DISGUISE

An illustration of how circumstance trumps resolve is that of suicide. You might think that if someone wants to end it all they will not be put off by an irritating glitch. Not so. Half all English suicides used to be by gas. The classic method in the 1950s was to put your head in the oven and succumb to carbon monoxide. With a cooker in every home it was convenient, it needed little courage, you could do it on a whim and you could change your mind halfway. But the replacement of coal gas by much safer North Sea gas in the 1960s and '70s removed the opportunity. Many desperate people found other ways to top themselves but the suicide rate came tumbling by 25 per cent and, in the main, stayed down. The same thing happened when catalytic converters were introduced which eliminated carbon monoxide from vehicle exhausts. Suicides by gassing dropped from over 2,500 in 1958 to just eight in 1997. The lesson was not lost on the authorities. One of the other most common ways to kill oneself was with painkillers. In 1998 new rules limited paracetamol to smaller packs and in 2005 co-proxamol was withdrawn altogether. By 2006 England had the lowest suicide rates since records began in 1910. Only after 2008 was there clear displacement as rates levelled and slowly began to climb again. So while the dark force of depression can tempt people to the brink, it takes opportunity to see it through.

There are many reasons why people are so easily put off. Even determined offenders are only prepared to put in so much time or effort to commit a crime, to take certain levels of risk or be nasty only to a certain extent. The harder and more hazardous you make it, the more will give up and the fewer will escalate to violence. Even determined crime like terrorism has limited resources and commitment. It is not a balloon which inevitably bulges in one place when squeezed in another.

And there are many reasons for the halo effect. We met quite a few of them in Chapter 14. Mending broken windows often works. We need the private sector, as well as the public one, to take these lessons to heart.

Ultimately, though, someone needs to *own* the crime problem as a whole. And surely the people to do so are the police.

21

POLICE

The police are the public and the public are the police; the police being only members of the public who are paid to give full-time attention to duties which are incumbent on every citizen in the interests of community welfare and existence.

– Robert Peel

So where does all this leave the police? The answer is, we need to re-invent them. They can go on being a servant of the courts, reaping any crime prevention benefits that incidentally flow. Or they could have a clear remit to forestall crime, using the courts as one of many options. Any change would have seismic political repercussions. It could only happen with broad and informed public consent which, given the traditions of British policing, would be hard to forge. But the alternative is that they go on muddling through, insufficiently resourced, juggling too many contradictory roles and mostly being judged by what goes wrong.

We need to go back to the beginning.

How the thin blue line got stretched

Once upon a time we all had a role in policing our communities.

We acquired professionals to do the business for us but we
have lost something precious on the way.

We have also lost sight of the original intention of policing.

Throughout the eighteenth century a long line of reformers
tried to create a regular force to curb rampant crime in Britain's
fast-expanding towns and cities. Robert Peel was not the first
to have the idea – and nor was the Metropolitan Police the
first professional force. That honour goes to the author Henry
Fielding, who sat as a JP at Bow Street magistrates' court. In
1749, with £200 of government money, Fielding began employing men to serve writs and make arrests – the so-called Bow
Street Runners. The first formal constabulary, the Marine Police,
came fifty years later, again inspired by magistrates. Its job was to
protect ship owners on the Thames from theft by dockers. Thus
the model of policing we have today had its roots in the protection of wealthy merchants rather than the community as a whole.

When the Met was finally established in 1829 the first
officers were rarely gentlemen. They had such ill-discipline
and drunkenness that Policeman Number 1 was sacked within
four hours, and they aroused such resentment that the first
'Rules for Police' warned: 'You must expect a hostile reception
from all sections of the public and be prepared to be assaulted,
stoned or stabbed in the course of your duties.'

There were several violent demonstrations between the
police and poorer sections of society and, tellingly, when PC
Robert Culley was killed in such a riot in 1833, the first of
the so-called 'Peelers' to die on duty, a jury returned a verdict
of justifiable homicide. Little wonder officers were sometimes
armed with cutlasses or guns.

But most significant was that as policing became established and new constabularies were formed across the country,
people gave up the age-old custom of keeping the peace for

themselves. Sir Robert Peel had said of his New Police, 'We're forming a body of men who will be paid to do what every citizen has a moral and legal obligation to do for themselves.' But by default rather than design we lost the tradition of hue and cry and its shared sense of responsibilities. The British people abandoned their rights and duties of involvement and eventually their withdrawal became so complete that for many years police warned, and people generally accepted, it was not sensible to 'have a go'.

The public retreat is profoundly important if only because there are so few police compared to the rest of us: perhaps, if we are lucky, one officer for every 420 citizens. In fact in any crowd you are more likely to meet a doctor than a copper. And if you set aside top brass, allow for holiday entitlements, sick leave, training, briefings, time spent booking prisoners into custody, cataloguing exhibits, typing up reports, court appearances, plus commitments to road safety, public order, lost property, stray dogs, serving warrants, assisting at accidents, breaking news of death to the bereaved and all the other duties police have to perform, you get to the reality of police patrols. At any one time in England and Wales there is one sergeant or constable available to watch over every ten square kilometres or so.

And that in turn leaves only one officer in every forty available to answer 999 calls, lending uncomfortable truth to the joke that: 'We live in an age when pizza gets to your home before the police.'

Detection has become impossibly stretched as well. In 1921 there were 57,000 police officers in England and Wales dealing with 103,000 recorded offences – fewer than two crimes per officer each year. In 2009, when police numbers reached an all-time high, there were 144,000 dealing with 4,655,000 recorded crimes – a sixteen-fold increase in their case load.

Nor are officers where the crime is. Policing has mostly been provided on the basis of population not crime rates – a distortion magnified at basic command level. Thus an offender in a crime hotspot generally has a bigger chance of getting away with it than his counterpart in a low-crime area.

To make matters worse, over the last hundred years technology has widened the gap between the grease and the squeak. The spread of traffic lights eliminated constables from busy road junctions and the widespread introduction of telephones, squad cars and two-way radios made police on the beat seem increasingly redundant. So began a retreat of the local bobby. In the 1960s an official inquiry proposed that each force should appoint a designated crime prevention officer but, though chief constables complied, the job had little status and was often a back door to retirement. With the advent of mobile phones the police became even more trapped in a reactive spiral, racing from one 999 call to the next, unable to keep up.

Two things follow.

Unless we reclaim our guardian role as citizens, controlling crime will always be beyond our reach.

And unless we can head off the volume crimes of tomorrow, the thin blue line will always be stretched to the point where it can barely cope.

Policing was not intended to be the way it is. In particular Robert Peel and other advocates of professional policing would be bewildered at how many tasks divert police from actually preventing crime. But they would be astonished at the extent to which officers who *are* available have been hijacked to make investigations on behalf of lawyers. This has all sorts of distracting effects which we outlined in Chapter 1, above all obliging them to focus on sins of the past more than guarding us from threats in the future. And it is not what policing was supposed to be about. On the contrary, the idea of a New Police had been opposed throughout the eighteenth century for fear of creating an army of state spies. Resistance only weakened after the success of privately financed river police to protect cargoes on the Thames. And importantly, the Marine Police had not employed investigators. Instead, with two magistrates in command and a thousand special constables patrolling the river, it had removed the opportunities for theft.

The Metropolitan Police was expected to do the same. Again there were two magistrates in charge, Colonel Charles Rowan and Richard Mayne (whom we met briefly in Chapter 1), and they made their objectives clear. Having found an office in Whitehall (which backed onto a courtyard known as Scotland Yard) one of the first things they did was to set down their 'Instructions, Orders etc.' which were issued with the approbation of the Home Secretary and furnished the most famous quote in policing history:

> It should be understood at the outset that the principal object to be attained is, 'the Prevention of Crime'. To this great end every effort of Police is to be directed. The security of person and property, the preservation of public tranquillity and all other objects of a Police establishment, will thus be better effected than by the detection and punishment of the offender after he has succeeded in committing the crime.

Ten years later a royal commission tasked with extending policing across England noted that its model for the task, the Metropolitan Police, had no powers to make even preliminary inquiries once a crime had taken place.

Of course there were many criminal investigations but, as

throughout most of British history, they were private. If Scotland Yard ever became involved it was at arm's length. For example, after a serious robbery in Welbeck Street in 1840, some 'active, intelligent men' were hired by police to trace the property but they were specifically not policemen. So how did the Peelers, unambiguously tasked with prevention rather than detection, turn into the paralegal service that we know today? There is a surprisingly contemporary ring to the answer: terrorism and sedition.

In 1842 politicians needed scapegoats. Parliament had snubbed the working classes by rejecting Chartist proposals for universal suffrage and, to make matters worse, wages had been slashed in a recession. There was a wave of strikes along with factory sabotage and riots. Troops were called in, four men died and some 1,500 people were imprisoned or transported to Australia. But some of the ringleaders proved elusive and Mayne and Rowan came under intense political pressure to play their role in law enforcement rather than just crime prevention. Reluctantly that year they set up a little investigative team – what Sir Richard Mayne called an experiment.

Over the next twenty-five years the experiment became quite a success. Contrary to Mayne's fears, his little band of state inquisitors did not provoke public disquiet. Far from it. Lawbreakers were so unused to investigation that the detectives were effective, even celebrated, feeding the growing Victorian appetite for newspaper stories and giving rise to a new genre of detective fiction. But it remained a very small-scale activity, with only eight detectives at Scotland Yard. And it might have stayed that way but for another threat of insurrection. This time it was the Fenians, the forerunners of the IRA.

In 1867 the public was becoming rattled and the government insisted the police should root out the conspirators. Mayne, now sole commissioner, resisted fiercely, pointing out that he had no will to go snooping on the public and no legal authority to do so. But he was increasingly seen as aloof and out of touch, and the following year he was outflanked by a Home Office committee which recommended the establishment of a large and permanent detective branch. Mayne died soon afterwards, angry and embittered.

His successor, Lt Colonel Edmund Henderson, did as his government paymasters asked and in 1873 the new 'Instruction Book for the Government and Guidance of the Metropolitan Police' subtly rewrote the objectives. No longer was prevention of crime 'better' than detection and punishment; instead the three aims morphed into a unitary task. The detective squad at Scotland Yard became a formal Criminal Investigation Department and was substantially enlarged.

Perhaps equally significantly, government ministers had shown that they could direct constabulary policy, especially under threat of terrorism, thereby greatly diluting the independence of the police.

Which brings us to where we are today. Nowadays the legal system is the tail that wags the dog. The police have become insulated from responsibility for bringing down the problem they were invented to resolve. There was a flurry of interest in crime prevention in the 1960s but it says much for the fatalism which gripped government that for many years its biggest investment in the field was the National Crime Prevention Centre, which essentially boiled down to a Portakabin in Stafford. Though it was eventually enlarged and moved to Yorkshire, where I formally opened the new facility, it closed soon afterwards when a review concluded that 'these services were not well enough resourced to have made a significant impact'.

Come to that, when the Association of Chief Police Officers

had a crime prevention committee, it was a subcommittee of the Crime Committee, not the other way around. The most senior rank ever achieved anywhere for a dedicated crime prevention officer was that of Inspector. Not surprisingly, crime prevention is often regarded by constables as peripheral or worse. The fun part of policing is responding to dramatic incidents, or engaging in detective work.

As it happens officers do engage in a huge amount of crime prevention work when it is exciting. For example, they might rush to reports of suspicious behaviour and will mount vigorous searches if a burglar may be on the premises. But the ardour tends to evaporate if an arrest is not on the cards.

Crime prevention, as such, is relegated to just one of the 190 training modules for police recruits. Even officers who want to get ahead don't need to know about how to bring down crime. The *Promotion Crammer for Sergeants and Inspectors* is essentially a law book. And the law has so many rules and requires such unqualified compliance that it soaks up an enormous proportion of police resources.

Has it ever occurred to you what a simple arrest involves for the officers involved? Take an elementary case of shoplifting, one of many whose aftermath I have witnessed while out with the police. Our patrol car is called to a supermarket where a customer has been detained, and it takes twenty minutes to get there through the rush-hour traffic. The man is terrified and admits he pocketed an item though he paid for everything else. He can't prove his identity so has to be cautioned and arrested. He is frisked, CCTV from the store is checked, arrangements are made to safeguard his bike, and he is led out to the car. The two officers have already been on the case for thirty-five minutes. But the nearest custody suite is full so the prisoner has to be taken through heavy traffic for a twenty-minute drive to the next police station – and eventually they will have a twenty-minute journey back. Custody suites are a pinch-point and the arresting officers often have to wait outside until space becomes available, which can take several hours. Then comes the paperwork: questionnaires on welfare considerations, fingerprints, DNA samples, photographs and an audit of the prisoner's property. Now they must 'do the notes', which means writing a statement of the arrest, which will take anything from five minutes to an hour, then spend thirty minutes or so keying in much of the same information to create a computerised crime report. An intelligence report comes next, often repeating information, which may take another ten or fifteen minutes, often followed by property logs, witness forms or missing person details, and admin paperwork for overtime or force initiatives. Meanwhile if the prisoner wants a solicitor it is up to the police to find one. That means calling round to local firms and waiting for a lawyer to arrive. Now, at last, the officers are allowed to interview their suspect. Things can be much more complicated if an ID parade is called for, if an interpreter is needed or if an 'appropriate adult' must be found to safeguard the interests of a vulnerable suspect. The typical shoplifting case I described was as simple as it gets, but it still took two officers off the streets for over three-and-a-half hours – in manpower terms, one officer for almost a day. A survey of officers' logs across England and Wales found this was average. The case resulted in a formal police caution.

Frankly, it need not be quite as bad as it is. I once witnessed a passenger falling from a train – or at any rate heard the door crash open and ballast flailing up against the floor. I found the guard, we stopped the train and the crew walked back and found the body. Knowing I would have to give a statement, I took names of fellow passengers, wrote up my contemporaneous account, and when I got home, typed it up and sent it to the police. But that is not how the system works. Two officers from the west of England where the incident happened had to travel up to London to interview me formally. Painstakingly they took down, longhand, everything I had to say, in a process that took just under two hours. They asked nothing that had not been in my written notes, and omitted much that was. Then they thanked me, and left for their three-and-a-half-hour journey home. Next day, no doubt, they would have to type their notes onto official forms. Some of this time-wasting is through lack of investment – it is hard to imagine a major corporation that is so scandalously outdated – but most of the red tape is imposed by the demands of the legal system.

But now take a case that goes to court. Before framing a charge the police must prepare a set of case papers, which will take at least an hour for the most elementary prosecution. Only then can they seek what is known as charging advice from the Crown Prosecution Service. If this can be done on the phone it might be sorted in less than twenty minutes; but more complex issues can mean booking an appointment with the lawyer, who might not be available for days. And the lawyer must be realistic. If a defendant is uncooperative, or plays a game, securing a conviction can be extremely long-winded, and very much harder than most members of the public seem to think.

Take another case I witnessed: an Albanian long known to the police as a drug dealer. Now he's been caught in the act. His apartment had been searched and enough cocaine was found for at least 400 lines. Six doses wrapped in yellow cling-film were in the jeans hanging in his closet, and another six wraps were in a jacket along with a golf-ball-sized lump from which the others had been cut. Dinner plates and a kitchen knife under belongings in his wardrobe showed traces of cocaine, and scientific tests proved that the cellophane drug wraps were chemically identical to a roll of cling-film in his drawer. The torn edges even matched precisely the cutter on his cling-film box. But despite the extensive forensic evidence the Albanian has an answer. He had a friend to stay, he says, and the clothes and drugs are his.

He is not entirely sure of the friend's name and has no contact numbers for him, even though they are supposedly intimate enough to hang their clothes together in the same closet. There is no trace of a guest having stayed in the one-room flat, and six months later no one has returned to retrieve the coat and jeans, nor has the friend made contact to inquire about his £1,500-worth of cocaine. But who can prove the friend does not exist? While the dealer is out on bail the Crown Prosecution lawyer agonises, and though she finally agrees to prosecute, she confesses she might not have done had I not been there as an observer. 'It might seem obvious,' she says, 'but it's really quite likely a jury will acquit.'

She is right. In the time it takes to come to court the dealer has a year to peddle drugs, is then acquitted, and doubtless goes back to peddle drugs again.

About a third of cases are considered not strong enough to go to trial and are abandoned. All those police inquiries are thus a waste of time and money. For the other two-thirds, getting the go-ahead to prosecute is just the halfway stage.

It takes on average nine-and-a-half days before things first arrive in court in England and Wales, which might be just a bail hearing. You can imagine how all-consuming a major case can be, one that may take months of detective work for dozens of officers followed by more months of court preparation and many weeks of trial. Apart from the vagaries of shift-working, with officers off sick, and others on light duties because of injury or pregnancy, consider the chance of being pulled off to help with a fatal accident inquiry or for extra anti-terrorist security. Or, just as likely, called to deal with some issue that is vexing journalists or politicians – what Lord Stevens, one of the most respected of police chiefs, describes as the 'three Ms': the demands of the moment, the demands of performance measures and the demands of the media.

True, in generations past police officers brought some of the bureaucracy down upon their own heads by 'fitting people up', roughing prisoners up in custody, being insensitive to mental frailties or failing to spot medical conditions. Sir Robert Mark, a former Met Commissioner, recalled how in the 1950s and 1960s suspects were half-drowned in lavatory bowls to extract confessions. But however we got where we are, what we have arrived at is plainly not fit for purpose if our purpose is reducing harm. It wastes police time.

Since prosecution has become an aim in itself, law enforcement agents often just ignore crimes that don't fit the legal paradigm. A resident might see a drugs deal going on outside her home and cannot understand why the police just shrug. The answer is it will not lead to an arrest. By the time a bobby gets there it will probably be over and in any case it would take a big operation to get enough evidence for court: ringing the area with officers so that people can be nabbed red-handed; video surveillance to prove the deal; and, if the dealer managed to throw away the drugs, forensic evidence to pin them specifically on him. Securing a conviction is very, very hard, and unless the evidence is overwhelming the case is almost certain to be dropped.

Accordingly it is more rewarding for police to go for easy meat. And this has been encouraged – even formalised – since at least the 1980s when Mrs Thatcher's fiscally conservative government started using detection rates as a proxy of police efficiency. This is still popularly regarded as a good measure of their success. After all, the conventional view is that catching bad 'uns is what policing is about. We all naturally and properly seek justice and I, like you, would be upset if we were victims and the police didn't do their best to arrest and prosecute the villain.

But apart from the risk of encouraging cops to fiddle the figures there is a bigger danger in this preoccupation. And a much more insidious one. For while we focus on detections we lose sight of the bigger picture. We are so busy totting up successes we fail to see what our real objective is. The blindness this induces becomes obvious if we drain the subject of emotion – crime caused by others – and look at offences where we ourselves are sometimes on the wrong side of the law.

Years ago my wife and I were driving out of London and, too late, saw a small sign warning there was no left turn at the junction ahead. We had missed a cut-through and would now have to go on a long detour through heavy traffic. It was far from clear why the left turn was forbidden, especially since the road we wanted was the main route out of London, and as we approached the traffic lights Sarah cajoled me into making the illegal turn: 'Don't be a wimp!' she joked. But just round the corner a police sergeant flagged me down and I joined a queue of motorists waiting to be given tickets.

It was embarrassing, not least because several people, and not just the officer, wanted my autograph – this was when I was on TV a lot. It got worse. More and more cars arrived and were flagged down. It turned out that this was a regular checkpoint and it harvested dozens of motorists each day.

But what was the point? If the left turn there was dangerous, why did the officer not stand at the junction to stop me breaking the law? Or, more to the point, why did he not get someone to improve the signage? If motorists knew of the earlier shortcut they would have been happy to take it, and there would be no cause for danger and no need to offend. In fact this is what happened some years later when enough people had complained, and through clear signage the problem was almost eliminated.

Here, on the road to Islington, was an exemplar of the police catching people after an offence had taken place instead of seeing their job as preventing the offence upstream. Doing their duty, upholding the law, unimaginative, fatalistic, punitive.

As usual, I was not the first to spot this.

POP: THE RADICAL IDEA THAT POLICE SHOULD
ACTUALLY SOLVE PROBLEMS

In 1953 a small army of observers was sent out across the United States to work out why the criminal justice system in American was 'so dreadfully slow'. One of the recruits was a young graduate called Herman Goldstein who hoped for a career in local government. Instead he found himself watching cops watching prostitutes watching would-be punters. Every now and then some of the girls would be arrested. There was no strategy or coordination and cases rarely went to court but street prostitution was thereby 'tackled'. It was the same with other crimes. Haphazard and reactive. If victims declined to file an official complaint no action was taken, so feuds, domestic disputes and serious injuries went unrecorded. The cops behaved as though they were omnipotent and yet were impotent in the face of rising crime. They had few if any partnerships with other agencies and while they were doing what was asked of them they were flailing around in a quite arbitrary way. Goldstein called it the Dark Age.

Goldstein did soon make it into local government but not as he intended. One of his senior colleagues was an ex-cop turned academic called Orlando Winfield Wilson and, when a few years later Wilson was hired to sort out Chicago's scandal-ridden police force, he brought in Goldstein as his executive assistant. It was an inspired partnership which reformed policing in the Windy City – indeed transformed it. But four years later when Goldstein left to become a law professor he was still vaguely dissatisfied. Policing was now fairer and more efficient, but what was it actually achieving? A radical idea was beginning to take root.

The following year, with crime a growing problem in America, a presidential commission exposed a clash of philosophies. One school thought the police should concentrate on 'real' crime like robbery and murder and stop trying to be social workers. The other view, championed by Goldstein, was that small offenders grew into big ones and that in any case so-called minor problems like youths massing in the street were often the ones that preoccupied the public. He wanted the police to be less reactive and more strategic. In his ambition police were not automatons enforcing the law but policy-makers and problem solvers.

Some of his views prevailed and helped pave the way for what happened later in places like New York. But still Herman Goldstein remained unfulfilled. The basis of police work remained the same – patrol, emergency call-outs, investigation and prosecution – a piecemeal response that was unable to stop crime growing and was becoming overwhelmed by the rising tide. 'Rushing around chasing crooks was never going to solve things.'

Finally, in 1979, his views came into blossom: POP. POP stands for Problem-Oriented Policing and Goldstein's book, *Improving Policing: a Problem Oriented Approach*, set out the two key features: prevention is preferable to emergency responding, and many elegant solutions are to be found outside the criminal justice system, often in partnership with others.

A US police chief describes policing in the years before she discovered POP: 'Paramilitary, hierarchical, protecting your butt. Leave your imagination at the door. As the call came in we'd go and answer it. No strategy, just response. It's what the public expect; but public expectations are bananas. There was no stake in seeing anything grow, succeed, or thrive.'

POP has since grown into a worldwide initiative and British bobbies excel at winning POP awards. But it remains essentially a side show. The ideas are out there, the will to implement them is not. Public expectations remain 'bananas'.

How do we change the priorities of British policing? The solution won't come from tinkering with policing structures. That is how politicians seek to show they have a grip on events: by rearranging furniture. Maybe it will emerge from elected crime commissioners – billed as the biggest idea in British policing for at least a century. But their need to whip up votes seems more likely to drive populism, parochialism and instant gratification. Our expectations of any institution are framed by what we know about its role, so there tends to be a circularity. Most people will tell you that they want the police to do roughly what they do, but better. To quote Henry Ford, 'If I'd asked people what they wanted they'd have asked for a better horse.'

Ultimately, in tackling crime we need to face up to a difficult choice about priorities. The big question is what we really want from the police. Neither Parliament nor voters have ever been invited to address that question and it deserves an informed debate. And the challenge boils down to whether we are more concerned about the future or the past.

Are we prepared to sacrifice justice for yesterday's victims in order to prevent tomorrow's victimisations? Unless you have unlimited resources there is an inevitable tension between these two objectives.

No one is suggesting we could or should abandon chasing after crooks. The question is strategic, about what we are trying to achieve. We have fudged the distinction between crime and punishment for too long. We need to rebalance police priorities. And there is an elegantly phrased vision statement for police waiting for us on a shelf where it was unceremoniously abandoned almost a century-and-a-half ago. It is the wisdom of Charles Rowan and Richard Mayne, and their key clause – that 'the principal object to be attained is "the Prevention of Crime".'

Once we have that firmly in our sights the rest will follow.

22

WHERE NEXT?

The principal object to be attained is 'the Prevention of Crime'.
– Charles Rowan and Richard Mayne

The police have a lot to do. And in all their major tasks but one they are expected to be ahead of the game. In crowd safety and maintaining public order, in security for big events and in road safety or disaster management, for countering terrorism or protecting diplomats and VIPs, there is a lot of forward planning. They seek to control events and they practise for all eventualities. But with crime they are almost always struggling to catch up. An intelligence-led approach was launched in the 1990s to disrupt prolific offenders, and CompStat-type reviews try to keep up with the latest trends. Police might sometimes infiltrate a gang or be forewarned by an informant so they can catch offenders in the act. They sometimes mount temporary campaigns against burglars or drink-driving. They rehearse how to handle major incidents like homicide or a missing child. But they are rarely in control of events.

The reason, as we've seen, is that detection has achieved supremacy and once a crime has been detected the task is done. A change of emphasis to crime prevention – if taken seriously – would be little short of revolutionary. And it would be transforming in at least five ways.

First it would give police a clear sense of direction. We should not underestimate how important clarity is in itself.

Second, it would liberate them from the box-ticking monopoly of lawyers. It is said that for a man with a hammer every answer is a nail. But now the police would have a whole new tool chest at their disposal and be free to explore a wide range of more constructive ways to tackle crime.

Third, it would require them to migrate from solving individual crimes to resolving underlying problems. Instead of pulling up weeds wherever they can find them they would make sure fewer seeds of crime get planted.

Fourth, it would move police higher up the food chain. Instead of subsistence farming, with hand-to-mouth ambitions, police would influence the ecosystem in which crime flourishes or struggles.

Fifth, it would help close the gap between them and us. Since police can't prevent crime on their own it would oblige them to work more closely with the rest of us, placing responsibilities on citizens, businesses and policy-makers to avoid polluting society with unnecessary temptations and opportunities for harm.

1. Clarity

You might imagine that the police know what they are doing when it comes to crime. They don't – and that's official. The Police Inspectorate, which regulates and monitors, has criticised the 'absence of clarity around a single mission for policing – forces all use different mission statements and these vary even across departments within a force. This undermines the legitimacy of both leadership and crime-fighting roles.'

Only one command unit was found by the Inspectorate to anticipate problems by drawing on work by crime scientists

– and that 'delivered significant burglary reduction in the areas concerned'. But for the most part, the report found, 'everything is a priority we just respond to the next call'.

If the police do not see crime prevention as their core role, who will? It can't be government, where freedom from crime is only one of many competing ambitions in a swirling galaxy of other noble hopes, hot-headed desires and political aspirations. If ever there is a minister with a driving passion to cut crime he or she will be here today and gone tomorrow. It can't be local government either. There was a brave attempt at this in 1998, requiring local authorities to have a crime reduction strategy in partnerships with other agencies, but with no one specifically in charge it rarely had much impact.

So the police are the natural guardians against crime. And once they have a no-nonsense strategy for crime reduction a lot of other things will change.

To quote ex-Met Chief Lord Stevens, 'For too long we have simply accepted the growing demands placed upon us. We must "front end" the business and not be a slave to the symptoms.'

2. Liberation

Ordinary citizens know that in civil disputes you go to court only *in extremis*. Companies or individuals understand that litigation is long-winded, capricious, horrendously expensive and to be avoided if at all possible. Yet in crime it is not just our first impulse; there is rarely a Plan B.

Some senior officers know this and many doubt that we could ever shift the balance to prevention. A few have called for a National Crime Reduction Service and one, a former Met Commander, Lawrence Roach, has even proposed that policing should be turned exclusively to crime reduction.

> A long-term permanent solution to the problems of the police requires them to withdraw from the investigation of crime, and the identification, detection and prosecution of offenders. In its place a national public prosecution department should be created within the Crown Prosecution Service under the direction of a public prosecutor supported by a staff of full-time crime investigators.

I think that goes too far. It would be hugely expensive, with inevitable gaps and duplications. In any case, certainty of detection is an important part of crime prevention. I am not arguing that cops should abandon arrests, much less that we should scrap the criminal justice system. Rather that, as with civil law, our last option should be to go to court and our first thought should be how to forestall the problem.

Thus, when there is a crime involved, every police officer needs to ask not just 'Who did it?' but 'How do I stop it happening again?' Sometimes a crime is so serious, or the offender so prolific, that the answers to both questions amount to the same thing. The culprit must be caught and brought before the courts. But even then there may be smarter ways to tackle more serious offenders than automatic prosecution. In fact sometimes a policy of with-holding prosecution can be as effective as going through with it.

SWORD OF DAMOCLES

With his long hair and beard, David Kennedy is an unlikely looking crime-fighter. Which is not surprising since he is a university professor. But in a series of dramatic interventions in gun and drug crime in US cities he has shown that not prosecuting gangsters can be more effective than sending them to prison. Starting with Operation Ceasefire in Boston, he and colleagues spent a year analysing an epidemic of shootings in city suburbs, eventually swooping on a small hard-core of trouble-makers while offering the great majority of gang members a way out. Youth homicides fell dramatically as a result.

He used the same technique to halt rampant drug deals in North Carolina. Police in High Point were frustrated at the seeming futility of arbitrary arrests and the resilience of the market. At Kennedy's direction they tried problem-solving rather than law enforcement. They used crime mapping to pinpoint hotspots, consulted residents, enlisted the support of all relevant agencies, and prepared for a day of reckoning. The police poured intelligence resources into the area, compiling evidence against everyone involved in the drug market. Just before D-day they arrested the three most dangerous offenders. Then they swooped on all the remaining dealers, showing them – and their relatives – photographic evidence of their crimes, but telling them they could avoid prosecution if they would come and talk things through. There was overwhelming compliance. But instead of one-on-one meetings the dealers were astonished to find themselves gathered with all the other drug-traders too.

The police told them their drug-dealing days were over. Social services explained how they would help the dealers to go straight, but this was a once in a lifetime opportunity. Then the prosecutor warned that he already had enough to send most of them to prison.

> I represent 2.5 million people but I'm more interested in you than any of them. I want you to succeed. But if you ever go back to dealing, ever, I promise you and I've told my pros-ecutors that if he or she doesn't do everything in their power to hit you with everything, then I'll fire them.

Finally they were told they had three days to clean up their business affairs; to sort out debts and get rid of drugs without being arrested.

The drug market ceased almost immediately and never reopened.

Nor was there noticeable displacement to other districts. And the housing estates that had once seethed with anti-police bravado became supportive. For as Professor Kennedy says, no community wants to be fearful, no mother or grandmother wants to see daughters turning to drug-addicted prostitution or sons at risk of being arrested or shot dead or finishing up with a walking stick and a colostomy bag. After years of trying to solve the problem through the courts, it was cured by not going through the courts.

Several academics, including Larry Sherman and ex-police chief Peter Neyroud, have explored ingenious ways of diverting people from the path to court. And when crime prevention, not law enforcement, becomes the principal objective for police, then cops will have to be more business-like in finding smarter strategies themselves.

Some already have. One policing unit posted simple warnings to put a stop to widespread internet fraud. Polite notes were hand-delivered to scammers telling them the authorities knew what they were up to. Perhaps unsurprisingly, realising the police were onto them the villains shut up shop and vanished from the world wide web. Organised gangs were tackled by civil law in an echo of how Al Capone was finally brought down for tax evasion. Money-laundering rules were used to seize their cash, their mansions, yachts and flashy cars.

In fact if criminal courts are seen only as a last resort it might even bring pressure on the justice system to reform, to be much cheaper, faster and more efficient, and to concern itself more with community safety than with blame. Maybe lawyers should take a lesson from auditors, whose bookkeeping has moved progressively from rules-based – which proved leaky and open to abuse – to principles-based accounting.

Until that happens the police should recognise that their role in crime prevention is generally different from the interests of the judiciary.

3. Solving problems not just crimes

The idea that police would see their role as problem-solvers is so straightforward, so obviously sensible, you might have imagined it would be central to our expectations of policing. Yet because we have seen criminals as the problem, not the symptom, police have never broken out of the circularity that so frustrated America's most famous cop, Bill Bratton: 'We're just stuck in this carousel that people get off of, then right back on again.'

And so long as police are measured on detection rates they can go on ignoring harms or go on round in circles reacting to calls for help without ever tackling the underlying ills – the real fundamentals that tempt people to act badly and then provide opportunities for them to do so.

WHY RESPONDING IS NOT RESOLVING

Take the example of a chronically sick woman who is terrified of the chaotic and possibly psychotic drug dealer who lives in the flat upstairs. Repeatedly she dials 999 because of violent arguments outside and sometimes death threats. Repeatedly the police arrive on blues and twos. But there is never any evidence to trigger an arrest and they lose interest. She is told to keep a diary, and for several months she cowers in her room noting down appalling intimidation, attempts to kick in her front door, fights and rows in the flat upstairs – but the police work to a threshold which requires a reasonable prospect of securing a conviction. It would be her word against his. The building is run by a housing association and the rents are paid for by the local authority – but no one has the will to solve the problem until we chance upon the horror of it all with a BBC film crew. Then, magically, she is rehoused and the dealer is evicted. What did the police think they were doing all those months? The answer is: responding. They did not take responsibility for the problem and they did not solve it. They defined their job by what would happen in court not what happens in real life. But given the unambiguous remit to take ownership of these sorts of problems, they could have, and should have, taken the lead with other agencies and solved things long before they became a running sore.

Problem-solving becomes king in a land where the principal object to be attained is *the Prevention of Crime* rather than feeding a conveyor belt to lawyers. Police would be free, in fact obliged, to think long-term. They would be motivated to lead alliances with businesses and local authorities and require them to mend the broken window issues in which disorder breeds.

4. Going higher up the food chain

The crime surge from the 1950s to the 1990s is testament to past failures of policing. They failed to forecast the surge in shoplifting, car crimes or muggings, mostly shrugged at whole swathes of white-collar and internet crime, and had to be shocked by public revulsion into understanding how to cope with race hate, sex crime or domestic violence. They were in the wake of events when they should have been our look-outs. We need a step-change in their sense of purpose.

All of this requires police to migrate higher up the food chain. They would be required to take a role akin to public health physicians and not just as emergency responders. They would have reason to use crime analysis not only to arrest a local troublemaker but to feed information so that wider patterns can be spotted. Instead of seeing evidence as lawyers do, they would have reason to collect the sort of data that show up weaknesses that lead to crime. They would be encouraged to feed local information for regional or national analysis and so spot common vulnerabilities and get early warning of emerging trends.

Accordingly the local fiefdoms of policing would have a natural incentive to collaborate nationally and even globally and to assert a crime prevention role by influencing product designs, policies and procedures which largely determine the rates of crime we suffer.

Like any business with objectives, they would have to invest money in research. The one group of scientists that does look for top-class evidence in crime reduction is the Campbell Crime and Justice Group. And it rightly despairs at the amateurishness of our approach to crime prevention.

We think it a major public policy failure that the government and the police have not invested greater effort and resources in identifying the specific approaches and tactics that work best in combating specific types of crime problems. The portfolio of studies that exists is at best serendipitous, and does not represent any concerted public effort to either assess the effectiveness of problem-oriented policing as an approach, or understand the mechanisms that would make it more successful.

Ideally we would follow the example of the NHS with its dedicated research arm and its constant search for cost-effectiveness. For the first time we could have a systematic approach to recidivism, with long-term randomised trials to assess the different options. There should be formal experiments to test out different forms of policing. Civilian analysts should be given much higher status as the boffins who help drive the whole crime reduction enterprise. Universities and business could be encouraged to collaborate in design against crime just as they do in medical science. Above all there must be horizon-scanning to head off trouble that is brewing on the skyline.

This means the police have to forestall crime not just at local level but by putting pressure on polluters far away. They need to be detectives of temptation and opportunity, seeking out emerging problems and demanding top-grade security for the next generation of services and products. If they won't who can, who will?

We should learn from other examples where public safety has been massively enhanced. Road deaths and workplace fatalities were both brought down by four-fifths – huge savings achieved by closing off the vulnerabilities that led to harm. Yet anachronistically we continue to treat crimes as largely discrete episodes rather than as a public health phenomenon.

THE GOOD SHEPHERD

Friday and Saturday nights are the busiest times for injuries at accident and emergency departments and most are associated with alcohol-related assault. As we saw in Chapter 9, very few patients tell the police, even when their wounds are serious, but a maxillofacial surgeon became so frustrated at stitching up people's faces that he began to treat the problem as a disease. Professor Jon Shepherd recruited help from hospitals around the country to build a picture of alcohol-related violence as doctors do routinely for some infections – but it was voluntary, had little official support and so compliance was patchy and results were inconsistent. Even so he found he could identify hotspots and risk factors, which in turn led to solutions. This is why Scotland declared a clampdown on cut-price booze. One of Shepherd's prescriptions was to persuade pubs in Cardiff to use plastic bottles and glasses, especially near football grounds on match days. Facial injuries plunged by 70 per cent.

We need to follow his example in many other areas of crime.

The massive drop in road deaths is a useful template for cutting crime. People have remained more or less the same since the bad days of the 1970s, and though drink-driving was targeted with highly visible campaigns, most of the gains were made because engineers made vehicles and highways more forgiving of human frailty.

We can learn from other big accident savings too. Manufacturers can no longer blame their customers if someone gets injured by their products. They are expected to build in safety as an integral part of the design. Yet when it comes to crime, companies routinely pass on vulnerabilities to consumers, polluting society as surely as a dirty factory dumping contaminants into a river and poisoning communities downstream.

Some of those businesses are owner-managed or have branches just around the corner, but who has access to the company's head office? Who can persuade the multinationals, the manufacturers and foreign institutions? As things stand, police have virtually no links, let alone close partnerships, with the companies that shape the future, such as Microsoft, Toyota or Visa, or even with industry trade bodies. We need to raise the sights of the police, from the pavement to the global boardroom and beyond. The answer is to go beyond problem-oriented policing which is mostly local to what we might call Problem Oriented Policing Version 2.0. One of the key responsibilities of the police must be to open channels of communication and contribute to a crystal-clear feedback of how their businesses affect our rates of crime. And that requires a whole new machinery for identifying trends and liaising across boundaries.

POP2 involves top-table access. Withdrawal from international crime treaties and policing institutions – as some urge on ideological grounds – would cut us off from influence and be a charter for more crime. We need closer collaboration not less. In fact the European Commission is often ahead of the game. Only indifference by national politicians has stymied a directive that 'products and services will not be vulnerable to crime risks that could reasonably have been addressed at the design stage'. That idea was part-authored by industry. And why not? Business is all about anticipation, forestalling competition, second-guessing regulation. It needs a level playing field and above all it needs incentives. We just have to remove excuses and find ways to harness the corporate selfish gene.

And what's sauce for the goose should be sauce for the gander: the public sector must stop polluting too.

THE POLITICS OF CRIME

Governments are among the greatest patrons of crime. This is partly because they handle so much money. Leaky tax policies and poorly supervised welfare payments between them probably haemorrhage £6 billion a year in scams. Occasionally promoting swindles is thought to be a price worth paying. VAT has always been an invitation to carousel fraud. Sometimes things are simply slapdash. For years the DVLA licensed vehicles in such a sloppy way that drivers could avoid excise duty and insurance. And politicians, like the rest of us, believe in law and order only when it suits them. One minister for example, on political grounds, chose not to tighten rules on selling used cars (as I had proposed and his senior civil servants recommended), with the result that thousands continue to disappear each year into a black economy.

There was a classic whiff of hypocrisy in 2001 when the government changed electoral rules to encourage postal voting. Ostensibly it was to broaden access to democracy. Coincidentally it was likely to swing elections to the party then in power. But postal ballots are vulnerable to 'personation' (stealing someone else's vote), forgery, bribery, intimidation, interception of the mail, patriarchal domination of a household and 'boss politics' where local power brokers can find themselves controlling hundreds of votes. There were objections from the Electoral Commission and from politicians who foresaw a scandal.

In the event electoral malpractice was so widespread, embracing all three parties, that one judge denounced 'evidence of electoral fraud that would disgrace a banana republic' and in another case the judge described the changes as 'lethal to the democratic system'. The Council of Europe was moved to comment that British elections had become 'childishly simple' to rig.

Not that European institutions can claim the moral high ground. EU agricultural tax breaks and subsidies may have encouraged more dishonesty than the Cosa Nostra. Supposedly high-minded politicians overrode advice to launch the €500 note, which is seven times more valuable than the highest denomination US dollar bill or Bank of England note and became the currency of choice for money launderers, forgers and drugs traffickers. The EU and the European Parliament Commission were swamped with so many expenses fiddles that you now have to go through a Kafkaesque bureaucracy to try reclaiming the cost of a train fare.

Whatever politicians say, tackling crime is not always top of their agenda.

5. Closing the gap between us and them

Given the unambiguous and relentless task of cutting crime, police would have to acknowledge that most of the factors that cause or curb crime are beyond their immediate control and so they would have to exert pressure on the rest of us to do our bit. As well as close collaboration with businesses and policy-makers it requires them to partner more openly with members of the public, who deserve to be treated as the most important stakeholders of all.

Police should experiment with local people taking key decisions about priorities. This is where they will find that, though from time to time we burn for justice, mostly we want to be safe rather than sorry and vengeful. And while in the abstract we want the police to do roughly what they do, responding to emergencies and catching villains, for the most part these things are a far remove from what concerns us in our daily lives. As we noted in Chapter 10, when communities are asked what bothers them, the priorities tend to be litter, pollution, noise, vandalism, speeding traffic, parking, inconsiderate neighbours, worrisome teenagers and dog mess. If crime, in a more conventional sense, is mentioned at all it is generally limited to hotspots on particular estates or in response to a spike in burglary or car crime. There are exceptions – in some towns poor estates endure gangs, drug dealing and a nasty atmosphere of violence where police and the community at large have lost control – but our personal experience rarely matches the big things that preoccupy police chiefs and politicians, let alone the drama in the news.

Just as banks are increasingly open-plan so police also need to be more open in every sense. Much of the secrecy of policing is unnecessary, as anyone who has attended routine briefing meetings will understand. Wanted posters adorn the walls but are marked 'Restricted' even when they contain nothing revelatory or actionable for defamation. In some parts of the US the media are invited to all CompStat gatherings, often exposed to intelligence reports, and, to my knowledge, there has never been a breach of security – or litigation from a suspect – as a result. In fact I learned from years on *Crimewatch* that senior investigating officers would often divulge secrets to me that they had kept from members of their own team. As one top detective put it, only half in jest, 'If you want something leaked, tell a policeman.'

All of which raises questions about why we need police to do policing.

Take that issue of confidentiality. Actually journalists are rather good at keeping secrets and will sometimes go to prison to protect their sources. Lawyers, tax inspectors, defence workers and many others also deal with privileged and sometimes potentially dangerous information with more integrity than some people in the service.

Or take detection. The likelihood of being caught remains key to reducing temptation. Yet despite our love of fictional sleuths like Sherlock Holmes we take it for granted that in real life, crime should be the sole reserve of the police. Why? A sadly short-lived national detective group, the Serious Organised Crime Agency, recruited widely from outside the police with great success. Cops have no monopoly on insight or integrity. Auditors, tax inspectors, customs and immigration officers, scientists, engineers, insurance claim examiners, crash or fire investigators and many others are detectives, not to mention investigative journalists. Cross-fertilisation would do more than introduce new analytic techniques. It would import inquiring minds less likely to regard a case as closed once a suspect has been caught, and keen to shut the stable door before other horses bolt. And diversity has been proved to work. There is one thing to bear in mind, though. British police are sitting on a brand name that is globally respected. It would be plumb crazy not to leverage it and give it truly national responsibilities: Scotland Yard.

Maybe the police should also try dropping rank. When policing first evolved it was natural to adopt a military hierarchy which reflected social class. Chief officers have continued to assume that square-bashing and rank are essential for keeping discipline, not least in crowd control or riots. I think they are trapped in their own presumptions. As management consultants point out, elephants can't be taught to dance. Few other safety-critical organisations are stuck with the old rigidities. In the nuclear power industry, or with special operations soldiers like the SAS, authority is often skill-specific. Surgeons defer to anaesthetists and in live TV, power passes naturally from series producer to studio director to floor manager to presenter depending on the circumstances. In any case leadership is increasingly about the capacity to inspire rather than the right to demand. Pecking orders stifle creativity.

The institutionalised canteen culture of policing has been less than enthusiastic about dissolving barriers between them and us. We have already opened up the police inspectorate to civilians but there is resistance to going further. Police have been reluctant to exploit outsourcing key activities, let alone experiment with privatisation. Yet commercial companies sort out our power and water, help supply and train our armies and keep our nuclear weapons safe. Why must we be trapped in a paradigm that says the police must be owned as well as guided by the machinery of state? In Denmark commercial companies operate the fire brigades, but the Danes baulk at shareholders running prisons. In Australia, Britain, Canada and the US it is the other way around. It is essentially a cultural bias. There are no more dangers of abuse in competitive enterprise than in a closed world of policing and it would be surprising if policing had nothing to gain from the disciplines of business.

Perhaps above all the police should level with us that there is only so much they can do. With every other field of public policy clamouring for money, they, and we, should make the case for transparent rationing. Britain's NHS got into an appalling mess by refusing to concede that it had limited capacity and funds. Admitting weaknesses helps create clarity and may actually create more political support. But more importantly it is one of the strongest arguments for change. It obliges us to look for what is most cost-effective. In the past the police have juggled resources through expedience – such as slashing road safety spending by a quarter, which may risk public welfare more than cutting back on murder squads. Transparent rationing would help make budgeting more rational. It will help police to see that that there are smarter ways to bring down crime than through the courts. It will help all of us – policy-makers, police and public – recognise that convictions and crime rates lead largely independent lives.

And with an emphasis on crime prevention rather than detection, the pressure will grow on all of us, as citizens or in our roles as designers, manufacturers, distributors, service providers and consumers, to make sure we arrange things so that we are not enablers of another's crime.

Let those who lead us into temptation deliver us from evil.

23

AFTERTHOUGHTS

We are left with a lot of unanswered questions. Some – like what we should do with offenders, or how to reform the courts – deserve a book in their own right. You will have to go online to www.thecrimebook.com to find more on this as well as sections on terrorism and tensions between policing and human rights.

But many things can become distractions if your main aim is to cut crime. The important message is that people, however weak or evil, are only one ingredient of crime. People need a motive before they do bad things. And then they need the opportunity to act.

Accordingly, we can cut crime more effectively by changing situations than by hoping to reform offenders. We *can* change individuals but our personalities are largely set in infancy and childhood. We would have to get in early. It is hard for later interventions to transform people's souls. It involves a lot of moral challenges too, especially if we are punitive or act without first-rate evidence that we are doing good.

Nor is it easy to change big things in society like poverty or morals. Even if we could agree on what to do, and do it quickly, it is far from clear that it would make a huge difference to how much crime we suffer.

What we *can* do is remove or diminish motives to act badly.

Our most effective answers will be found not in abstract theory but close in time and space to the actual offence. We can make ourselves aware of what tempts people to do wrong and so remove or mask unnecessary provocation. We can think ahead and eliminate needless opportunities for harm. Each crime we prevent means we conscript fewer people into the habit of behaving badly. Thereby we create a virtuous circle. We will never eradicate crime. It will continue to hurt us and we will find that like disease it constantly mutates. But we can make big inroads.

And we can recruit the techniques of science to test our assumptions, to shunt false ones to the sidelines, and to make our products and services more resilient.

Already more academics and policy-makers are pressing for better scientific evidence. Experimental criminologists and crime scientists are leading the way.

Hopefully we will not have to twist the arms of the police. Their best strategists have already seen the problems and are grasping for the solutions. According to Chris Sims, chief constable of Britain's second biggest force, 'The criminal justice system belongs in a domain of serious crime. We do it no favours if we clutter it up with things that are better dealt with by other means.'

And in his valedictory address in 2012 the Chief Inspector of Constabulary, Sir Denis O'Connor, made an open plea for radical change. 'Preventative policing has ebbed and flowed over my forty years-plus in the Service. It now needs to be nurtured [otherwise] we will be looking not at reform but at decline.'

After years of strategic initiatives coming and going we have a new National Crime Agency, and much depends on the direction it now chooses. If it emphatically sets crime reduction as its goal it will have to overcome entrenched ideologies and old politics. But politicians will change their tune if voters do.

It's up to us.

We need to be aware that so much of what we're told is wrong. We have reduced crime dramatically, almost without recognising our achievement. We now know how we did it, and we now know how to cut crime in future.

www.thecrimebook.com

APPENDIX

Criminology, like sociology and despite its grand Greek suffix, is a rag-bag of different approaches, few of which would pass muster in the natural sciences like physics or biology.

The term appears to have been used first in the late nineteenth century (in 1885 there was a book called *Criminology* by Raffaele Garofalo) and from the start it rejected the classical approach of philosophers like Cesare Beccaria (1738–94) and Jeremy Bentham (1748–1832) who thought that criminals are basically rational and will break the law if the rewards exceed the pain. Instead criminology has two quite different roots, the first of which was the assumption that criminals are abnormal.

Since time immemorial crime had been ascribed to badness, and no doubt people had always portrayed villains as villainous-*looking*, but from about the sixteenth century it became popular to think that you really could tell who were wicked people just from their appearance. *Physiognomists* studied corpses and claimed convicts were 'shifty-eyed' and had distinctive facial features. The trouble was, different physiognomists could not agree. Some said criminals had small noses, fleshy lips, small ears and weak chins; others that they had arrogant noses, narrow lips, protruding ears and bushy eyebrows. *Phrenologists* were more interested in the skull and they insisted that various shapes and bumps on the head indicated abilities and even moralities.

It was the view that criminality is physical, inherent and incurable that, for three-quarters of a century, led to mass transportation of offenders to Botany Bay in newly discovered Australia – a process that, at its height, removed a greater proportion of young men than imprisonment ever did before or since.

Towards the end of the nineteenth century, influenced by Lamarck and Darwin, people began to think these 'deformities' were inherited, and Cesare Lombroso (1835–1909), an Italian doctor, coined the term 'born criminal'. He performed autopsies which revealed to him, 'all of a sudden, lighted up as a vast plain under a flaming sky', that criminals had small heads but large faces and receding foreheads more like monkeys and chimpanzees. Plainly they were throwbacks to a primitive stage of human evolution. Eventually he produced a list of eighteen characteristics of the poorly endowed criminal (a list which bizarrely included tattoos – something of a giveaway that not all these features could be inherited) and opined that female criminals were physically like men.

Given that all this was so deterministic, sexist and condescending, it is not without irony that Lombroso is still sometimes known as the father of criminology. His findings were roundly refuted by a British doctor, Charles Goring (1870–1919), who pointed out that Lombroso had only studied convicts and not compared them to anybody else. Goring matched 3,000 English prisoners with thousands of soldiers, and in 1913 published a damning refutation of Lombroso's work. (The failure to compare is sometimes known as the 'Lombrosian fallacy'. Sadly Lombroso's canard helped lead to an equally ill-considered notion, clung to by many of today's criminologists, that *no* biological explanations for crime have anything to offer.)

But the idea of innate degeneracy lived on, shifting to body proportions as a whole and thus the view that criminals are physically inferior in almost every respect. After the Lombroso fiasco these opinions were based on comparative studies, but they did not always compare like with like – prison inmates were disproportionately poor and black so it is unsurprising that warning signs of criminality included big chests, waists and forearms, and 'Negroid' foreheads. This school of *constitutionalists* became popular in the 1920s and '30s and was significant in the US well into the 1950s.

Given the failings of this physiological approach to crime (sometimes known as criminal anthropology), with its racist, sexist and eugenic overtones, you may be surprised to know that early sociology was given to similar views. In fact it was an American social investigator, Richard Dugdale (1841–83), who captured the public's imagination with a damning study of a degenerate family in upstate New York. His report, *The Jukes: A Study in Crime, Pauperism, Disease and Heredity* (1875), traced a family (Jukes was a pseudonym) back to colonial times and demonstrated a clear lineage of crime, prostitution and disease. He estimated the cumulative cost to the public purse of housing, imprisoning and dealing with the family was almost $1.5 million. In 1911 Dugdale's manuscript was found and led to a follow-up by Arthur H. Estabrook which renewed public outrage and was hailed by the eugenics movement as a study of hereditary feeble-mindedness and immorality.

Around the same time a psychologist, Henry Goddard, published *The Kallikak Family: A Study in the Heredity of Feeble-Mindedness* (1912), which was equally damning, and Goddard campaigned openly for policies to rid the world of these 'bad genes'. This has become known as the 'bad seed' approach, and even though some of the studies have been shown to be flawed (Goddard was accused of inventing much of his data), it contributed to enforced sterilisation of thousands of Americans (the practice was only stopped by the Supreme Court in 1942) and gave pseudoscientific credibility to the Nazi ideology which, in Europe in the 1940s, led to the murder of millions.

In stark contrast to all this biological determinism was an idea that was much more sympathetic to offenders: that criminals were caused by society. This is the approach that came to dominate criminology overwhelmingly and, rather as Charles Darwin (1809–82) had enthused the physiologists, his contemporary Karl Marx (1818–83) inspired the sociologists. Their greatest proponent was another man often called the father of sociology, the French academic Émile Durkheim (1858–1917). Durkheim was brilliant, highly politicised, socialist and (though secular) Jewish, and at odds with the dutiful Catholic nationalism which dominated France after the Franco-Prussian war. In 1895 he published a manifesto for sociology called *Rules of the Sociological Method*, and founded the first European department of sociology (at the University of Bordeaux). If the anthropologists saw crime as the inevitable outcome of genes, Durkheim saw it as the inevitable outcome of people's roles in society. Remember, this was a time of entrenched class divisions when many middle-class commentators, including Charles Dickens (1812–70) and Henry Mayhew (1812–87), had long expressed concern at harsh conditions suffered by the poor. According to Durkheim, a community was like an organism and each individual was allocated a function in the division of labour. In stable societies there were strong social norms, and if anyone broke the rules the purpose of the law was to restore the equilibrium. But in rapidly changing communities there was less organic solidarity, there were fewer norms to regulate behaviour (a state which Durkheim called 'anomie') and the law was generally repressive.

Durkheim's analysis was ground-breaking and hugely influential, and it was his sociological (not to say socialist) approach that so dominated criminology during its explosive growth in the latter part of the twentieth century. In the US it was taken up by people like Edwin H. Sutherland (1883–1950), whose formidable 1924 text, *Criminology*, asserted the importance of social standing, class and social disorganisation. Sutherland also insisted that the problem in criminology is to explain the criminality of behaviour, not the behaviour as such, thereby entrenching the view that it was not the crime that mattered, nor the victim, so much as the social forces weighing down upon the perpetrator. In Europe especially, all this gave birth to a colourful variety of theories and tied criminology firmly to a left-wing perspective that saw the state as generally repressive. Over millennia crime had been blamed on just about everything: the gods or demons, the influence of planets, illness, feeblemindedness, physical degeneracy and mental illness. Over the last century, following Durkheim's lead, criminology has embraced an almost equally exotic range of causes: class structures, poverty, male cultural dominance, childhood deprivation, Freudian subconsciousness and much more besides. It has given rise to various competing schools of thought, including 'postmodernism' (a widely applied but rather pretentious and ill-defined rejection of 'modern' truths and explanations which, in its criminological incarnation, equates criminality with exclusion from power), the Frankfurt school (neo-communist), the Chicago school (crime is caused by the failure of city institutions), strain theory (people turn to crime because they can't achieve the American Dream), symbolic interactionism (they turn to crime because they are labelled as troublemakers), left realism (the law suppresses the poor) and right realism (we need more individual responsibility and punishment) and several more; but almost all of them are critiques of society rather than of crime.

It is such a shame. For a brief time, around the 1920s, there was a chance that British criminology might have been practical and scientific. The first university lectures in criminology were to medical students in 1921; it was a doctor, Hamblin Smith, who seems to have been the first Briton to call himself a criminologist; and interest was driven by forensic psychiatry and educational psychology. But theory and politics began to swamp the infant discipline, as it had done in the USA. Although claims to scientific principles continued to feature strongly, pseudoscience and ideology rather than experiment were at the root of what became Britain's criminological Establishment. In 1931 an 'Association for the Scientific Treatment of Criminals' was formed in London to promote alternatives to prison, largely through psychoanalysis (the doctor and theorist Sigmund Freud and the spiritualistic Carl Jung were leading lights). The Association soon became an Institute and in 1953 it set up a 'scientific' forum to debate criminality, though there was little scientific methodology. It was this group of like-minded reformers which, in 1961, changed its name to the British Society of Criminology.

Politicisation soon followed, fanned by two radical Americans. In 1967 a Chicago sociologist, Howard Becker, delivered a call to arms claiming criminology had to take sides with the under-dog, prompting an influential response from a colleague, Alvin Gouldner, who insisted the question was not whose side social scientists should be on but *how* they should take up the battle. The next few years saw a wholesale rejection of the 'straitjacket' of science and the 'blandness' of nonpartisan inquiry.

Thus, criminology is mostly a liberal or leftist philosophy rather than an 'ology' in the sense that so impressed the grandma in that 1980s TV ad. And as we saw in Chapter 15, where it does attempt experiment, its political heritage is far more powerful than its scientific one. But for now the important issue is that most criminology has been politicised, preferring to focus on the criminal rather than the crime, and tending to see the offender as a victim of what society had done to him. None of this is very helpful to those who want to cut victimisation caused by crime.

REFERENCES AND NOTES

For all the references, notes and more background go to **www.thecrimebook.com**.

Type into the search window a few words from the phrase you wish to interrogate.

There is the option to report errors, omissions or broken links.

www.thecrimebook.com also has additional sections on terrorism and other crime for political motives, on civil liberties and more.

www.thecrimebook.com

INDEX